Economic Welfare and Inequality in Iran

Mohammad Reza Farzanegan • Pooya Alaedini
Editors

Economic Welfare and Inequality in Iran

Developments since the Revolution

palgrave
macmillan

Editors
Mohammad Reza Farzanegan
Center for Near and Middle
Eastern Studies
School of Business & Economics
Philipps-Universität Marburg
Marbug, Germany

Pooya Alaedini
Department of Social Planning
Faculty of Social Sciences
University of Tehran
Tehran, Iran

ISBN 978-1-349-95024-9 ISBN 978-1-349-95025-6 (eBook)
DOI 10.1057/978-1-349-95025-6

Library of Congress Control Number: 2016960899

Printed on acid-free paper

This Palgrave Macmillan imprint is published by Springer Nature
The registered company is Nature America Inc.
The registered company address is: 1 New York Plaza, New York, NY 10004, U.S.A.

Acknowledgments

In the preparation of this book, we were supported by a number of individuals. As editors, we would like to thank all our chapter authors for their contributions. Our further gratitude goes to two anonymous referees who read the original project proposal; Professor Sang-Hyop Lee, Ahmed Mohamed Badreldin, and Dalia Fadly for giving valuable comments on certain chapters; and Sven Fischer for providing an excellent assistance on the preparation of the manuscripts. We would also like to extend our appreciation to Sarah Lawrence, Commissioning Editor, Economics and Finance, at Palgrave Macmillan/Springer Nature, for encouraging us from the beginning to the end of this project. Allison Neuburger at Palgrave Macmillan/Springer Nature further deserves a special mention for her professional assistance. Last but not least, we are thankful to our families who supported us with a great deal of patience.

Mohammad Reza Farzanegan and Pooya Alaedini

ACKNOWLEDGEMENTS

Contents

List of Figures

List of Tables

List of Contributors

Pooya Alaedini is Associate Professor of Social Planning at the Faculty of Social Sciences, University of Tehran. Over the past decade, he has served as a consultant for several international development projects in the Middle East, Central Asia, and Africa. His publications include monographs, a number of peer-reviewed articles in Persian and English, and several full-length reports produced for international organizations. He holds a Ph.D. in Urban Planning and Policy Development from Rutgers University. Email: palaedini@ut.ac.ir

Hamid Reza Ashrafzadeh is Associate Professor at the Institute for Trade Studies and Research in Tehran with a long record of research and publication. He has authored a number of books, articles, and research reports on various economic issues, particularly trade and industrial development in Iran. His main interests include econometrics, macroeconomics, international trade, and export-oriented industrial development. He studied at the University of Tehran as well as Beheshti University and earned his Ph.D. from Tarbiat Modares University in Tehran. Email: shrashrafzadeh@gmail.com

Mitra Babapour is a Ph.D. student in economics at Allameh Tabatabai University in Tehran. She has conducted research on income distribution, poverty, and mobility and has several publications to her record, including refereed journal articles and book chapters. Email: babapour.mitra@yahoo.com

Nadereh Chamlou is currently an International Development Advisor. She is a retired Senior Advisor to the Chief Economist of the World Bank's Middle East and North Africa (MENA) Region. In over three decades with the World Bank, she held technical, coordination, managerial, and advisory positions across the organization in such areas as economic management, private sector development, financial markets, knowledge economy, environmental sustainability, infrastructure, corporate governance, and gender and development. Her experience extends to Latin America, East Asia and Pacific, Eastern Europe, and MENA. She has a number of seminal publications, some of which were translated into other languages. Her research focuses on entrepreneurship and private sector development, particularly on talent pool and knowledge economy, stressing competitiveness and growth through diversity, and gender inclusion. She is a frequent speaker at regional and international conferences, serves on several boards, and was a 2015 recipient of The Global Alliance for Women's "Making a Difference" award. Email: nchamlou@gmail.com

Sajjad Faraji Dizaji is Assistant Professor of Economics at Tarbiat Modares University of Tehran. He teaches econometrics as well as macroeconomics and microeconomics with a mathematical approach. His main research interests are political economy of oil, sanctions, international economics, and empirical methods. He has published in the *Journal of Peace Research*, *International Tax and Public Finance*, *Economic Modelling*, *Money and Economy*, and several peer-reviewed economics journals in Persian. He holds a Ph.D. in Economics from Tarbiat Modares University. Email: s_dizaji@modares.ac.ir

Mohammad Reza Farzanegan is Professor and Departmental Chair of Economics of the Middle East at the Center for Near and Middle Eastern Studies, Philipps-Universität Marburg, in Germany. He is also affiliated with MACIE (Marburg), CESifo (Munich), and ERF (Cairo). He obtained his Ph.D. in Economics from Technische Universität Dresden in 2009. His research interests include political economy of natural resources, demographic transition, and impact of sanctions. His publications have appeared in *Applied Economics*, *Defence and Peace Economics*, *Ecological Economics*, *Energy Economics*, *European Journal of Political Economy*, *International Tax and Public Finance*, *Journal of Peace Research*, and *World Development*, among other research journals. He is on the Advisory Board of the *Middle*

East—Topics & Arguments (*META Journal*). Email: farzanegan@uni-marburg.de

Hassan F. Gholipour is Lecturer in Economics at Swinburne University of Technology in Australia. Prior to joining Swinburne, he was a postdoctoral researcher in real estate economics and finance at Universiti Teknologi Malaysia (UTM). He holds a Ph.D. in International Finance from Universiti Sains Malaysia (USM). His research interests include real estate economics and finance, tourism economics, and social economics as well as the economies of the Middle East region. He has published over 30 peer-reviewed journal articles. Email: hgholipour@swin.edu.au

Mohammad Mohammadi Khabbazan is Associate Researcher and Scientific Programmer at Cluster of Excellence "Integrated Climate System Analysis and Prediction" (CliSAP), Center for Earth System Research and Sustainability (CEN), University of Hamburg. He teaches GAMS, conducts and supports projects, and co-supervises graduate students. He earned his Ph.D. in Economics from Tarbiat Modares University of Tehran in 2015, having written a dissertation titled "The Economic Effects of Sanctions on Iran's Economy." His areas of interest are international economics, economics of climate change, and general equilibrium theory. Email: mohammad.mohammadi@uni-hamburg.de

Majid Koosheshi is Assistant Professor of Demography at the Faculty of Social Sciences, University of Tehran. He also chairs the Division of Population Research at the University of Tehran's Institute for Social Studies. His research in the past few years has focused on the demography of aging in Iran. In particular, he has conducted research on the health status of the elderly, elderly abuse, coresidency in old age, and social and family support of the elderly. He is the coauthor of "Population Ageing in Iran: Socio-economic, Demographic and Health Characteristics of Elderly" (published by UNFPA, 2012). He holds a Ph.D. in Demography from the University of Tehran. Email: kooshesh@ut.ac.ir

Jeremy Nguyen is Lecturer in Economics at the Swinburne Business School. He holds a Ph.D. in Economics from the Australian National University. Prior to the current position at Swinburne, he was an Economist with the Reserve Bank of Australia, held teaching positions at the Australian National University and Griffith University, and was a Visiting Fellow at the

Brookings Institution, Washington, DC. His research interests include applied econometrics and quantitative methods, macroeconomics, economics of happiness and life satisfaction, income inequality, population aging, and innovations in the teaching of economics and business. Email: jdnguyen@swin.edu.au

Hossein Raghfar is Associate Professor of Economics and Director of the Institute for Economic and Social Studies at Alzahra University in Tehran. His areas of research include income distribution, poverty, social security, and social economics in which he has a long record of publications. He holds a Ph.D. in Economics from the University of Essex. Email: raghfar@alzahra.ac.ir

Hossein Sadeghi is Associate Professor of Economics at Tarbiat Modares University in Tehran. He received his Ph.D. in Economics from the same university in 1994. His main research interests are energy economics, economics of natural resources and environment, economics of defense, and the underground economy. He is the author or coauthor of over one hundred papers either published in peer-reviewed journals or presented at various conferences. Email: sadeghih@modares.ac.ir

CHAPTER 1

Introduction

Mohammad Reza Farzanegan and Pooya Alaedini

Why Study Inequality?

In a recent survey of 1767 leaders from academia, business, government, and nonprofits, the World Economic Forum's Global Agenda Council found *increasing income inequality* to be the top global concern in 2015, followed by increasing joblessness, and lack of leadership across countries (WEF 2015). Inequality indeed matters and there is a rich literature investigating its relationship with economic development. Okun (1975) argues that in pursuing increased economic efficiency, trade-offs in terms of increased inequality may be necessary to facilitate capital accumulation and technological innovation and encourage economic agents to invest in education and health. There is a larger body of literature, however, that highlights the long-term negative effects of increasing income inequality on sustainable and inclusive development. In their study of 174 countries, Berg and Ostry (2011) contend that countries with lower income inequality enjoy higher growth rates in the long run, after controlling for market

M.R. Farzanegan (✉)
Center for Near and Middle Eastern Studies, School of Business & Economics, Philipps-Universität Marburg, Marbug, Germany

P. Alaedini
Department of Social Planning, Faculty of Social Sciences, University of Tehran , Tehran, Iran

M.R. Farzanegan, P. Alaedini (eds.), *Economic Welfare and Inequality in Iran*, DOI 10.1057/978-1-349-95025-6_1

structure and other institutional factors. Bénabou (1996) also shows that economic growth in countries with high income inequality is slower than economies with lower levels of inequality. It has been further argued that inequality is associated with business recessions and economic crises. For example, income inequality and the ratio of debt to income saw rapid increases before both the Great Depression of the 1930s and the 2007–2008 Great Recession (Kumhof et al. 2015). By increasing concentration of income, inequality can reduce aggregate demand in an economy, leading to recession. This is mainly due to the lower marginal propensity to consume associated with the wealthy in comparison to middle- and lower-income groups (Carvalho and Rezai 2014). In explaining the global financial crisis of 2007–2008, deepening income inequality has indeed been highlighted as a major culprit (see Stiglitz 2012). Inequality affects the poor by reducing their ability to invest in their health and human capital formation (Galor and Moav 2004; Aghion et al. 1999). It also influences social mobility across generations, as children's future earnings are significantly affected by their parents' earning profiles (Corak 2013). Finally, it has been shown that inequality damages economic growth through intensifying conflicts and political stability. Increasing inequality reduces the opportunity cost of engaging in conflicts (Lichbach 1989).

Aside from the effects of inequality on socioeconomic variables, there is also a relatively extensive literature examining inequality's drivers. What are the possible causes of inequality? Part of the literature investigates the role of socioeconomic and political factors behind changes in inequality across countries. One key factor is education. Enhancing education and skills can increase potential access to more promising job opportunities, higher income, and economic security. An educated generation is increasingly able to cope with technological change that can potentially lead to rapid economic growth. Higher levels of education influence occupational choices and signal higher productivity to the job market (Dabla-Norris et al. 2015). Yet, the net effect of education on inequality depends on the degree of access to quality educational opportunities and the rate of return on education (see Mincer 1958; Becker and Chiswick 1966). Globalization, with increasing trade openness and higher degrees of foreign direct investment (FDI), is also probed in the literature as a potential driver of inequality—yielding mixed results. Expansion of trade can increase demand and wages for abundant lower-skilled workers in emerging economies and raise purchasing power (Dabla-Norris et al. 2015). This indicates that globalization is *negatively* associated with income inequality. However, there are also studies that underscore the negative consequences of globalization and trade openness. Financial globalization in the form of higher FDI may act to increase income inequality. When FDI is concentrated in sectors with skill- and technology-intensive activities, the effect can be a widening wage gap in an economy (see Freeman 2010). Financial deepening, in the form of greater liquidity in the economy, can increase access to funding opportunities for households and firms. Combined with an inclusive financial market, financial deepening might, at first glance, be expected to lead to decreases in income inequality. However, Greenwood and Jovanovic (1990) suggest a nonlinear relationship between financial deepening and inequality. At earlier stages of financial development, we may observe a worsening of income distribution. Yet, after a certain threshold, financial development may benefit most of the population and lower income inequality. This said, Claessens and Perotti (2007) show that those who have more assets and capital also have greater access to financial markets. Financial deepening in such societies implies higher growth in the skill premium and potentially higher returns to capital.

Why Study Inequality in Post-revolutionary Iran?

Over the past half a century, Iran has experienced a series of momentous political economic events with significant implications for its income distribution and social development. Thanks to increasing oil revenues, between 1960 and 1977, Iran's GDP per capita grew at impressive rates that averaged 9.6 percent per year (Amuzegar 1993: 5). An undesirable consequence of rapid economic growth was a sharp increase in inequality—as suggested by the rise in the Gini coefficient as well as the ratio of the richest decile to the poorest decile (CBI 2015). Inequality reached its peak in 1976—with a Gini coefficient of 0.502. However, it started to decline two years before the 1979 Revolution, possibly due to "trickle down" effects of large investment expenditures directed at the poorer sections of the society (Salehi Esfahani and Pesaran 2009).

The main message of the 1979 Revolution incorporated the goals of social justice, addressing the plight of the downtrodden, and representing the lower social strata in the government. It also included the aims of reducing the country's overreliance on oil revenues and self-sufficiency. The Revolution was followed by an eight-year war with Iraq, postwar privatization and economic liberalization initiatives carried out under the

Rafsanjani and Khatami administrations, the ascendance of a populist economic platform under the Ahmadinejad administration, and most recently the lifting of energy and financial sanctions in January 2016 under the Rouhani administration.

In the immediate aftermath of the 1979 Revolution, an idealistic social justice agenda was adopted by the new establishment. The Constitution of the Islamic Republic requires the government to provide adequate shelter, employment, and means of subsistence for all citizens. The socioeconomic objectives of the Constitution also extend to uprooting regional imbalances and especially tending to rural populations. Major activities undertaken to fulfill these promises over the last three and a half decades have included the provision of basic services in rural areas as well as inner-city low-income neighborhoods, extensive subsidies on various commodities and amenities, direct cash transfers, and land allocations for housing. At the dawn of the post-revolutionary period, Ayatollah Ruhollah Khomeini, the undisputed leader of the Revolution, decreed the establishment of several large foundations—such as *Bonyad-e mostaz'afan* (Foundation of the Downtrodden), *Bonyad-e shahid* (Foundation of the Martyrs), and *Komiteh-ye emdad-e Emam Khomeini* (Imam Khomeini Relief Foundation). The creation of these foundations was financed by large-scale confiscation of property belonging to those associated with the *ancien régime* as well as through donations. These extra-governmental institutions have been active in providing a wide range of social services to their target groups. For example, the Imam Khomeini Relief Foundation, established just 22 days after the victory of the 1979 Revolution, was mandated to uproot poverty, support the deprived, and provide relief to the oppressed. Apart from claiming a share of the government's annual budget, this para-statal organization funds its programs through receiving religious taxes as well as from donations deposited in charity boxes installed at every corner.[1]

A major post-revolutionary episode with serious economic consequences was the eight-year Iran-Iraq War. The war period, which lasted through August 1988, was associated with significant reductions in per-capita incomes and high rates of subsidies provided by the state to control inflation (Nikou 2010).[2] The war inflicted tremendous damage on the Iranian economy. Privatization and economic liberalization efforts spearheaded by the Rafsanjani administration after the war diluted some of the earlier social justice goals in favor of new economic opportunities, a major part of which was reaped by individuals and groups with tight political connections to the establishment (see Klebnikov 2003; Bjorvatn and Selvik 2008).

The most important features of the subsequent Khatami administration included efforts toward international détente as well as political and cultural reforms. Yet, lack of adequate attention given to economic issues as affecting the lower-income strata of the society arguably had damaging political consequences for the reformists (Farzanegan 2009b). Specifically, neoconservative forces grabbed the opportunity to present their own alternative, new in one sense and associated with the 1979 revolutionary slogans in another (Ehteshami and Zweiri 2007: 46).

Oil-income redistribution under the populist administration of Ahmadinejad was carried out in a number of forms. One was through the establishment of *Sanduq-e mehr-e Emam Reza* (Imam Reza Charity Fund) in 2005, officially claimed to be used to help young people secure jobs, afford marriage, and purchase homes (see Dolat-e Bahar 2014; Farzanegan 2009b). Another program under the title *Saham-e edalat* (Justice Shares) was implemented under the Ahmadinejad administration to distribute shares of government-owned companies among lower-income individuals. Other initiatives included the creation of additional funds for employment generation and rural development as well as a banking account scheme facilitating the marriage of young people. Yet, in November 2008, a group of 60 Iranian economists voiced their concern about the negative consequences of these populist programs by ironically highlighting the increasing inequality as one of their side effects as well as lack of economic growth, increasing unemployment, runaway inflation, and a crisis in the capital market (Deragahi 2008). International sanctions imposed on Iran during the last years of Ahmadinejad's presidential term were an additional burden, with far-reaching consequences for the country's economy. Significant falls in oil revenues, investment, and production were accompanied by severe inflationary pressure, reappearance of a black market premium for hard currencies, and increasing unemployment rates (Farzanegan 2013). The populist government's tenure ended as Iran's economic and financial systems were coming under mounting pressure due to international sanctions as well as domestic mismanagement and corruption. At the time of this writing, a deal concerning Iran's internationally disputed nuclear program, negotiated under the Rouhani administration with the governments of major world powers, has paved the way for the removal of most economic and banking sanctions. Iran is thus experiencing a re-opening with potentially significant consequences for its economy and society. Needless to say, these consequences can be both positive and negative.[3]

Real per-capita income growth, employment, labor force participation rate, and measures to control inflation have been disappointing in post-revolutionary Iran. Furthermore, inequality, which decreased just after the Revolution and fluctuated between 1981 and 1984, has not experienced significant changes since 1985 (Salehi Esfahani and Pesaran 2009; Salehi-Isfahani 2009). Yet, there have been improvements in a number of human development indicators in Iran since the 1979 Revolution. Health indicators and especially literacy and educational attainment have seen steady improvements. Although at present nearly one-fifth of the population over 15 years of age remains illiterate and illiteracy rates are some 10 percent higher for females than males, levels of educational attainment have been on the rise in both rural and urban areas while this rise has been quite steep over the last two decades and in the case of tertiary education (SCI 2015).

Against the backdrop of these developments as well as the original social justice agenda of the 1979 Revolution, this book deals with economic inequality and welfare in post-revolutionary Iran. Employing a variety of perspectives and methodological approaches, scholars across different social science fields, who are intimately familiar with Iran, examine the issue at hand in the book's nine chapters. Before providing an overview of these chapters in a separate section, however, it is only fair to discuss some of the volume's limitations.

A commonly used measure of economic inequality is the income (or expenditure) Gini coefficient, which is employed extensively in most of our chapters. The income Gini coefficient is a valuable tool in tracking the overall profile of income distribution in a country, but it is not without shortcomings. To begin with, the Gini coefficient may turn out to be the same for different structures of income distribution. Collecting the required data for its calculation may also be problematic, especially in developing countries with relatively extensive informal economic (unregistered) activities—as is the case for Iran. Furthermore, inequality indexes based on income sources may not be able to show a comprehensive picture of disparity in terms of "well-being," particularly in economies where the government maintains extensive subsidy programs—as has been the case in Iran.

The above limitations notwithstanding, inequality of income or expenditure does not necessarily reflect inequality of wealth or opportunity. These are much more difficult to track—particularly due to the scarcity of data—and we have relegated an attempt at probing them to future endeavors. Yet, inequalities in wealth and opportunity are likely to be associated with monopolies, corruption, and rent-seeking activities. Certain institutions reward accumulation of wealth through such practices rather than creation of wealth that can generate jobs and new productive investments (see Mehlum et al. 2006). The existence of a large shadow economy (see Schneider and Enste 2000) both undermines redistributive taxation and distorts the picture of inequality based on the distribution of reported income in a country like Iran as well. Iran's post-revolutionary economy has indeed experienced significant distortions, leading to accumulation of wealth and opportunities by politically connected individuals and entities (Farzanegan 2012). Furthermore, persistently high inflation has encouraged investment in fixed assets, especially real estate whose prices and rates of return have risen even faster as a result. Yet, widespread illegal land takeovers, referred to as *zamin-khari* (land grabbing or literally land eating) in the local media, have also become a common feature of the country's contemporary political economy.[4] All these hint at the existence of a complex structure of wealth and opportunity in Iran, whose analysis should be pursued by careful studies in the future.

Overview of the Chapters

Chapter 2, coauthored by Pooya Alaedini and Hamid R. Ashrafzadeh, examines the determinants of income distribution and middle-class size in post-revolutionary Iran. It first underscores the social justice agenda adopted by the post-revolutionary government, especially through its Constitution, to set the stage for a discussion of income distribution and social development. It highlights the fact that despite improvements in social service delivery, human capital, and life expectancy attributable to the government's programs, including large-scale subsidies and transfers, the country has continued to face two-digit inflations rates, high rates of unemployment, very low rate of labor force participation rate especially for the youth and women, and stagnant per-capita incomes. Furthermore, the overall inequality has stayed more or less the same after its initial post-revolutionary decline. Yet, the middle class, if defined in terms of income and in a global sense, has continuously increased its share in the population. The second half of Chap. 2 is dedicated to an empirical analysis of factors influencing income distribution and the size of the middle class in association with two other endogenous variables, namely urbanization and manufacturing exports, in a system of four simultaneous equation panel data model. The estimation results show complex relationships among Iran's social, economic, and political structures and especially highlight the negative role of urbanization and the positive role of human capital as influencing both income distribution and the size of the middle class.

In Chap. 3, Hossein Raghfar and Mitra Babapour examine poverty, inequality, mobility, and vulnerability in Iran among different generations over time. They set a threefold task for themselves. The first is to discuss the changing shape of poverty and inequality for different generations. The second is to probe mobility and decomposition of expenditures and unemployment rate. The third is focused on determining the vulnerability of households to poverty. They employ a pseudo-panel that combines 31 years of cross-sectional surveys from 1984 to 2014. Their findings suggest very low absolute and conditional mobility. Furthermore, their analysis of the determinants of vulnerability to poverty underscores the significance of gender and education of household head as well as regional effects and household characteristics such as the number of children. They further show that unemployment rate is rising for cohorts born after 1971.

How have oil rents in Iran shaped inequality and what has been the role of political institutions in this nexus? Sajjad Faraji Dizaji strives to answer this double question in Chap. 4 by introducing the role of political institutions as an important concept in shaping the income inequality effects of oil rents in Iran. He uses time-series data from 1969 to 2012 to examine how and why political institutions can shape oil rents-inequality nexus. His empirical analysis shows that an increase in oil and gas rents has an increasing effect on income inequality in Iran. However, this increasing effect is reduced when the quality of political institutions is improving. In other words, the final inequality effects of oil rents in Iran depend on the quality of democratic institutions. Based on this analysis, GDP per capita and money supply have negative and positive effects on inequality, respectively. There is also some evidence for the existence of an inverted U-shaped relationship between inequality and income per capita. In contrast to the aggravating effect of military spending on inequality, education and social expenditures are found to have improved income distribution. Furthermore, financial development in Iran has widened the income gap between the rich and the poor.

In Chap. 5, Mohammad Reza Farzanegan, Hassan F. Gholipour, and Jeremy Nguyen focus on the influence of the real estate market on income inequality in post-revolutionary Iran. Increasing housing prices have been associated with a range of socioeconomic ills, such as land grabs and increasing fragility of family structures. Against this background, the authors of this chapter are prompted to investigate the impact of rising home prices on income inequality by employing cointegrating regression and using time-series data for 1982–2012. Their main result indicates an increasing and statistically significant association between housing prices and income inequality. This result is robust after controlling for other drivers of inequality such as income per capita, government spending, trade and financial openness, population size, inflation rate, and quality of political institutions.

Iran has progressively narrowed disparities in human capital between men and women. Yet, its gap between male and female employment and labor force participation has been among the highest in the world and is indicative of institutional and legal barriers that women face in accessing economic resources. Naderh Chamlou starts Chap. 6 with a review of the recent literature on the significant association between gender inequality and income inequality. She argues that addressing gender-based inequalities in a country like Iran can tackle inequality in a deeper way and in turn lead to workforce development, improved access to economic resources, and growth—as the economic power of women is tapped. She calls for equality of opportunities and removal of obstacles that prevent women from having full economic participation, which will have considerable impact on the distribution of income and upward mobility of families.

Iran's elderly population is growing in absolute and relative terms as a result of improving life expectancies, an earlier period of rapid population growth, and declining fertility rates in the more recent periods. Chapter 7 by Majid Koosheshi and Pooya Alaedini investigates the implications of Iran's socio-demographic developments for elderly women. It probes gender gaps in employment, economic activity, literacy rate, and marriage rate among the current elderly population of the country as well as their significance for those who will join the elderly population in the future. The chapter then employs the approach of National Transfer Accounts to investigate gender gaps in generational terms for a number of parameters, including labor income, asset income, and pension receipts as well as inter-household and other types of flows for elderly women. It then highlights two sets of serious challenges faced by the current and future population of elderly women.

Chapters 8 and 9 treat the effects of oil and banking sanctions, respectively, on the welfare of Iranian households. In Chap. 8, Mohammad Reza Farzanegan, Mohammad Mohammadi Khabbazan, and Hossein Sadeghi underscore oil sanctions as the most prominent sanctioning policy imposed against post-revolutionary Iran and examine its macroeconomic and household welfare consequences. They use a computable general equilibrium model based on a social accounting matrix to simulate selected scenarios in which exports of oil from Iran to the rest of the world are banned. Their main results show that, under oil sanctions, higher-income households in both urban and rural areas lose more welfare than lower-income households. Total imports, exports, private consumption, and GDP fall in response to oil sanctions. Interesting is the increase in net indirect taxes at the time that oil revenues fall when real exchange rate appreciates. In addition, labor income increases, whereas capital income falls in response to oil sanctions in Iran. These simulations are in line with the reality of the Iranian economy after the oil sanctions began.

Whereas oil sanctions can impose significant economic pressure on Iran, some of the harmful effects may be alleviated through adjustment processes such as increasing non-oil exports (as suggested in Chap. 8). This adjustment process can be interrupted when banking sanctions are taken into account. In the final chapter, Mohammad Mohammadi Khabbazan and Mohammad Reza Farzanegan examine this effect on Iranian household welfare. Using a stylized computable general equilibrium model, they simulate recently imposed banking sanctions against Iran and investigate the effects of sanctions on both macro-indicators and the welfare of households. They further divide banking sanctions into three sub-banking sanctioning scenarios—export-only, import-only, and financial-only. Their main results show that banking sanctions have significant consequences in terms of pushing the country toward autarchy. As households experience welfare loss, the country faces inflation, a soaring exchange rate, and reductions in GDP. In addition, Iran's economy becomes inflexible when banking sanctions are tougher. In both urban and rural areas, higher-income households lose more welfare than lower-income households. Furthermore, decomposing the effects of banking sanctions shows that Iranian households are more vulnerable to bans on exports than to embargos on imports and foreign investments.

Notes

1. Article VIII of the Bylaws of Imam Khomeini Relief Foundation mentions the financial resources of the foundation as support from the supreme leader; allocated budget and assistance from the Islamic Republic Government; assistance and donations of people,

institutions, organizations, and foundations inside and outside the country; alms and other religious contributions; and income resulting from the economic activities of the organization foundation itself after the approval of the qualified authorities (IKRF 2016).

2. According to the World Bank's World Development Indicators, inflation in the first five years of war with Iraq was reduced significantly from 20.6 percent in 1980 to 4.3 percent in 1985 (World Bank 2016).
3. For example, Farzanegan (2009a) shows that, in the case of Iran, trade openness at the presence of low quality of institutions and lack of transparency can have negative consequences in terms of increased illegal trade.
4. Administrative and political corruption is suspected of playing a main role in such activities in Iran (see Sharq 2015; Iran Daily 2015). Yet, the scale of the problem is reflected in the speech delivered by Iran's Supreme Leader, Ayatollah Ali Khamenei, to environmental officials on March 8, 2015, quoted in Al-Monitor (2015): "It's painful that through cleverness or manipulating the law, and lately by buying off a few weak-minded officials in a certain institution, [its possible] to turn public wealth into personal wealth." He continued by adding that the "issue of land-grabbing has slowly turned into mountain-grabbing... When I see what is happening north of Tehran, one becomes very disappointed. I've talked about this issue many times to city and administration officials, and they've made efforts, but they need to act decisively."

References

Aghion, P., Caroli, E., & Garcia-Penalosa, C. (1999). Inequality and economic growth: The perspective of the new growth theories. *Journal of Economic Literature, 37*, 1615–1660.

Al-Monitor. (2015, March). Khamenei warns against destruction of Iran's forests. *Al-Monitor*. Retrieved April 24, 2016, from http://www.al-monitor.com/pulse/originals/2015/03/iran-land-grabbing-khamenei-environment.html#

Amuzegar, J. (1993). *Iran's economy under the islamic republic*. London: I.B. Tauris.

Becker, G. S., & Chiswick, B. R. (1966). Education and the distribution of earnings. *American Economic Review, 56*, 358–369.

Bénabou, R. (1996). Inequality and growth. *NBER Macroeconomics Annual, 11*, 11–74.

Berg, A., & Ostry, J. D. (2011). Inequality and unsustainable growth: Two sides of the same coin? IMF Staff Discussion Note 11/08. International Monetary Fund, Washington, DC.

Bjorvatn, K., & Selvik, K. (2008). Destructive competition: Factionalism and rent-seeking in Iran. *World Development, 36*(11), 2314–2324.

Carvalho, L., & Rezai, A. (2014). *Personal income inequality and aggregate demand.* Working Paper No. 2014-23. Department of Economics, University of São Paulo, São Paulo.

CBI [Central Bank of Iran]. (2015). Time series data tables. Retrieved December 5, 2015, from www.tsd.cbi.ir

Claessens, S., & Perotti, E. (2007). Finance and inequality: Channels and evidence. *Journal of Comparative Economics, 35*, 748–773.

Corak, M. (2013). Income inequality, equality of opportunity, and intergenerational mobility. *Journal of Economic Perspectives, 27*, 79–102.

Dabla-Norris, E., Kochhar, K., Suphaphiphat, N., Ricka, F., & Tsounta, T. (2015). Causes and consequences of income inequality: A global perspective. IMF Staff Discussion Note SDN/15/13. International Monetary Fund, Washington, DC.

Deragahi, B. (2008). Economists in Iran criticize Ahmadinejad. *Los Angeles Times.* Retrieved March 24, 2016, from http://articles.latimes.com/2008/nov/10/world/fg-iran10

Dolat-e Bahar. (2014). Dolatebahar news website. Retrieved March 25, 2016, from http://www.dolatebahar.com/print-31317.html

Ehteshami, A., & Zweiri, M. (2007). *Iran and the rise of its neoconservatives.* London: I.B.Tauris & Co Ltd.

Farzanegan, M. R. (2009a). Illegal trade in the Iranian economy: Evidence from structural equation model. *European Journal of Political Economy, 25*, 489–507.

Farzanegan, M. R. (2009b). *Macroeconomic of populism in Iran.* MPRA Paper No. 15546, Munich.

Farzanegan, M. R. (2012). Dark side of trade in Iran. In C. C. Storti & P. de Grauwe (Eds.), *Illicit trade and globalisation* (pp. 73–118). Cambridge, MA: MIT Press.

Farzanegan, M. R. (2013). Effects of international financial and energy sanctions on Iran's informal economy. *The SAIS Review of International Affair, 33*, 13–36.

Freeman, R. B. (2010). Does inequality increase economic output? In D. Grusky (Ed.), *Controversies about inequality.* Stanford, CA: Stanford University Press.

Galor, O., & Moav, O. (2004). From physical to human capital accumulation: Inequality and the process of development. *Review of Economic Studies, 71*, 1001–1026.

Greenwood, J., & Jovanovic, B. (1990). Financial development, growth, and the income distribution. *Journal of Political Economy, 98*, 1076–1107.

IKRF [Imam Khomeini Relief Foundation]. (2016). Official website of imam Khomeini relief foundation. Retrieved March 23, 2016, from http://www.emdad.ir/en/constitution.asp

Iran Daily. (2015, March 10). 15 officials arrested over land grab. *Iran Daily*. Retrieved April 27, 2016, from http://www.iran-daily.com/News/113566.html

Klebnikov, P. (2003). Millionaire mollahs. *Forbes Magazine* (July 21). Retrieved March 15, 2016, from http://members.forbes.com/global/2003/0721/024.html

Kumhof, M., Romain, R., & Pablo, W. (2015). Inequality, leverage, and crises. *American Economic Review, 105*, 1217–1245.

Lichbach, M. I. (1989). An evaluation of 'does economic inequality breed political conflict?' studies. *World Politics, 41*, 431–470.

Mehlum, H., Moene, K., & Torvik, R. (2006). Cursed by resources or institutions? *World Economy, 29*, 1117–1131.

Mincer, J. (1958). Investment in human capital and personal income distribution. *Journal of Political Economy, 66*, 281–302.

Nikou, S. (2010). Iran's subsidies conundrum. *Peace Brief*, 49, Washington, DC: United States Institute of Peace. Retrieved March 24, 2016, from http://purl.fdlp.gov/GPO/gpo36332

Okun, A. M. (1975). *Equality and efficiency: The big trade-off.* Washington, DC: Brookings Institution Press.

Salehi Esfahani, H., & Pesaran, M. H. (2009). The Iranian economy in the twentieth century: A global perspective. *Iranian Studies, 42*, 177–211.

Salehi-Isfahani, D. (2009). Poverty, inequality, and populist politics in Iran. *Journal of Economic Inequality, 7*(1), 5–28.

Schneider, F., & Enste, D. (2000). Shadow economies: Size, causes, and consequences. *Journal of Economic Literature, 38*, 77–114.

SCI [Statistical Center of Iran]. (2015). Excel data tables on literacy. Retrieved August 24, 2015, from www.amar.org.ir

Sharq. (2015). Nam-e zamin-kharan azhar men al-shams ast [Names of the land grabbers are known to everyone]. *Sharq*, No. 2257. Retrieved April 27, 2016, from http://www.magiran.com/npview.asp?ID=3126211 (in Persian).

Stiglitz, J. E. (2012). *The price of inequality: How today's divided society endangers our future.* New York: W.W. Norton & Company, Inc..

WEF [World Economic Forum]. (2015). Outlook on the global agenda 2015. Retrieved April 26, 2016, from http://reports.weforum.org/outlook-global-agenda-2015/

World Bank. (2016). World development indicators. Retrieved March 5, 2016, from http://data.worldbank.org/data-catalog/world-development-indicators

CHAPTER 2

Iran's Post-revolutionary Social Justice Agenda and Its Outcomes: Evolution and Determinants of Income Distribution and Middle-Class Size

Pooya Alaedini and Hamid R. Ashrafzadeh

Introduction

A major part of the discourse associated with Iran's 1979 Revolution revolved around rising economic inequality and the goal of social justice in the name of the lower strata of the society (Parsa 1989: 82–85; Nowshirvani and Clawson 1994: 229; Behdad 1996: 99; Amuzegar 2014: 66). At the same time, the middle class had a leading role (Amirahmadi 1990: 1–9) or at least a significant presence (Keddie and Richard 2006: 222–225; Parsa 1989: 126–127; Ashraf and Banuazizi 1985: 25; Abrahamian 1982: 496–524) in the coalition of forces responsible for the revolutionary events. Against this background, our main concern in this chapter is to investigate how income distribution and the middle class have been affected since the Revolution.

P. Alaedini (✉)
Department of Social Planning, Faculty of Social Sciences, University of Tehran, Tehran, Iran

H.R. Ashrafzadeh
Institute for Trade Studies and Research, Tehran, Iran

M.R. Farzanegan, P. Alaedini (eds.), *Economic Welfare and Inequality in Iran*, DOI 10.1057/978-1-349-95025-6_2

We first describe the post-revolutionary government's social justice agenda and point out its overall mixed outcome. Based on the available evidence, we then highlight the relative stability of income distribution following its improvement in the first few post-revolutionary years. We next turn to Iran's middle class and examine its evolution through the Revolution and the post-revolutionary period. If defined in income terms and a global sense, the middle class has expanded since the Revolution despite a general stagnation of per capita incomes. The general picture that thus emerges is that whereas the post-revolutionary social and political economic structures have been less than conducive to improving the overall income distribution, they have helped the income middle class to expand. This prompts us in the second half of the chapter to employ an empirical model aimed at probing the determinants of both income distribution and size of the income middle class in Iran. Our analysis relates Iran's social, economic, and political structures through a simultaneous equation panel data model aimed at contributing to discussions on Iran's political economy.[1] The main variables defining the social structure are Gini coefficient, middle-class size in income terms, and urban population. The economic structure is particularly represented by a panel of manufacturing subsector variables as well as variables for the agriculture and service sectors and the macroenvironment. Furthermore, the government's role in the economy—including its current and development expenditures, the taxes it collects, the compensations it makes to its employees, and the oil revenues at its disposal to exert its authority—is taken to signify the political structure. By probing the interactions of these variables, we are able to show the complex relationship among Iran's social, economic, and political structures and especially highlight the negative role of urbanization and the positive role of human capital as influencing both income distribution and size of the income middle class.

Post-revolutionary Social Justice Agenda and Its General Outcomes

The Constitution of the Islamic Republic of Iran is highly reflective of the major slogans of the 1979 Revolution concerning social justice and the cause of the downtrodden (*mostaz'afan*).[2] Its preamble states that the government's responsibility is to create "equal opportunities" and "work for all." Under its Article 3, a main duty of the government is declared as "planning for a just economic system" that provides for general welfare, eliminates poverty, and ends deprivation in terms of food, shelter, work, healthcare, and social safety. Furthermore, Article 43 of the Constitution calls for the provision of basic amenities for all citizens, including "shelter, food, clothing, medical treatment, education, and the necessary means for the establishment of a family" as well as "employment opportunities for everyone." Although, Chapter IV of the Constitution on the Economy and Financial Affairs does not give enough clues as to how the above goals would be achieved, in practice the Iranian government (as well as a number of para-governmental revolutionary foundations) has carried out an array of programs, especially as part of its five-year national plans and annual budgets (Amirahmadi 1990: 99–131; Mofid 1987), to provide the types of services and opportunities envisaged in the Constitution. These measures have included the provision of social services—especially education, healthcare, and social insurance—as well as significant subsidies and transfers on housing, food, and energy. Public policy orientation from the early revolutionary years through the Iran-Iraq War, postwar reconstruction efforts, and several contrasting presidential terms has not been immune to swings between left-leaning statist and right-leaning mercantile tendencies (Pesaran 2011). Nor have various measures carried out by successive post-revolutionary administrations been without significant strategic, planning, and implementation management shortcomings. Yet, social justice has endured as a major public policy goal to feature prominently in the "2025 Vision Document of the Islamic Republic" (Majles 2003), which further highlights "appropriate income distribution," "equal opportunities," and "poverty alleviation." As such, social justice has also remained a political issue on which Iran's competing ruling factions have often capitalized to gain popular support.

For example, President Mahmoud Ahmadinejad (2005–2013) ran on a platform of compassion (*mehrvarzi*), and his administration was adamant about initiating several significant socioeconomic projects—at least two of which aimed directly at social justice. One has been named "Justice Shares" (*saham-e edalat*). It has provided shares of government-owned companies to low-income strata in pursuit of "relative economic justice," "balanced wealth distribution," "generation of long-term income for low-income households," and so on (IPO 2016). While the shares have been granted to a wide range of beneficiaries and not just low-income groups, they may not be traded and the fate of the program is at best unclear under the current administration. Another scheme, dubbed "Compassion Housing" (*maskan-e mehr*), has entailed granting preferential housing finance and construction tax exemptions to homes constructed on designated public lands for low-income households (Alaedini and Fardanesh 2014: 52–54; MRUD 2016). Notwithstanding the various shortcomings of the scheme—including remoteness of designated locations from urban and employment centers, unaffordability to lowest income groups, lack of urban social services, and low-quality construction that are regularly featured in the Iranian press—a majority of its planned housing units have been delivered to applicants. Furthermore, despite the program's hardly bearable costs incurred to the government's troubling finances in recent years, President Rouhani's administration has reluctantly committed to the delivery of the rest of the housing units while also considering an alternative low-income housing program for the future (MRUD 2015).

Large-scale and largely untargeted subsidies and transfers have been a prominent feature of Iran's post-revolutionary economy and a major reflection of the government's social justice agenda. For instance, between 1999 and 2009, subsidies and transfers accounted for an annual average of 31.5 percent of public expenses (World Bank 2015). This said, reforming the subsidy system in Iran has also been a major policy goal of the government. A bill was approved by Iran's Islamic Consultative Assembly in 2010 to initiate subsidy reforms covering a number of items—particularly energy. Indeed, energy subsidies are believed to have encouraged waste and diverted investment in oil and gas production to consumption (IMF 2010). They further tend to benefit the well-to-do with higher consumption rates as compared to the lower-income strata of the society. Thus, another important scheme, also initiated originally during President Ahmadinejad's tenure, has comprised replacing part of the energy subsidies by yet another untargeted social program entailing direct cash transfers to every Iranian citizen. This scheme has placed tremendous pressures on the public budget and has been criticized for being wasteful, for not directly focusing on reduction of poverty or on improving income distribution, and for potentially having a range of negative economic and social impacts (ILSS 2013). Yet, the current administration has chosen to continue the transfers albeit with a very small reduction in the erstwhile universal pool of beneficiaries. The Rouhani administration is further striving to expand the coverage of the social security system and to unify its structure (which comprises both governmental and para-governmental actors).

There have been significant improvements in a number of development indicators in Iran since the Revolution, and their connection to the government's social programs cannot be downplayed. There was a strong emphasis on rural development in the initial post-revolutionary years, which resulted in the improvement of service delivery to Iran's disparate villages (Shakoori 2001: 71–77). The percentage of rural households with access to piped water and electricity increased from low- to mid-teens at the time of the Revolution to close to 90 and 99 percent, respectively, by 2004—in turn resulting in dramatic rises in ownership rates for refrigerators, television sets, and other household appliances as well as in health indicators (Salehi-Isfahani 2009b: 19). Life expectancy at birth has improved greatly in both rural and urban areas—increasing from 54.1 to 75.4 years between 1980 and 2014 (UNDP 2015). Literacy rates for women and men also experienced respectable rises and closed their gap while the mean number of school years increased from 2.3 to 8.2 between 1980 and 2014 (Ibid.). The expansion of Iran's tertiary education has been much more dramatic both in absolute and comparative international terms. For example, enrollment in institutions of higher education increased from 1,284,668 in 1995 to 4,8040,37 eight years later in 2013 (SCI 2015).

Rapid population growth (resulting in a very young population) and urbanization since the Revolution may have shared the positive influences on some of the above outcomes, but population pressure in the cities is also likely to have limited the wider economic impact of the improvements. According to figures from the Statistical Center of Iran (SCI 2015), the country's population grew from 33.7 million to 75.1 million between 1977 and 2012 (at an average annual rate of 2.32 percent). In the same period, Iran's urban population rose from 15.85 million to 53.65 million (at an average annual rate of 3.54 percent) and the number of cities with more than 100,000 inhabitants increased to over 80 (Ibid.). Economic and urban policies have not been able to keep up with these extraordinary developments. Despite large-scale urban land allocations by the government after the Revolution, the price of land and housing continued to rise and shelter affordability for low-income families deteriorated—a trend continued to this day even with the housing scheme mentioned above (MRUD 2015). Unable to afford housing inside the city proper, especially across larger urban areas, poor households—including migrants from rural areas and smaller towns—have found shelter in informal settlements and other types of slums. It is now estimated that close to 10 million persons in Iran live in urban informal settlements, where a range of social and urban services may be missing (Alaedini 2015).

Significant unemployment and underemployment as well as very low rates of labor force participation—especially for the youth, women, and recent college graduates—have also become a permanent feature of the Iranian economy, and their sheer magnitude is creating a serious crisis in the recent period (see Fig. 2.1). Yet, social security programs and especially the cash transfer scheme mentioned above may have alleviated the extreme poverty of those simultaneously lacking assets and jobs. Available evidence indeed generally suggests that poverty has declined in the post-revolutionary period and is below the average of comparable developing countries (Salehi-Isfahani 2009a; Salehi-Isfahani 2009b: 16–17), which is attributable to the types of policies mentioned above. Table 2.1 provides the World Bank's figures on poverty headcount and gap in Iran in the last two decades, which suggest respectable declines in poverty rates. However, high unemployment

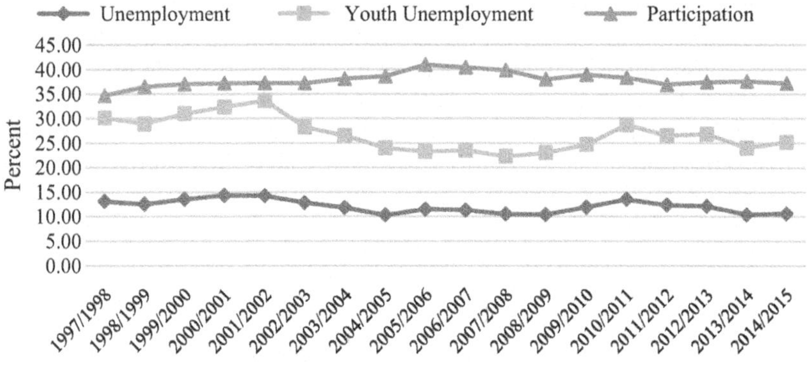

Fig. 2.1 Rates of unemployment, youth unemployment, and labor force participation. *Source*: Statistical Center of Iran, Time series data, 2015

Table 2.1 Poverty headcount and gap in Iran

Year	*1986*	*1990*	*1994*	*1998*	*2005*	*2009*	*2013*
Poverty headcount ratio at $3.10 a day (2011 PPP) (% of population)	17.6	17.03	11.61	11.52	11.17	3.05	0.66
Poverty headcount ratio at $1.90 a day (2011 PPP) (% of population)	5.84	5.32	2.28	2.21	2.61	0.26	0.08
Poverty gap at $3.10 a day (2011 PPP) (%)	5.31	5.05	2.8	2.76	2.78	0.54	0.12
Poverty gap at $1.90 a day (2011 PPP) (%)	1.33	1.34	0.44	0.35	0.54	0.05	0.03

Source: World Bank, World Development Indicators (2015)

and low labor force participation rates severely restrict opportunities—for individuals by seriously affecting their livelihoods and hampering their upward mobility and for the national economy as a whole by negatively affecting growth potentials and per capita incomes. It is no surprise then that the highest post-revolutionary per capita figure, registered in 2011 at US $3758 (in constant 2005 prices), was only 80 percent of its 1977 level just prior to the Revolution (World Bank 2015).

Industrialization and especially manufacturing export promotion have constituted a major area of emphasis in Iran's post-revolutionary plans with the aim to reduce the country's over-reliance on oil exports that could also potentially reduce unemployment, raise stagnant per capita incomes, and positively impact the income structure of the society. The First and Second Five-year Economic, Social, and Cultural Development Plans of the Islamic Republic (adopted in 1990 and 2004, receptively)[3] called for efforts to increase the share of non-oil commodities in total exports by providing export incentives and streamlining the procedures—which resulted in the establishment of the Export Guarantee Fund of Iran (EGFI 2016) among other institutions. Furthermore, the Third Development Plan Law (adopted in 2000) dedicates five of its nine articles on industry, mine, and commerce to the promotion of non-oil exports. The Fourth and the Fifth Plans (adopted in 2005 and 2011, respectively) have also given special attention to the goal of non-oil exports. While experiencing much fluctuation, the export value of manufactured products from Iran, which stood at US$606 million right after the Iran-Iraq War in 1988–1989, indeed began to increase and reached its highest level in 2011–2012 (Persian calendar year 1390) at US$29.1 billion (CBI 2015). It thus grew at an average rate of 18.2 percent during the period from 1988–1989 through 2011–2012 (this figure has been reduced in the last three years most likely due to the impact of sanctions). Yet, the monetary value of Iran's manufacturing exports has been dominated by upstream petrochemicals, whose production is highly capital-incentive and its direct employment impact and by extension positive income distribution effects are likely to be small.

Inequality After the Revolution

There were significant shifts in fortunes as a result of the 1979 Revolution. Nowshirvani and Clawson's (1994) findings are thus not surprising, which indicate that Iran's income disparities narrowed in the immediate aftermath of the event—especially in urban areas. According to their calculations

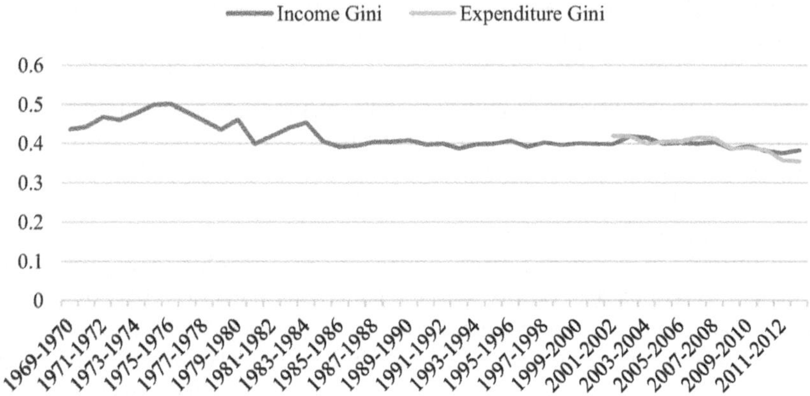

Fig. 2.2 Inequality trends in Iran in terms of Gini. *Source*: Income Gini from CBI (2015); Expenditure Gini from SCI (2014)

based on the household expenditure surveys of the Statistical Center of Iran, those in the four bottom expenditure deciles increased their share of total expenditures to such an extent that it more than offset the overall falling average expenditures (with the top two deciles conversely experiencing a significant decline in their share of total expenditures). Examining trends in Iran through 2005, Salehi-Isfahani (2009a) reports a relatively stable level of inequality—with an expenditure Gini in the 0.43–0.45 range—following an initial post-revolutionary decline. He uses general entropy measures to further probe income differences at the tail of distributions, which reveal that the initial post-revolutionary decline in inequality was due to an upper-tail compression presumably caused by upheavals affecting the top section of the society most negatively.

Time series for a few inequality measures are available from the Central Bank of Iran and the Statistical Center of Iran that run through the last decade. The graphs in Fig. 2.2 are drawn based on CBI's (2015) 1969–2012 income Gini figures and SCI's (2014) 2001–2012 expenditure Gini data. Furthermore, Fig. 2.3 depicts two graphs based on data from CBI and SCI on the share of highest income/expenditure deciles divided by the share of the lowest income/expenditure decile. These graphs show the same general trends, that is, initial post-revolutionary decline of inequality, its relative stability thereafter, and a slight decline in inequality in the last years of the period ending in 2012.

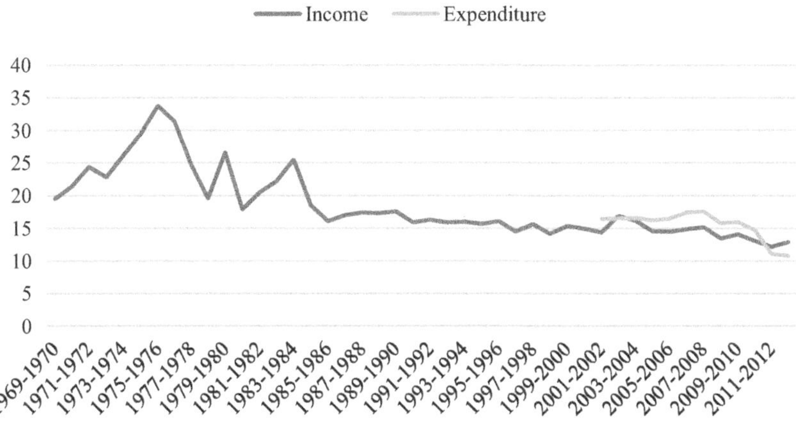

Fig. 2.3 Income/expenditure share of highest decile divided by income/expenditure share of lowest decile. *Source*: Income data from CBI (2015); Expenditure data from SCI (2014)

Iran's Middle Class Through the Revolution

The genesis and development of the middle class in Iran has been treated in a few studies (e.g., Bill 1963; Adibi 1975; Ashraf and Banuazizi 1985; Eyvazi 2001; Liaghat 1980; Keddie and Richard 2006). They commonly refer to a traditional stratum and a modern stratum in the Iranian middle class prior to the Revolution. For example, Liaghat (1980) draws a distinction between the "new middle class" and the "old middle class." The former is said to have been made up of craftsmen, artisans, small farmers, small producers, self-employed professionals, and so on (i.e., the petty bourgeoisie) and the latter to have comprised professionals and technocrats (emerging as a result of industrialization and modern education). As mentioned in the introduction, the middle class has generally been identified as a leading or at least an important force in the movement that carried out the 1979 Revolution. Amirahmadi (1990), for instance, calls the 1979 event a Third World "middle class revolution" with a "cross-class ideology," which as such had a "limited transforming potential."

Studies available on the middle class after the 1979 Revolution also distinguish between its two strata—modern and traditional (e.g., Bashiriyeh 2002; Rabbani 2006; Rabiee 2011; Keshavarz 2011; Rajabloo and Tahmasebi 2011; Masodnia and Mohammadifar 2011). These studies generally suggest that the religious component of the 1979 revolutionary coalition with roots in the old middle class managed to outcompete liberal nationalists and leftists originating in the modern middle class. For example, Masodnia and Mohammadifar (2011) assert that members of the modern middle class—comprising persons with a middle societal position, a high level of education, and a modern cultural outlook—were pushed and kept outside Iran's post-revolutionary ruling political structure. It is true that the post-revolutionary government tried to promote the sociopolitical culture of the traditional middle class based on its own roots. Yet, the modern middle-class/traditional middle-class dichotomy has not remained static through the post-revolutionary period either. The position of those with more education certainly deteriorated in the immediate aftermath of the Revolution in Iran. As Nowshirvani and Clawson (1994: 251) show (based on urban households' expenditure and income survey data from the Statistical Center of Iran), the likelihood for those with university education to fall in the bottom four income deciles was six times higher in 1985 as compared to 1977. Similarly, the number of government employees, which was 849,085 persons right after the Revolution, experienced some reductions through 1986 due to widespread purges and early retirements. But it rose rapidly thereafter to reach the figure of 2,147,195 persons (including those with either permanent or renewable contracts) by 2006 (SCI 2015). Rajabloo and Tahmasebi's (2011) study, which examines occupational stratification data, provides further empirical evidence for the reassertion of the professional and technocratic elements of the middle class between the first and second post-revolutionary decades. Thus, through creating new groups of bureaucrats and technocrats (as well as modern businessmen) out of some members of the traditional, lower middle, and lower classes—aided especially by the rapid expansion of the tertiary educational system as suggested earlier—the post-revolutionary government has also given impetus to the growth of a modern middle class.

In the private sector, the number of small-scale stores, associated with petty bourgeoisie, also witnessed a steep rise after the Revolution. The number of retail and wholesale workshops with 5 or fewer workers more than doubled between 1986 and 2002 from 706,466 to 1,456,131, whereas the number of those employing more than 50 workers declined from 439 to 371 during the same period (SCI 1988, 2003). These developments may have been influenced by rapid urbanization on the one hand and the social roots of the post-revolutionary cadre in the traditional bazar and petty bourgeoisie on the other. They nonetheless point to the expansion of the middle class. Furthermore, as suggested earlier, public-sector subsidies and transfers have been more likely to benefit the middle class. For example, large-scale public-sector land allocations in urban areas are believed to have benefited mostly government employees (who would be in the best position to access government-allocated land by establishing housing cooperatives), those with connections, and the middle class (World Bank 2004: 61; Ehsani 2009: 61). Yet, as the price of urban land and housing has soared dramatically in the past decades (MRUD 2015), access to them by itself could shift the standing of some households from the lower to the middle class through its wealth effect.

Behdad and Nomani (2009) probe the dynamics of Iranian social classes through three periods—1976–1986, 1986–1996, and 1996–2006. They associate the first period, coinciding with the first post-revolutionary decade, with the disruption of capitalist relations. According to them, the class structure in the latter two periods reveals a reversal, which they call "de-involution." They employ a decomposition technique to differentiate between changes resulting from structural reconfiguration of classes and those stemming from increases in the absolute size of the labor force. Their definition of the middle class is quite narrow and includes only those who work—with some authority and autonomy—in administrative-managerial and professional-technical positions for the state or the private sector. Thus, in their analysis, part of the middle class in terms of income is actually included under either petty bourgeoisie or the capitalists or political (including military and paramilitary) functionaries. Despite this, some of their findings shed light on the middle class as a whole. Their calculations show that, in the first period, the number of middle-class employees of the private sector declined, whereas the number of those belonging to the categories of middle-class employees of the state and petty bourgeoisie grew in absolute and relative terms. The number of traditional capitalists, a large part of whom actually would fall in the middle class in terms of income, also increased. Political functionaries grew rapidly in number, a large part of whom belonged to the military and paramilitary forces engaged in the Iran-Iraq War. These increases absorbed a significant portion of the working class whose share of employment declined significantly. Yet, in the second period, the growth rate of the middle-class employees in the private sector bounced back. In the category of petty bourgeoisie, only the modern stratum continued to grow. Furthermore, with the end of the Iran-Iraq War, the size of military and paramilitary forces in the category of political functionaries shrank significantly. However, the number of middle-class

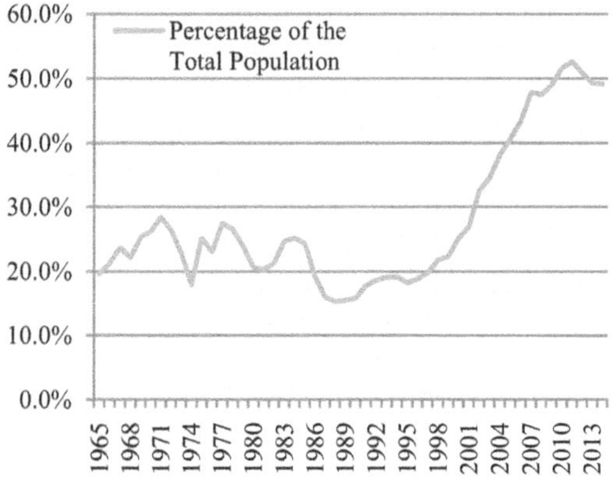

Fig. 2.4 Iran's income middle class as percentage of the total population. *Source*: Data from Brookings Institution (2015), Development, aid and governance indicators

employees of the state increased. All in all, their analysis hints at the growth of the middle class through both periods, with an emphasis on its traditional stratum in the first and its modern stratum in the second period.

Available evidence further indicates the expansion of the middle class in terms of income throughout the post-revolutionary period. We have drawn Fig. 2.4 using middle-class data from the Development, Aid and Governance Indicators of the Brookings Institution (2015). It has defined the income middle class in absolute terms and globally, by using US$10 per day (2005 Purchasing Power Parity (PPP)) for its lower bound and US$100 (2005 PPP) for its upper limit. This definition with an upper bound of US$100 (2005 PPP) includes persons who may be considered rich locally, but has the advantage of being both a global and absolute measure. The graph shows that despite stagnant per capita incomes and stability of inequality in Iran as suggested earlier, the defined income middle class has continually expanded after the Iran-Iraq War.

Potential Factors Influencing Income Distribution and Size of the Middle Class

In this section, we briefly review potential economic and social factors influencing the size of the income middle class and inequality in order to develop our empirical model to test for some of them in the case of Iran.

A relatively large body of literature on income distribution has been preoccupied with the growth-inequality debate—as initiated by Kuznets (1955)—across advanced and developing countries. The Gini coefficient for income or consumption is employed as the most common measure of inequality (e.g., Deininger and Squire 1998; Barro 2000). A few of such studies have also been conducted for the case of Iran. For example, using an endogenous growth model and Iranian development and income distribution data through 2008, Bakhtiari et al. (2010) examine the impact of income distribution on economic growth in the country to show that inequality hinders economic growth, while economic growth has positive effects on employment, investment spending, technological progress, and human capital.

A smaller number of studies have been concerned, wholly or partially, with the determinants of inequality in developing countries. Focusing on a single country, Blejer and Guererro's (1990) empirical study indicates that income distribution worsens due to inflation, underemployment, and government spending and improves by gains in productivity, real interest rate, and real exchange rate. Better income distribution has also been correlated with more democratic regime types (an early review of this literature may be found in Sirowy and Inkeles 1990). Bourguignon and Morrison's (1998) cross-country study highlights macroeconomic dualism—proxied by the ratio of labor productivity in agriculture to that of the rest of the economy—as a major determinant of country differences in income distribution. Treating five Latin American countries, Jiménez and Ruedi (1998) examine income distribution among urban households and identify some of the major sources of income inequality as lower employment remuneration due to educational access disparities, higher unemployment rates, and lower labor force participation rates as well as predominance of certain demographic characteristics among the lowest income deciles. Criticizing econometric studies concerned with institutional determinants of income distribution for not considering a more complete range of factors, Durham (1999) specifically provides empirical evidence for a relationship between fiscal federalism and equitable income distribution. Li et al. (2000) show that inequality is high with low as well as high levels of corruption. Odedokun and Round (2004) use data for 35 African countries to identify the attained level of economic development, regional factors, size of government budget and its share allocated to subsidies and transfers, phase of economic cycle, share of agricultural sector in total labor force, and human and land resources endowment as affecting income distribution.

The causal relationship between the main development variables and inequality is likely to be bidirectional as the original Kuznets' paper also implicitly suggested. That is, some of the determinants of inequality may in turn affect income distribution. Recognizing this, Fielding and Torres (2005) employ a set of simultaneous equations and cross-country data to show the complex interactions of income inequality with a number of social and economic development variables—including per capita income, average educational level, average level of health, per capita physical capital stock, factor efficiency, cost of investment in education (net of its consumption benefits), cost of investment in health (net of its consumption benefits), interest rate, institutional indicators, per capita natural resource stock, ethno-linguistic diversity, cultural characteristics, and mean annual temperature. Their study indicates that the causal relationship between improvements in income distribution and other development variables runs from income inequality to average income and life expectancy.

Unlike the case of inequality for which a number of well-known measures—especially the Gini coefficient—have been widely employed, the middle class has been defined in broader social, cultural, and economic terms. Sociocultural definitions notwithstanding, relative economic measures have been used especially to track the shifting shares of the middle-class income over time. Absolute measures, which can be employed to determine the size of the middle class, have been suggested using various definitions (e.g., Banerjee and Duflo 2008; Birdsall 2007; Bussolo et al. 2009; Kharas and Gertz 2010; Kharas 2010). The measure used by Kharas and Gertz (2010) and Kharas (2010), employs US$10 per day (2005 PPP) for the lower bound which is the poverty line in the poorest advanced countries and US$100 (2005 PPP) for the upper limit which is twice the median income of the richest advanced countries. Earlier, we provided the graphical representation of the middle-class data for Iran using this measure (based on data from Brookings Institution 2015).

As distinct from inequality, the middle class has been highlighted for both positively influencing and being positively influenced by economic development. All developed countries have large middle classes now, while it has been observed that the early expansion of the middle class gave impetus to industrialization (Landes 1998: 217–218). A number of studies have shown that a small middle class impacts growth negatively (e.g., Galor and Zeira 1993; Alesina and Rodrik 1994; Presson and Tabellini 1994). Easterly (2001) emphasizes the relationship between growth on the one hand and size of the middle class and its share of income on the other. It has also been argued that without a large enough middle class, it is unlikely to escape the middle-income trap (Kharas and Gertz 2010; Kharas 2010). Poverty may also be reduced by the expansion of the middle class (Ravallion 2009). The middle class has been further identified with entrepreneurial activities as well as accumulation of human capital and savings (Banerjee and Duflo 2008).

This brief review underscores the lack of a specific model in the literature to describe the determinants of income distribution or size of the middle class. Yet, a number of factors have been treated in the literature as impacting income distribution that may be potentially considered for the size of the middle class as well. These include macroeconomic and labor market indicators, productivity and efficiency measures, sectoral outputs, subsidies and transfers, and human capital measures as well as land and mineral resources endowments and institutional factors such as political regime, cultural characteristics, and ethno-linguistic diversity—the latter group being more suited for cross-country rather than single-country analyses. The choice of factors to include in any empirical model of the determinants of inequality and size of the middle class in a developing country like Iran should nonetheless be determined through insight and justification on the one hand and the availability of data on the other.

Empirical Model and Data

We now suggest an empirical model to probe the drivers of both income distribution and size of the middle class in Iran. While our variable choices are greatly constrained by time series data availability, our model allows us to probe the interaction of a number of social and political economic variables directly relevant to our analysis. The model consists of a system of four simultaneous equations. Dependent variables in the first two equations are income inequality and size of the income middle class, respectively, which constitute our main concern in the model. For income inequality, we employ the Gini coefficient which—despite some of its disadvantages (see Cowell 2011; Atkinson 1983)—has been widely used and for which time series data are readily available for Iran. For the size of the income middle class, we employ the Brookings Institution (2015) Development, Aid and Governance Indicators' data and definition—between US$10 per day (2005 PPP) and US$100 (2005 PPP).

We further view rapid population growth and urbanization as central to Iran's socioeconomic development dynamics. As mentioned, Iran's total population, urban population, and number of cities with more than 100,000 residents have grown rapidly since the Revolution. With an increasing population in ever-expanding urban areas, more people have gained access to better services, higher-paying occupations, and further social, cultural, and economic opportunities. Yet, since access to these benefits is uneven, income distribution and the size of the middle class are likely to have been impacted by them differently. Thus, apart from including total population among our independent variables, we have specified an additional equation for urban population in the model as an endogenous variable. Furthermore, home- and land-ownership in larger cities often constitute major wealth, especially as their prices have increased steadily in Iran over the years. Yet, the expansion of informal settlements may be an indication of unaffordability of housing to the urban poor and unequal access to public-sector land and housing schemes. To probe these effects, we have included the price of urban land as an independent variable in our model. As cost of food in addition to shelter comprises a major part of household expenditures for lower-income households, food price inflation is also introduced as an independent variable in our model.

As a major factor potentially influencing both income distribution and size of the middle class, human capital is proxied by education expenditure and number of high school students. While educational opportunities have expanded steadily in Iran since the Revolution, their effects on income distribution and the size of the middle class are likely to be mixed. For one thing, the two-digit unemployment rates—also included in our model as an independent variable—and low rates of labor force participation have possibly checked the impact of improving human capital. Human capital in our model is augmented with the number of patents as a measure of knowledge capital. We capture the monetary system effects by including one- and five-year interest rates (invoking consumption and investment purposes, respectively), ratio of liquidity (M2) to nominal GDP as a measure of financial depth, and amount of loans provided to the private sector among the independent variables in our model. The effects of trade openness—measured by sum of exports and imports divided by GDP—and oil exports are also considered in our model. Moreover, two independent variables are also introduced for the agricultural sector, namely, agricultural value added and ratio of agricultural value added to land area under cultivation as a measure of land productivity. The effect of the service sector is further taken into account by including its value added. As time series for subsidies and transfers are lacking, we have proxied their effect by including the price of gasoline, which has been targeted by the government for subsidy reform. We consider this as a rough but good proxy, since a number of occupations, including an array of petty jobs and by expansion livelihoods, involve the use and depend on the price of gasoline. Yet, the government's influence on the model's dependent variables is further probed by including the total compensation to government employees as a proxy for public-sector employment. Three other important parameters included for the government in the model are current expenditures, development expenditures, and tax receipts.

The last equation in our model is specified for manufacturing exports. Its promotion has been a major focus of Iran's national development plans, with the assumption that increasing exports would lead to economic development, higher welfare levels, and social justice. We have assembled our large panel data covering the period 1996–2013 by using information on Iran's manufacturing subsectors—available for 101 four-digit ISIC (International Standard Industrial Classification) codes—including export value, number of firms, value added, labor force size, and wage. Information on manufacturing export values for the 101 subsectors is from Iran's Customs Administration (after converting HS classification into ISIC), while the rest of our manufacturing data are from the Survey of Manufacturing Establishments conducted by the Statistical Center of Iran.

The model is specified below while definitions and data sources for the variables are given in Table 2.2:

$$(1)\ \text{lgini}_t = \alpha_1\text{lexdreal}_{it} + \alpha_2\text{lcapexpr}_t + \alpha_3\text{lliqgdp}_t + \alpha_4\text{lagrvalad}_t + \alpha_5\text{lurbanpop}_t + \alpha_6\text{lpoptotal}_t + \alpha_7\text{lcompgov}_t + \alpha_8\text{lcurexp}_t + \alpha_9\text{lfdinf}_t + \alpha_{10}\text{lserval}_t + \alpha_{11}\text{lmid}_t + \alpha_{12}\text{ltradopn}_t + \alpha_{13}\text{loil}_t + \varepsilon_{1it}$$

$$(2)\ \text{lmid}_t = \beta_1\text{lcapexpr}_{it} + \beta_2\text{ll}_{it} + \beta_3\text{lwager}_{it} + \beta_4\text{lprod}_t + \beta_5\text{lagrvalad}_t + \beta_6\text{lexdreal}_{it} + \beta_7\text{lpoptotal}_t + \beta_8\text{lurbanpop}_t + \beta_9\text{ldevexp}_t + \beta_{10}\text{lcurexp}_t + \beta_{11}\text{lgini}_t + \beta_{12}\text{loil}_t + \beta_{13}\text{ltax}_t + \varepsilon_{2it}$$

$$(3)\ \text{lurbanpop}_t = \gamma_1\text{lcapexpr}_t + \gamma_2\text{lpatent}_t + \gamma_3\text{unemprate}_t + \gamma_4\text{lloan}_t + \gamma_5\text{lpland}_t + \gamma_6\text{lpoptotal}_t + \gamma_7\text{lagrvalad}_t + \gamma_8\text{lexdreal}_{it} + \gamma_9\text{lpgasoline}_t + \gamma_{10}\text{lgini}_{t\ +}\ \gamma_{11}\text{lcurexp}_t + \gamma_{12}\text{lcompgov}_t + \gamma_{13}\text{lmid}_t + \varepsilon_{3it}$$

$$(4)\ \text{lexdreal}_{it} = \varphi_1\text{lstudent}_t + \varphi_2\text{ln}_{it} + \varphi_3\text{intoney}_t + \varphi_4\text{intfivey}_t + \varphi_5\text{lgini}_t + \varphi_6\text{lurbanpop}_t + \varphi_7\text{lmid}_t + \varphi_8\text{ly}_{it} + \varepsilon_{4it}$$

The unbalanced panel data model allows us to probe interactions of the social structure—comprising income distribution, size of the middle class,

Table 2.2 Variable definitions and sources of data

Variable name	*Definition*	*Data source*
$lgini_t$	Log(1+Gini/100)	CBI (2015)
$lexdreal_{it}$	Logarithm of export values in real prices for 101 three-digit ISIC manufacturing subsectors (conversion made to ISIC from harmonized system—HS)	CAI (2015)
$lcapexpr_t$	Logarithm of total education expenditures in constant 2000 US dollars (adjusted using US consumer price index) divided by number of students	World Bank (2015)
$lliqgdp_t$	Logarithm of ratio of liquidity (M2) to nominal GDP as a measure of financial depth	CBI (2015)
$lagrvalad_t$	Logarithm of agriculture-sector value added in constant 2004–2005 (Persian calendar year 1383) Iranian rials	CBI (2015)
$lurbanpop_t$	Logarithm of urban population	World Bank (2015)
$lpoptotal_t$	Logarithm of total population	CBI (2015)
$lcompgov_t$	Logarithm of total compensation to government employees in Iranian rials	CBI (2015)
$lfdinf_t$	Logarithm of food price inflation	CBI (2015)
$lserval_t$	Logarithm of service-sector value added in constant 2004–2005 (Persian calendar year 1383) in Iranian rials	CBI (2015)
$ltradopn_t$	Logarithm of sum of non-oil exports and imports divided by GDP (all in Iranian rials) as a measure of trade openness	CBI (2015)
$loil_t$	Logarithm of oil exports value in current US dollars	CBI (2015)
$ldevexp_t$	Logarithm of government's development expenditures in Iranian rials	CBI (2015)
$lcurexp_t$	Logarithm of government's current expenditures in Iranian rials	CBI (2015)
$ltax_t$	Logarithm of government's total tax receipts in Iranian rials	CBI (2015)
$lmid_t$	Logarithm of number of persons with income between US \$10 per day (2005 PPP) and US\$100 (2005 PPP) as a measure of the size of the middle class	Brookings Institution (2015)
ll_{it}	Logarithm of labor force for 101 manufacturing subsectors	SCI (2015)
$lwager_{it}$	Logarithm of real wages for 101 manufacturing subsectors, calculated using workers' remuneration figures	SCI (2015)
$lprod_t$	Logarithm of ratio of agriculture-sector value added to land area under cultivation as a measure of agricultural land productivity	World Bank (2015)
$lpatent_t$	Logarithm of number of patents of residents as a measure of knowledge capital	World Bank (2015)
$unemprate_t$	Rate of unemployment	CBI (2015)
$lloan_t$	Logarithm of amount of loans provided to the private sector	CBI (2015)

(*continued*)

Table 2.2 (continued)

Variable name	*Definition*	*Data source*
$lpland_t$	Logarithm of average price of one square meter of urban land in Tehran	CBI (2015)
$lpgasoline_{it}$	Logarithm of price of gasoline	Ministry of Energy (2015)
$lstudent_t$	Logarithm of number of high school students as a measure of human capital	World Bank (2015)
ln_{it}	Logarithm of number of firms for 101 manufacturing subsectors as a measure of scale economies	SCI (2015)
$intoney_t$	One-year interest rate	CBI (2015)
$intfivey_t$	Five-year interest rate	CBI (2015)
ly_{it}	Logarithm of value added for 101 manufacturing subsectors	SCI (2015)
ε	Residuals	–

and urban population—with the government's role in the economy and manufacturing exports as the driving force of economic development.

Estimation Results

Our model has four endogenous variables, is overidentified, and has a large panel of variables for manufacturing subsectors. We employ 3SLS (three-stage least squares) and EC3SLS (error-component three-stage least squares) to estimate the model as a system of equations (Baltagi 2008). Thus, simultaneity, endoegeneity, heterogeneity, and cross-equation correlation are addressed. All variables are de-meaned so that fixed effects are removed from the system (Hsiao 2014). Estimation results are provided in Table 2.3.[4] We can safely accept the 3SLS results in which all variables are highly significant. The predominantly large *t*-statistics are associated with applying fitted values from first estimates on the other regressors.

Results concerning the first equation, specified for the Gini coefficient, indicate that population growth has the strongest positive effect on income distribution (reduces inequality the most). Conversely, urbanization has the strongest aggravating impact on inequality. These two findings together may indicate that rural-urban migrants face increasing challenges in realizing relative improvements in their means of subsistence in the cities. After total population, per capita education expenditures have the largest effect on reducing income inequality. As expected, the government's current

Table 2.3 3SLS and EC3SIS estimation results (T=18, N=101, sample period: 1996–2013)

Eq.	*Parameter*	*Coefficient symbol*	*Estimated coefficient*	*3SLS*		*EC3SLS*	
				t-*statistic*	P-*value*	t-*statistic*	P-*value*
Gini	$lexdreal_{it}$	α_1	−0.365805E-02	−38.4011	[0.000]	−4.32046	[0.000]
	$lcapexpr_t$	α_2	−0.595810	−48.7110	[0.000]	−5.48042	[0.000]
	$lliqgdp_t$	α_3	0.030759	137.075	[0.000]	15.4221	[0.000]
	$lagrvalad_t$	α_4	0.752707E-02	40.9647	[0.000]	4.60889	[0.000]
	$lurbanpop_t$	α_5	2.83905	117.588	[0.000]	13.2296	[0.000]
	$lpoptotal_t$	α_6	−3.82592	−116.429	[0.000]	−13.0993	[0.000]
	$lcompgov_t$	α_7	−0.649073E-02	−10.5440	[0.000]	−1.18629	[0.236]
	$lcurexp_t$	α_8	−0.019957	−94.2973	[0.000]	−10.6093	[0.000]
	$lfdinf_t$	α_9	0.015049	57.6346	[0.000]	6.48440	[0.000]
	$lserval_t$	α_{10}	−0.082831	−56.7888	[0.000]	−6.38924	[0.000]
	$lmid_t$	α_{11}	−0.032365	−25.0707	[0.000]	−2.82067	[0.005]
	$ltradopn_t$	α_{12}	0.364644E-02	32.7064	[0.000]	3.67975	[0.000]
	$loil_t$	α_{13}	0.662273E-02	115.011	[0.000]	12.9397	[0.000]
Middle class	$lcapexpr_{it}$	β_1	6.24364	14.3437	[0.000]	1.61379	[0.107]
	ll_{it}	β_2	1.00815	37.7776	[0.000]	4.25031	[0.000]
	$lwager_{it}$	β_3	0.392090	32.5931	[0.000]	3.66701	[0.000]
	$lprod_{it}$	β_4	−0.508851	−22.6178	[0.000]	−2.54470	[0.011]
	$lagrvalad_t$	β_5	0.917501	25.5950	[0.000]	2.87967	[0.004]
	$lexdreal_{it}$	β_6	0.178855	18.9597	[0.000]	2.13313	[0.033]
	$lpoptotal_t$	β_7	80.2163	18.5370	[0.000]	2.08558	[0.037]
	$lurbanpop_t$	β_8	−43.8491	−15.5379	[0.000]	−1.74815	[0.080]
	$ldevexp_t$	β_9	0.201523	34.8733	[0.000]	3.92355	[0.000]
	$lcurexp_t$	β_{10}	−0.312821	−30.8034	[0.000]	−3.46565	[0.001]
	$lgini_t$	β_{11}	−647.139	−22.6678	[0.000]	−2.55033	[0.011]
	$loil_t$	β_{12}	0.038641	15.4396	[0.000]	1.73709	[0.082]
	$ltax_t$	β_{13}	−0.077259	−27.7936	[0.000]	−3.12702	[0.002]

Urbanization	$lcapexpr_t$	γ_1	0.186154	298.229	[0.000]	33.5534	[0.000]
	$lpatent_t$	γ_2	0.485905E-03	98.3050	[0.000]	11.0602	[0.000]
	$unemprate_t$	γ_3	−0.637535E-03	−398.328	[0.000]	−44.8153	[0.000]
	$lloan_t$	γ_4	−0.281832E-02	−156.197	[0.000]	−17.5736	[0.000]
	$lpland_t$	γ_5	0.369321E-02	242.282	[0.000]	27.2589	[0.000]
	$lpoptotal_t$	γ_6	1.66646	1604.37	[0.000]	180.505	[0.000]
	$lagrvalad_t$	γ_7	0.013974	366.170	[0.000]	41.1973	[0.000]
	$lexdreal_{it}$	γ_8	0.133615E-02	281.256	[0.000]	31.6438	[0.000]
	$lpgasoline_{it}$	γ_9	−0.678618E-03	−142.624	[0.000]	−16.0464	[0.000]
	$lgini_t$	γ_{10}	0.496479	360.909	[0.000]	40.6054	[0.000]
	$lcurexp_t$	γ_{11}	0.405488E-02	567.681	[0.000]	63.8691	[0.000]
	$lcompgov_t$	γ_{12}	0.732672E-02	225.530	[0.000]	25.3741	[0.000]
	$lmid_t$	γ_{13}	−0.035696	−297.843	[0.000]	−33.5100	[0.000]
Man. exports	$lstudent_t$	φ_1	2.42102	24.7622	[0.000]	2.78596	[0.005]
	ln_{it}	φ_2	−2.51296	−27.4026	[0.000]	−3.08303	[0.002]
	$intoney_t$	φ_3	1.19786	37.9668	[0.000]	4.27160	[0.000]
	$intfivey_t$	φ_4	−0.951440	−39.0931	[0.000]	−4.39832	[0.000]
	$lgini_t$	φ_5	−39.9935	−27.0031	[0.000]	−3.03809	[0.002]
	$lurbanpop_t$	φ_6	−38.3559	−32.5256	[0.000]	−3.65942	[0.000]
	$lmid_t$	φ_7	10.9473	39.5284	[0.000]	4.44730	[0.000]
	ly_{it}	φ_8	1.47796	22.6138	[0.000]	2.54426	[0.011]

expenditure and compensation to its employees also reduce inequality, but the effect of the latter is relatively small. Somewhat surprisingly, our estimation results show that whereas service-sector value added and manufacturing exports positively influence income distribution, agriculture-sector value added aggravates inequality. The positive and negative effects of manufacturing exports and agriculture-sector value added on income distribution are both small. While activities across the three sectors may provide significant employment to lower-skilled workers, the adverse impact of value added associated with agriculture on inequality may hint at a higher level of unevenness in the distribution of benefits for this sector. As for the rest of the parameters in the first equation, increasing financial depth aggravates inequality, while trade openness, oil receipts, and food price inflation also have small negative impacts on income distribution. As expected, growth of the middle class and inequality move in the opposite direction.

As log(1+gini/100) gives very small values that are scaled to the large figures for the dependent variable in the model, estimation results for the second equation register an extremely large aggravating impact of inequality on size of the middle class. Aside from this, the largest positive influences on size of the middle class are from total population and per capita education expenditures. Yet, the increasing urban population has the most pronounced negative effect on size of the middle class. Urbanization may allow for higher levels of access to services, but the scarcity of decent-paying jobs and other barriers to opportunities in the cities may have more than offset this effect during the period under consideration. Curiously, whereas agriculture-sector value added acts relatively strongly to expand the middle class, higher productivity of agricultural land contracts it. A preliminary interpretation of the latter finding—which calls for additional investigation—is that increased productivity of land in rural areas is benefiting the rich. The positive impacts of employment, real wages, and exports of the manufacturing subsectors on middle-class size are relatively strong. Furthermore, the government's development and current expenditures have opposite influences on the size of the middle class, affecting it in positive and negative ways, respectively. In a similar way, the small effects of oil receipts and taxes on middle-class size are, respectively, positive and negative.

Urbanization, probed through the third equation of the model, is most positively affected by total population growth. Intriguingly, further impetus is given to urbanization by increased income inequality and a smaller income middle class as well as by higher urban land prices in a minor way.

Higher levels of agriculture-sector value added also influence urbanization positively. The effects of the rest of the independent variables on urbanization are relatively small. Urbanization is positively influenced by government employment and current expenditures as well as by education expenditures and number of patents, which proxy human and knowledge capital, respectively. Manufacturing exports and agriculture-sector value added also have positive effects on urbanization. Yet, loans provided to the private sector impact urbanization negatively. So do unemployment and higher gasoline prices, as expected.

Exports from manufacturing subsectors in the final equation are most positively (and expectedly) affected by the expansion of the middle class, reductions in income inequality, and increases in the number of students. In contrast, urbanization has a strong negative effect on exports—likely via increasing consumption at the expense of selling abroad. Furthermore, whereas value added associated with 101 manufacturing subsectors has a relatively strong positive influence on exports, higher numbers of manufacturing subsector firms reduce manufacturing export values through decreasing scale economies. One-year and five-year interest rates, associated with consumption and investment, respectively, also have somewhat strong impacts on exports. Whereas the former reduces the tendency to sell manufacturing goods abroad via its consumption effect, the latter enhances exports.

Discussion and Conclusion

In this chapter, we started out by underscoring the significance of the middle class in the Iranian Revolution. We further pointed out the continued prominence of a social justice agenda in the post-revolutionary government's policy initiatives carried out in the name of the downtrodden. These have comprised an array of service delivery programs as well as significant subsidies and transfers concerning healthcare, education, food, energy, and housing. We then showed that a number of development indicators relevant to the government's social justice agenda have indeed improved since the Revolution, including those related to health, education, municipal services, and poverty reduction. Yet, against the backdrop of rapid population growth and urbanization as well as government's efforts to promote industrialization and especially non-oil exports, we also cited major development shortcomings in terms of housing challenges and slum proliferation in urban areas, unemployment and low rates of labor force participation, and stagnant per capita incomes. Furthermore, we suggested untargeted subsidies and transfers, particularly those related to housing and energy, were likely to have a middle-class bias. Available evidence also shows that whereas income distribution has stayed more or less the same following an initial decline in the immediate aftermath of the Revolution, the size of the middle class has doubled through the post-revolutionary period.

We then empirically tested for the effects of a number of variables on income distribution and size of the middle class by employing four simultaneous equations that connected Iran's social, political, and economic structures. The Gini coefficient, size of the middle class, and urban population defined the main components of the social structure, while the economic structure was represented especially by a panel constructed for 101 manufacturing subsectors, but also agriculture and service sectors as well as a number of macrovariables. The government's role in the economy was probed through the inclusion of variables for public-sector employment, government's current and development expenditures, taxes, and oil receipts. The government exerts its political authority by way of these as its prerogative to reward or penalize certain individuals and segments of the society. The three structures whose relationship was examined through our model have profound implications for Iran's socioeconomic conditions including its income distribution, middle-class size, and urbanization trends. The results of our empirical analysis are interesting as well as encouraging in that they lead to a number of conclusions about Iran's social structure and political economy.

To begin with, improvements in income distribution strongly benefit the size of the middle class. Apart from this, an intriguing finding based on our estimation results concerns urbanization. Income distribution is most positively affected by population growth and most negatively influenced by urbanization. Urbanization also has a strong negative impact on middle-class size (as well as on exports), while a worsening income distribution and a shrinking middle class give impetus to urbanization. Interestingly enough, increasing agriculture-sector value added worsens income distribution as well. Furthermore, although increasing agriculture-sector value added has a moderately strong impact on expanding the middle class, increasing agricultural land productivity acts to reduce its size in a moderately strong way. This constitutes a feedback loop working through urbanization with highly negative socioeconomic consequences. Increasing income inequality accompanied by a structure of agricultural production disfavoring better income distribution increases urbanization. Higher unemployment rates only act weakly to curb urban population growth, whereas higher urban land prices have a positive—albeit minor—effect on urbanization. Yet, the growing urban population strongly acts to increase inequality which in turn gives impetus to further urbanization. Urbanization also has a strong negative impact on manufacturing exports, while lower manufacturing exports in turn curb urbanization in a relatively small way—which nonetheless translate into a worsening income distribution and a shrinking middle class directly as well as indirectly via higher levels of inequality. The price of gasoline has a minor role in checking urbanization and by extension income inequality.

The role of human capital is also worth highlighting separately. Its effects (as probed through per capita education expenditures) on expanding the middle class and lowering income inequality are strong and moderately strong, respectively. Human capital (as measured by the number of students) also has a relatively strong impact on manufacturing exports that in turn directly enhances income distribution and size of the middle class. It also enhances urbanization with indirect negative consequences for income distribution and size of the middle class. But these effects are rather small, as is the indirect negative impact of human capital on income distribution and size of the middle class resulting from increased urbanization via higher levels of manufacturing exports.

Thus far, we have highlighted the strong to moderate effects of total population growth, urbanization, and human capital on income distribution. We have also touched upon the relatively small positive effect of manufacturing exports as well as the minor negative (yet illuminating) influence of agriculture-sector value added on income distribution. Better income distribution and higher levels of exports have a direct bidirectional positive relationship—with the effect running from the latter to the former being quite strong (although urbanization plays a negative mediating role between manufacturing exports and income distribution in both ways). Service-sector value added also reduces income inequality with a moderate effect. Yet, trade openness and oil exports both have negative—although minor—impacts on income distribution. Increasing financial depth also aggravates income inequality in a small way. Furthermore, the direct influence of the government on reducing income inequality is relatively small through current expenditures and minor via public-sector employee compensation. The government's current expenditures even have a moderate impact on shrinking the middle class, although the government's development expenditures expand it. Aside from the influence of the government on the middle class as well as that of human capital and the agriculture sector highlighted earlier, manufacturing exports expand the middle class, while a growing middle class leads to increasing manufacturing exports. This bidirectional relationship is facilitated through increased manufacturing production as measured by value added and lower long-term interest rates presumably used for investment. Higher wages as well as higher employment levels across the manufacturing subsectors also expand the middle class with moderate effects. Finally, the relationship between urbanization and size of the middle class does not constitute a strong feedback loop similar to the case of income distribution. Although the size of the middle class is affected by urbanization directly, negatively, and strongly and is further reduced in a small indirect way via the negative impact of urbanization on income distribution and manufacturing exports, its growth has a small to moderate influence on reducing urbanization itself.

One shortcoming of our analysis concerning the government's role is lack of adequate information on subsidies and transfers. We introduced gasoline prices in our model as a rough proxy for subsidies and transfers for which we do not have data during the period under consideration. Yet, gasoline subsidies comprise only one part of the government's transparent as well as hidden subsidy package and have not proven particularly illuminating in our analysis. Furthermore, our analysis concerning the middle class could improve if time series data for the number of government employees as well as the number of retail stores were to become available. Finally, our only measure of inequality in this study has been the Gini coefficient while we have made use of a global definition of the income middle class with high lower and upper bounds. Employing additional inequality measures and trying out a carefully thought-of definition of the income middle class suited to Iran can further enhance the analysis.

Notes

1. Systematic discussions on Iran's political economy were initiated especially by Katouzian (1981) as well as Karshenas (1990).
2. English translations of the Constitution of the Islamic Republic of Iran may be accessed through the website of the World Bank's Financial Disclosure Law Library (http://publicofficialsfinancialdisclosure.worldbank.org/sites/fdl/files/assets/law-library-files/Iran_Constitution_en.pdf) as well as the website of WIPO (http://www.wipo.int/edocs/lexdocs/laws/en/ir/ir001en.pdf). See further Amuzegar (1993: 16–23), Nowshirvani and Clawson (1994: 230–231), and

Amirahmadi (1990: 99–101) for discussions on the post-revolutionary Constitution and its social justice agenda.

3. The Persian texts of all laws for Iran's first through fifth national plans are available through the website of Majles [Islamic Consultative Assembly] at http://rc.majlis.ir
4. Credit goes to the program provided by Clint Cummins, used with TSP 4.3.

References

Abrahamian, E. (1982). *Iran between two revolutions.* Princeton: Princeton University Press.

Adibi, H. (1975). *Jameashenasi-e tabaqat-e ejtemai* [Sociology of social classes]. Tehran: Faculty of Social Sciences, University of Tehran.

Atkinson, A. (1983). *The economics of inequality* (2nd ed.). Oxford: Clarendon Press.

Alaedini, P. (2015). CITIES vi. Urban informal settlements in modern Iran. *Encyclopædia Iranica*, online edition. Retrieved September 11, 2015, from http://www.iranicaonline.org/articles/cities-06-settlements

Alaedini, P., & Fardanesh, F. (2014). *From shelter to regeneration: Slum upgrading and housing policies in I.R. Iran.* Tehran: Urban Development and Revitalization Organization.

Alesina, A., & Rodrik, D. (1994). Distributive politics and economic growth. *Quarterly Journal of Economics, 108*, 465–490.

Amirahmadi, H. (1990). *Revolution and economic transition: The Iranian experience.* Albany: State University of New York Press.

Amuzegar, J. (1993). *Iran's economy under the islamic republic.* London: I.B. Tauris.

Amuzegar, J. (2014). *The islamic republic of Iran: Reflections on an emerging economy.* London: Routledge.

Ashraf, A., & Banuazizi, A. (1985). The state, classes and modes of mobilization in the Iranian revolution. *State, Culture, and Society, 1*(3), 3–40.

Bakhtiari, S., Meisami, H., & Soleimani, M. (2010). Income distribution and economic growth: Evidence from islamic republic of Iran. *Journal of Third World Studies, 27*(2), 135–147.

Baltagi, B. H. (2008). *Economic analysis of panel data* (4th ed.). West Sussex: John Wiley & Sons, Ltd.

Banerjee, A., & Duflo, E. (2008). What is middle class about the middle classes around the world? *Journal of Economic Perspectives, 22*(2), 3–28.

Barro, R. J. (2000). Inequality and growth in a panel of countries. *Journal of Economic Growth, 5*(1), 5–32.

Bashiriyeh, H. (2002). *Jame'ashenasi-e syasi—naqsh-e niruha-ye ejtemai dar zendegi-e syasi [Political sociology—Role of social forces in political life]*. Tehran: Nashr-e ney.

Behdad, S. (1996). The post-revolutionary economic crisis. In S. Rahnema & S. Behdad (Eds.), *Iran after the revolution: Crisis of an islamic state* (pp. 97–128). London: I.B. Tauris.

Behdad, S., & Nomani, F. (2009). What a revolution! Thirty years of social class reshuffling in Iran. *Comparative Studies of South Asia, Africa, and the Middle East, 29*(1), 84–104.

Bill, J. A. (1963). The social and economic foundations of power in contemporary Iran. *Middle East Journal, 17*(4), 400–418.

Birdsall, N. (2007). *Reflections on the macro foundations of the middle class in the developing world*. Working Paper No. 130. Center for Global Development, Washington, DC.

Blejer, M. I., & Guerrero, I. (1990). The impact of macroeconomic policies on income distribution: An empirical study of Philippines. *Review of Economics and Statistics, 72*, 414–423.

Bourguignon, F., & Morrisson, C. (1998). Inequality and development: The role of dualism. *Journal of Development Economics, 57*, 233–257.

Brookings Institution. (2015). Development, aid and governance indicators (developed by Kaufmann, Kharas and Penciakova). Retrieved September 15, 2015, from http://www.brookings.edu/research/interactives/development-aid-governance-indicators

Bussolo, M., De Hoyos, R. E., & Medvedev, D. (2009). The future of global income inequality. In A. Estache & D. Leipziger (Eds.), *Stuck in the middle: Is fiscal policy failing the middle class?* (pp. 54–74). Washington, DC: Brookings Institution Press.

CAI [Customs Administration of Iran]. (2015). Data tables for manufacturing export values.

CBI [Central Bank of Iran]. (2015). Time series data tables. Retrieved November 5, 2015, from www.tsd.cbi.ir

Cowell, F. (2011). *Measuring inequality* (3rd ed.). Oxford: Oxford University Press.

Deininger, K., & Squire, L. (1998). New ways of looking at old issues: Inequality and growth. *Journal of Development Economics, 57*(2), 259–287.

Durham, J. B. (1999). Econometrics of income distribution: Toward more comprehensive specification of institutional correlates. *Comparative Economic Studies, 41*(1), 43–74.

Easterly, W. (2001). The middle class consensus and economic development. *Journal of Economic Growth, 6*(4), 317–335.

EGFI [Export Guarantee Fund of Iran] (2016). EGFI website. Retrieved January 11, 2016, from egfi.ir

Ehsani, K. (2009). The urban provincial periphery in Iran: Revolution and war in Ramhormoz. In A. Gheissari (Ed.), *Contemporary Iran: Economy, society, politics* (pp. 38–76). Oxford: Oxford University Press.

Eyvazi, M.R. (2001). *Tabaqat-e ejtemai va rejim-e pahlavi* [Social classes and the Pahlavi regime]. Tehran: Markaz-e asnad-e enqelab-e eslami.

Fielding, D., & Torres, S. (2005). A simultaneous equation model of economic development and income inequality. *Journal of Economic Inequality, 4*(3), 279–301.

Galor, O., & Zeira, J. (1993). Income distribution and macroeconomics. *Review of Economic Studies, 60*(1), 35–52.

Hsiao, C. (2014). *Analysis of panel data*. Cambridge: Cambridge University Press.

ILSS [Institute for Labor and Social Security]. (2013). *Goftogu piramun-e yaraneha-ye naqdi* (collection of essays in response to a request made by Deputy Minister Ahmad Meydari for suggestions on the optimal reforms of the cash transfer program). Tehran: Ministry of Cooperatives, Labor, and Social Welfare.

IMF [International Monetary Fund]. (2010). IMF Country Report No. 10/74. Retrieved February 3, 2016, from http://www.imf.org/external/pubs/ft/scr/2010/cr1074.pdf

IPO [Iranian Privatization Organization]. (2016). Official information on "Justice Shares." Retrieved February 5, 2016, from http://ipo.ir/index.aspx?siteid=81&pageid=214

Jiménez, L. F., & Ruedi, N. (1998). *Determinants of inequality among urban households. CEPAL Review 66*. Santiago, Chile: UN-ECLAC.

Karshenas, M. (1990). *Oil, state, and industrialization in Iran*. Cambridge: Cambridge University Press.

Katouzian, H. (1981). *Political economy of modern Iran: Despotism and pseudo-modernism, 1962–1979*. New York: New York University Press.

Keddie, N. R., & Richard, Y. (2006). *Modern Iran: Roots and results of revolution*. New Haven: Yale University Press.

Keshavarz, B. (2011). Social classes and forces—Role and situation in Iran in 1981–2001. *[University of Tehran] Political Quarterly, 41*(3), 263–247. (in Persian).

Kharas, H. (2010). *The emerging middle class in developing countries*. Working Paper No. 285. OECD Development Centre, Paris.

Kharas, H., & Gertz, G. (2010). The new global middle class: A cross-over from West to East. In C. Li (Ed.), *China's emerging middle class: Beyond economic transformation* (pp. 32–53). Washington DC: Brookings Institute Press.

Kuznets, S. (1955). Economic growth and income inequality. *American Economic Review, 45*, 1–28.

Landes, D. (1998). *The wealth and poverty of nations*. New York: Norton.

Li, H., Xu, L. C., & Zou, H. (2000). Corruption, income distribution, and growth. *Economics & Politics, 12*(2), 155–182.

Liaghat, G. (1980). Changes in a new middle class through the analysis of census data: The case of Iran between 1956–1966. *Middle East Journal, 34*(3), 343–349.

Majles [Islamic Consultative Assembly]. (2003). Chashm-andaz-e jomhuri-e eslami-e Iran dar ofoq-e 1404-e hejri-e shamsi [2025 Vision Document of Islamic Republic of Iran]. Retrieved November 4, 2003, from http://rc.majlis.ir/fa/law/show/132295

Majles [Islamic Consultative Assembly]. (2016). Texts of five-year economic, social, and cultural development plans in the post-revolutionary period. Retrieved February 11, 2016, from http://rc.majlis.ir

Masodnia, H., & Mohammadifar, N. (2011). The new middle class in Iran—Threat or opportunity. *Political and Economic Ettelaat, 283*, 60–73. (in Persian).

Ministry of Energy. (2015). Gasoline price statistics. Retrieved September 7, 2015, from www.moe.gove.ir

Mofid, K. (1987). *Development planning in Iran: From monarchy to islamic republic.* Cambridgeshire: MENAS Press.

MRUD [Ministry of Roads and Urban Development]. (2015). Tarh-e jame'-e maskan: 1393–1405 [Draft of combined summary of Comprehensive Housing Plan, released for comments]. Retrieved February 1, 2016, from http://www.mrud.ir/portal/File/ShowFile.aspx?ID=93c8ca54-dac2-4fe4-add4-bc77a2cc89cd

MRUD [Ministry of Roads and Urban Development]. (2016). Official information on "Compassion Housing." Retrieved February 5, 2016, from http://maskanmehr.net/

Nowshirvani, V. F., & Clawson, P. (1994). The state and social equity in postrevolutionary Iran. In M. Weiner & A. Banuazizi (Eds.), *The politics of social transformation in Afghanistan, Iran, and Pakistan* (pp. 228–269). Syracuse: Syracuse University Press.

Odedokun, M. O., & Round, J. I. (2004). Determinants of income inequality and its effects on economic growth: Evidence from African countries. *African Development Review, 16*(2), 287–327.

Parsa, M. (1989). *Social origins of the Iranian revolution.* New Brunswick: Rutgers University Press.

Pesaran, E. (2011). *Iran's struggle for economic independence: Reform and counter-reform in the post-revolutionary era.* London: Routledge.

Presson, T., & Tebellini, G. (1994). Is inequality harmful for growth? *American Economic Review, 84*, 600–621.

Rabbani, R. (2006). *Jame'eshenasi-e qeshrha va nabarabariha-ye ejtemai [Sociology of social strata and inequality].* Esfahan: University of Esfahan Press.

Rabiee, A. (2011). Income gap a security concern for countries in transition: Case study of Iran. *Rahbord Journal, 57*, 155–180. (in Persian).

Rajabloo, A., & Tahmasebi, Z. (2011). The development excursion of social stratification of urban society in two decades of the Islamic Republic of Iran

(1980s–1990s). *[Tarbiat Modares University] Journal of Historical Sociology, 3* (1), 3–22. (in Persian).
Ravallion, M. (2009). The developing world's bulging (but vulnerable) middle class. *World Development, 38*(4), 445–454.
Salehi-Isfahani, D. (2009a). Poverty, inequality, and populist politics in Iran. *Journal of Economic Inequality, 7*(1), 5–28.
Salehi-Isfahani, D. (2009b). Oil wealth and economic growth in Iran. In A. Gheissari (Ed.), *Contemporary Iran: Economy, society, politics* (pp. 3–37). Oxford: Oxford University Press.
SCI [Statistical Center of Iran]. (1988). *Salnameh-ye amari-ye Iran (1367) [Statistical yearbook of Iran].* Tehran: Statistical Center of Iran.
SCI [Statistical Center of Iran]. (2003). *Salnameh-ye amari-ye Iran (1382) [Statistical yearbook of Iran].* Tehran: Statistical Center of Iran.
SCI [Statistical Center of Iran]. (2014). Towzi'-e daramad dar khanevarha-ye shahri, rustai, va koll-e keshvar, 1380–1391 [Income distribution for urban and rural households and nationwide]. Retrieved August 12, 2015, from http://amar.org.ir
SCI [Statistical Center of Iran]. (2015). Time series excel tables. Retrieved November 8, 2015, from www.amar.org.ir
Shakoori, A. (2001). *The state and rural development in post-revolutionary Iran.* New York: Palgrave.
Sirowy, L., & Inkeles, A. (1990). The effects of democracy on economic growth and inequality: A review. *Studies in Comparative International Development, 25*(1), 126–157.
UNDP [United Nations Development Programme]. (2015). *Human development report 2015.* Retrieved January 5, 2016, from http://hdr.undp.org/en/2015-report
WIPO [World Intellectual Property Organization]. (2016). Constitution of the islamic republic of Iran. Retrieved February 19, 2016, from http://www.wipo.int/edocs/lexdocs/laws/en/ir/ir001en.pdf
World Bank. (2004). Islamic republic of Iran: Strategies for the housing sector. Report No. 28983. Retrieved July 23, 2015, from http://www-wds.worldbank.org/external/default/WDSContentServer/WDSP/IB/2004/06/08/000112742_20040608142402/Rendered/PDF/HSS0v30revised010final.pdf
World Bank. (2015). World development indicators [Data on Iran]. Retrieved December 22, 2015, from http://data.worldbank.org/country/iran-islamic-republic
World Bank [Financial Disclosure Law Library]. (2016). Constitution of the islamic republic of Iran. Retrieved February 19, 2016, from http://publicofficialsfinancialdisclosure.worldbank.org/sites/fdl/files/assets/law-library-files/Iran_Constitution_en.pdf

[illegible]

CHAPTER 3

Poverty, Inequality, and Income Mobility in Iran: A Pseudo-Panel Approach

Hossein Raghfar and Mitra Babapour

Introduction

Iran has experienced various social, economic, and political upheavals and structural changes over the past four decades. They have included an Islamic Revolution, an imposed war, economic sanctions, a series of demographic transitions, and rapid fluctuations in oil revenues. These economic and political developments have arguably had differential influences across generations and stages of life—hence, a variety of welfare conditions experienced by different age groups. In this chapter, we look at the dynamics of income distribution across generations over the last three decades. We specifically probe poverty, inequality, income mobility, and vulnerability associated with various generations. Major questions to be answered in this chapter are thus as follows: What is the behavior of consumption expenditure for different age groups and how has it changed through the years? How do poverty and inequality change among different generations according to gender and educational attainment of the household head? What is the speed of income convergence and are households able to improve their standing after negative income shocks? What are the effects

H. Raghfar (✉)
Institute for Economic and Social Studies, Alzahra University, Tehran, Iran

M. Babapour (✉)
Allameh Tabatabai University, Tehran, Iran

M.R. Farzanegan, P. Alaedini (eds.), *Economic Welfare and Inequality in Iran*, DOI 10.1057/978-1-349-95025-6_3

of the unemployment rate as an important factor influencing consumption expenditures? Have younger generations faced greater rates of unemployment compared to the age groups who lived their youth prior to the Revolution? Which household characteristics have influenced the vulnerability rate?

We use the Foster-Greer-Thorbecke (1984) poverty indicators and Gini index to respectively measure poverty and inequality associated with various generations. We further employ the Deaton and Paxson (1994) method—widely used in probing intergenerational behavior—to analyze consumption expenditures and unemployment rates for different generations. We treat income mobility and vulnerability by utilizing fixed and random effects and a probit model. Cross-section data from Iran's household surveys between the years 1984 and 2014 are combined to construct a pseudo-panel as an alternative to long-term panel data which is not available.

The chapter is organized in the following way: In the next section, we define poverty, inequality, and mobility as well as vulnerability by briefly reviewing the literature. We then explain the use of repeated cross-sections in constructing our pseudo-panel to overcome the lack of panel data. In another section, we describe our estimation methodology. We subsequently present the estimation results and provide our conclusions in the final section.

Poverty, Inequality, Mobility, and Vulnerability: A Brief Review

There is no consensus on the definition of poverty. In the most general sense, poverty may be defined as inability to meet different needs. Needs however vary from one person to the next. Yet, average income and income inequality are the most widely used measures of income distribution. A large body of literature has probed poverty and inequality for various countries using different methods and data sets (which unfortunately make comparative analyses exceedingly difficult). As an example, Chen and Ravallion's (2007) study investigates absolute poverty for developing countries by employing 1981–2004 household survey data. It reveals decreasing trends in the percentage of absolutely poor people with uneven progress across regions as well as mixed success in reducing the total number of poor.

Several studies on poverty and inequality are also available for the case of Iran. Assadzadeh and Paul's (2001) study focuses on rural and urban poverty in Iran in the ten-year period between 1983 and 1993. It shows that poverty decreased slightly in rural areas but increased by 40 percent in the cities. Raghfar et al. (2016) provide a wide spectrum of poverty profiles for different groups at different geographical levels for over three decades in Iran. In this study, absolute and severe poverty are estimated for male and female household heads as well as children. It indicates that after two decades of declining poverty, the trend has been reversed in the last decade. Using Theil, Atkinson, and Gini indexes, Raghfar et al. (2012) measure within-group and between-group income inequalities for nine regions of Iran during the period 1984–2010. Their findings reveal differential inequality trends across regions in the investigated period as well as the prominence of within-group inequality. Salehi-Isfahani and Majbori (2013) treat Iran's mobility and poverty dynamics for the period 1992–1995. They show that chronic and transient poverty are higher among the youth, female-headed households, and households headed by less educated men. They further indicate that Tehran as well as rural areas often experience transitory poverty more than chronic poverty, and that education can directory influence chronic and transitory poverty.

Raghfar and Babapour (2014) probe poverty dynamics in Iran, by investigating the behavior of household consumption expenditures in the life-cycle model as one of the determinant factors of welfare. To this end, they construct pseudo-panel data that combine 29 years of cross-sectional household surveys from 1984 to 2012. They show that, in spite of many upheavals and structural breaks in the economy, inequality figures are relatively stable which may indicate that public policies failed to fulfill social justice promised. The results of cohort effects suggest that between age 25 and 37 there is no significant differences in the unemployment rate of those born between 1926 and 1970, but the cohort effects are rising for cohorts born after 1971.

Raghfar et al. (2015) focus on the impact of economic growth on poverty and inequality in relation to different socioeconomic development programs in Iran during 1989–2013. They decompose the elasticity of poverty into growth and inequality effects and calculate the outcome of the economic growth using Kakwani and Son's (2008) poverty equivalent growth rate. They show that the effect of neutral growth on poverty is negative, while the neutral effect of inequality has positive and negative fluctuations. Their analysis of poverty equivalent growth rate index in association with economic and social development programs in Iran indicates the lack of effective policies to achieve sustainable welfare.

The significance of mobility in inequality analysis has been underscored in the literature (Fields 2006; Antman and McKenzie 2005). Although mobility and inequality are considered related concepts, they are quite distinct. The concept of inequality focuses on the income distribution of individuals at specific points of time, whereas mobility reflects on the extent of movement of income (ups and down) between two or more points in time. People's welfare is different in two societies having the same inequality level but quite different mobility patterns. Individuals in societies with higher mobility are more likely to be motivated to elevate their positions in the income distribution in comparison with members of low-mobility societies. Furthermore, mobility is associated with equality of opportunities while high degree of inequality and its persistence are consistent with low degree of mobility (Cuesta et al. 2007).

Empirical studies on mobility have employed panel as well as pseudo-panel data. Utilizing panel data, Scott and Litchfield's (1994) study measures mobility and inequality for rural households in Chile between 1968 and 1986. It treats the determining factor in income change through a linear regression and a logit model. Age, educational attainment of household head, land ownership, and per capita income of household in the initial year are found to be among the most important factors in changing to higher ranks. Employing a pseudo-panel approach based on household head's year of birth and level of education, Antman and McKenzie (2005) examine income trends for various generations in Mexico from 1987 to 2001. Their estimation results indicate little absolute convergence between the rich and the poor, thus suggesting the persistence of high level of inequality during the investigated period. However, they find conditional mobility to be high for their case, which indicates quick recovery of households from earnings shocks.

By imposing the threat of slipping into poverty on individuals, vulnerability is associated with downward absolute mobility along the welfare distribution. The risks that poor individuals face as a result of their circumstances are the apparent causes of their vulnerability. Yet, a deeper cause is their inability to reduce or mitigate risks or cope with shocks, which influences and is affected by other dimensions of poverty. From a different perspective, the underlying cause of vulnerability is the inability of the public sector or community to develop mechanisms for reducing or mitigating the risks that poor people encounter.

A number of studies have focused on vulnerability and its interaction with poverty. Pritchett et al. (2000) is an example that uses panel data to investigate vulnerability in Indonesia in terms of gender, level of education, urban/rural residence, land ownership, and household activity. It suggests that while many households may not be poor, they are nonetheless vulnerable to poverty in the face of illness, loss of job, unexpected expenses, or economic recession. It further indicates much higher levels of vulnerability in rural (especially for those associated with agricultural activity) versus urban areas, higher level of vulnerability among female-headed households, and lower levels of vulnerability among households headed by more educated individuals. For the case of Iran, Raghfar and Sanei (2010) employ a logit model to measure vulnerability of Tehran residents to poverty in the period 1993–2007. Their findings show that the bigger the family size, the more vulnerable is the family to poverty. Yet, having a job as well as having more education makes people less vulnerable, while loss of job, age, and gender can also influence vulnerability, as revealed in their study.

Data and Methodology

Pseudo-Panel Approach

Panel data are most suited for specific dynamic analyses of poverty, inequality, and mobility, as they allow observation of the same household over time. Unfortunately, in most countries including Iran, long-term panel data are either unavailable or subject to attrition. Moreover, nonrandom loss of data can cause serious problems of bias even in the case of high-quality data sets. Pseudo-panel data created from repeated cross-section (RCS) data can be used as a substitute for panel data. RCS data can be generated from the more broadly available household surveys conducted regularly—once or twice a year (Deaton 1997). In RCS data, there is no possibility of following the same individual through time. For respondents in each period are not necessarily the same. To address this shortcoming, Browning et al. (1985) and Deaton (1985) suggest converting individual-level data into cohort-level data. It is then possible to track cohorts of individuals through time. A cohort is defined as a group with a fixed membership—individuals identified as they show up in surveys (Deaton 1985). For every cohort, the mean value for each variable is calculated across time periods. These averages have many of the properties associated with panel data, as they relate to the same group of people. Time series of these averages for each cohort create the pseudo-panel data. The variable tracked across time is typically of an average value (although medians or percentiles can also be used). Deaton (1985) counts several advantages for pseudo-panel data. First, in generating pseudo-panel data, data from different sources can be combined and there is no need to collect data from the same households or to repeat the survey. Second, because samples can be renewed in every period, attrition problems may be minimized. Third, pseudo-panel data that relate household behaviors and national-level aggregates minimize inconsistencies between macro and micro analyses as well as allow linkages between macro analyses and income distribution. Yet, pseudo-panels are not without limitations. One of the main deficiencies of the pseudo-panel is the cross-section nature of the data which provides no information about intra-cohort dynamics for two adjacent periods; it is not possible to relate the joint distribution of characteristics of the cohorts (Deaton 1997).

Measuring Poverty and Inequality

Cross-sectional analyses can describe the incidence, depth, and severity of poverty. They are however unable to explore the incidence, depth, and severity of poverty among the same groups through time. The use of pseudo-panel data in exploring poverty and inequality over a period of time among different groups addresses these shortcomings. In this study, we conduct an estimation of the absolute poverty line—the level of income necessary for people to buy goods (both food and nonfood) that allow them to maintain the minimum standard of a decent living. We derive cost-of-basic-needs poverty lines. Food cost is the cost of buying a basket of food containing 2080 kilocalories intake per adult per day—calculated by Iran Institute for dietetics. Using Engle coefficient, costs of nonfood goods are estimated. As households have heterogeneous compositions, their consumption levels must be made comparable by making use of equivalent scales. Furthermore, since each cohort contains both poor and the non-poor households, poor households are identified and marked. This serves to identify the poor, once we construct the cohorts.

Once the poverty line is specified, the next step is to decide on an appropriate summary measure of aggregate poverty. Foster-Greer-Thorbecke (1984) is the most popular set of poverty indexes, defined in the following way. The headcount index (P_0) measures the percentage of the population with consumption or income below the poverty line. The poverty gap index (P_1) measures the extent to which individuals fall below the poverty line as a proportion of the poverty line. The sum of these poverty gaps gives the minimum cost that is needed to eliminate the poverty, provided that transfers are flawlessly targeted. The poverty severity index (P_2) averages the squares of the poverty gaps relative to the poverty line and gives more weight to the very poor. The class of Foster-Greer-Thorbecke poverty measures has a general formula with a parameter α, poverty aversion, which takes the value of zero for the headcount ratio, one for the poverty gap, and two for the squared poverty gap. If we have a population n, in which q people are poor, then:

$$P_\alpha = \frac{1}{n}\sum_{i=1}^{q}\left[\frac{z - y_i}{z}\right]^\alpha$$

where z and y refer to poverty line and income, respectively.

Inequality is a broader concept than poverty as it is defined over the entire population rather than the poor only. The most commonly employed measure of inequality is the Gini coefficient which ranges from 0 (perfect equality) to 1 (perfect inequality). A large number of mathematical expressions have been suggested for the Gini index. A highly useful expression is based on the covariance between the income of an individual or household (Y) and the rank that the individual or household holds in the distribution of income (F). $\widetilde{Y}$ in the following formula is mean income; therefore, the standard Gini index is given by:

$$\text{Gini} = \frac{2\text{cov}(Y, F)}{\widetilde{Y}}$$

For this study, the Foster-Greer-Thorbheck measures and the Gini coefficient have been estimated and the results are discussed in the results section.

Mobility

Employing pseudo-panel data and some of the estimation models proposed by Antman and McKenzie (2005),[1] the degree of income mobility in Iran is estimated during a 31-year period between 1984 and 2014. In keeping with the consistency conditions required by McKenzie (2004), the least square method is used for the estimations.

A simple mobility measure (the slope coefficient in an income regression over its lagged value) is chosen to establish the magnitude of temporal dependence of incomes as well as the way incomes converge or diverge with respect to the mean value in the long term. An absolute convergence with homogeneity of parameters among the cohorts has thus been estimated.

The first model is determined without considering fixed effects through the following equation:

$$\bar{Y}_{c(t),t} = \alpha + \beta \bar{Y}_{c(t-1),t-1} + \varepsilon_{c(t),t}. \tag{1}$$

If $\bar{Y}_{c(t),t}$ indicates the income level of households belonging to cohort c observed in time t, then $\beta < 1$ will show that a household with income below the mean in period $t-1$ experiences faster income growth than richer households. For instance, a value of $\beta = 0.9$ reveals that a ten percent difference in income between two persons would be nine percent after one year. Estimation of Eq. (1) gives *absolute mobility*. It shows the extent to which households move around in the overall income distribution, as mobility can lower lifetime inequality and provide equality of opportunity. It captures the influence of current income in determining the evolution of its future values.

Income differences among people can be due to differences in individual capacities to earn income. The second model, considering the fixed effects, is thus determined by the following equation (see Antman and McKenzie 2005):

$$\bar{Y}_{c(t),t} = \alpha_c + \beta \bar{Y}_{c(t-1),t-1} + \varepsilon_{c(t),t}. \tag{2}$$

Estimation of Eq. (2) provides a measure of *conditional mobility*. Including the individual fixed effects, certain differences are allowed to exist among incomes. Individual differences such as level of education, health status, and so on are included in α_c. These characteristics can affect individual abilities in accessing opportunities and higher incomes. Given the personal characteristics, the value of β measures the speed in returning to the level of their average incomes of people that, due to their capability, can earn more or less (Antman and McKenzie 2007). In this case, β relates to the mobility around the mean incomes for each household. A value of β smaller than one indicates that households below their own mean incomes will have quicker income growth than others. If conditional mobility is very low, shocks to household incomes will cause more inequality of income, since incomes are not able to recover to the level corresponding to their characteristics.

As Antman and McKenzie (2005) show, for better interpretation, the model can be rewritten as follows:

$$Y^{*}_{i,t} = \alpha_i + \beta Y^{*}_{i,t-1} + u_{i,t} \tag{3}$$

The current household income thus consists of three terms:

$$Y^{*}_{i,t} = \alpha_i \left(\frac{1-\beta^t}{1-\beta}\right) + \beta^t Y^{*}_{i,0} + \left(\sum_{s=0}^{t-1} \beta^s u_{i,t-s}\right) \tag{4}$$

The first term reflects household fixed effects on income growth, the second is related to the effects of primary differences in household income, and the last explains the growing impact of shocks to income. This allows us to compare incomes of households *i* and *j* in this way:

$$\mathrm{Y}^{*}_{i,t} - \mathrm{Y}^{*}_{j,t} = \left(\alpha_i - \alpha_j\right)\left(\frac{1-\beta^t}{1-\beta}\right) + \beta^t\left(\mathrm{Y}^{*}_{i,0} - \mathrm{Y}^{*}_{j,0}\right) + \sum_{s=0}^{t-1} \beta^s \left(u_{i,t-s} - u_{j,t-s}\right) \tag{5}$$

It is clear that differences in income can remain because of differences in any of the three terms; high rates of conditional mobility suggest that if household *j* has lower current income than household *i* for having lower initial income, household *j* will have faster income growth than household *i*. Increasing beta in $0<\beta\leq 1$, $\alpha_i > \alpha_j$ will cause a growth in income gap between the household *i* and *j* in every period. In case, $\beta = 0$ the initial differences and shocks in income do not have any effects on the income differences; but incomes will continue to be different due to the difference between α_i and α_j. Therefore, the faster conditional mobility lowers the divergence in incomes which is because of the existed differences in fixed effects but never omits it.

Regarding cross-sectional variances of Eq. (4) reveals implications for inequality:

$$var_i\left(Y^*_{i,t}\right) = \mathrm{var}(\alpha_i)\left(\frac{1-\beta^t}{1-\beta}\right)^2 + \beta^{2t}\mathrm{var}_i\left(Y^*_{i,0}\right) + \mathrm{var}_i\left(\sum_{s=0}^{t-1}\beta^s u_{i,t-s}\right) \quad (6)$$

This shows that a high degree of conditional mobility reduces inequality by lessening differences in initial incomes and in earnings shocks, but inequality may still remain high if there is considerable variation in the fixed effects among households.

Finally, a vector of independent variables was presented to determine which factors affect mobility. In this case, the estimation model will be:

$$\bar{Y}_{c(t),t} = \alpha + \beta\bar{Y}_{c(t-1),t-1} + x'_{c(t),t}\delta_c + \varepsilon_{c(t),t} \quad (7)$$

where the vector x holds control variables such as average age of the cohort and the square of such variables as well as the size of the cohorts.

We provide estimates of the behavior of mobility for periods of different lengths and discuss our interpretations for the three measures in the results section.

Decomposition of Expenditures and Unemployment Rate

The common indexes of income distribution—such as Gini and headcount indexes—are widely employed but provide an imperfect depiction of income distribution as they summarize an entire distribution with one value. A cohort analysis (Deaton and Paxson 1994) is used to examine the lifetime profiles of consumption. In this part, the expenditure behavior of various cohorts using the method of Deaton (1997) which is one of the most referenced methods in considering intergeneration behavior is discussed. In this method, expenditure is decomposed to three parts: age, cohort, and year effects. Age effects offer the typical age profile. Cohort effects are related to the secular trends that bring about differences in the positions of age profiles for various cohorts. Year effects are indicative of shocks that have influenced the consumed expenditure in various years. In order to decompose the effects of age, cohort, and year, various methods are employed, among which use of dummy variables is most common. The following relation explains this decomposition:

$$y = \beta + A\alpha + C\gamma + Y\psi + u \tag{8}$$

where A is a matrix of age dummies, C is a matrix of cohort dummies, and Y is a matrix of year dummies while y is the stacked vector of cohort-year observation (Deaton 1997).

In decomposing year, age, and cohort effects, these assumptions are made: (1) the sum of year effects is zero, (2) year effects are orthogonal to time trend, and (3) the determinants of the studied variables are age and cohort effects and year effects capture cyclical fluctuations (Deaton and Paxson 1994; Deaton 1997).

Furthermore, the unemployment rate—that can affect household consumption through decreasing current income and labor income—is considered as a factor influencing consumption expenditures in this study.

Vulnerability

In order to analyze vulnerability, a probit model is used in which the probability of being poor in selected cohorts in 2005 and 2010 is explained by a set of variables reflecting household characteristics. The goal of performing regressions for two different years is to evaluate the importance of those variables in changing the possibility of being poor through years. Focusing on cohorts separately allows the relevance of each variable to be tracked across time for each group. The specification is as follows:

$$y_i = \alpha + \beta X_i + y Z_i + \gamma G_i + \varepsilon_i, \tag{9}$$

where i indicates households in each cohort, and y_i is 1 when the household average per adult equivalent expenditure is below the poverty line and zero otherwise. X_i is a vector of household head characteristics—employed/ unemployed, gender (1 for men), and education (1 for high school and higher education). Z_i is a vector of household characteristics, including the dependency ratio (ratio of individuals 17 or younger to the number of those in the 18–60 age range in the household). G_i is a vector of geographic variable, including nine region.[2]

Data and Construction of Cohorts

To investigate poverty, inequality, and mobility in Iran, we use 31 rounds of the Household Expenditure and Income Survey (HEIS) conducted annually by the Statistical Center of Iran (SCI 1984 through 2014). In these surveys, the sampling unit is household. New samples of households are interviewed for each year. The survey is thus not designed as panel and does not allow for the tracking of households over time. HEIS provides a wide range of economic and socio-demographic information, such as different sources of income, education, and other social indicators, but its main focus is on expenditures. In this study, we use expenditure rather than income data as they allow for a better comparison of economic wellbeing. All expenditure figures are deflated by Consumer Price Index (published by Central Bank of Iran) to make them comparable across years and to measure all values in 2011 prices. We also adjust all expenditures figures to reflect household composition and size. For this purpose, the following equivalence scale is used[3]:

$$\text{Equivalence Scale} = (N_a + 0.4N_c)^{.85}$$

where N_a and N_c are the number of adult and children, respectively.

Our period of analysis spans 1984 through 2014. Between 2670 and 20,196 urban households have been surveyed during these years, with specifics provided in Table 3.1. For the dynamic analysis, we need to follow cohorts. In this study, we use birth year of household head as the principle characteristic. Expenditure data are available only for households whose compositions may change often. Thus, when we track households labeled by the age of the heads, it is not always certain that we are sampling from the same population in successive years. In spite of these problems, as Deaton and Paxson (1994) argue, working with households is preferable to any attempt at conversion to individuals through assignment rules. Our cohorts are defined in five-year bands, starting with those born between 1926 and 1930 and ending with those born between 1976 and 1980. This manner of construction prevents the problem of low number of observations in each cell. The middle points of the bands define the age of the cohort. Each cohort enters the sample at age 25; for example, the youngest cohort is not included until 2003. This restricts our sample to households with heads aged 23–70 years of age. Tables 3.2 and 3.3 present age and annual observations (number of households included) for cohorts. We also calculate average year of education for every cohort (Table 3.4). This measure does not vary much across years, but it does change across cohorts. The average years of education are higher for the younger cohorts, which is

Table 3.1 Data coverage of cross-section HEIS

	Coverage	*Individual*	*Household*
1984	Urban	73,894	14,728
1985	Urban	70,684	13,976
1986	Urban	13,426	2670
1987	Urban	13,984	2748
1988	Urban	20,590	3987
1989	Urban	28,136	5492
1990	Urban	46,918	9095
1991	Urban	47,216	9168
1992	Urban	31,112	6268
1993	Urban	33,146	6775
1994	Urban	60,224	12,116
1995	Urban	10,0842	20,196
1996	Urban	52,721	10,977
1997	Urban	52,096	10,968
1998	Urban	39,130	8285
1999	Urban	60,658	12,731
2000	Urban	55,675	12,320
2001	Urban	55,178	12,337
2002	Urban	66,708	15,114
2003	Urban	48,180	10,959
2004	Urban	49,900	11,619
2005	Urban	54,278	12,925
2006	Urban	57,986	14,175
2007	Urban	60,662	15,018
2008	Urban	77,271	19,381
2009	Urban	74,398	18,665
2010	Urban	72,441	18,701
2011	Urban	71,461	18,727
2012	Urban	69,567	18,535
2013	Urban	68,058	18,881
2014	Urban	67,482	18,886

Source: Authors' calculations based on HEIS data files

consistent with the general educational improvements in Iran over the years. Our cohort analysis is carried out for the totality of cohorts. Yet we also divide household cohorts according to educational levels of the household head—below high school and high school and above—as well as gender for certain demonstrations.

Table 3.2 Age of cohorts

Birth-year of household head	*1926–1930*	*1931–1935*	*1936–1940*	*1941–1945*	*1946–1950*	*1951–1955*	*1956–1960*	*1961–1965*	*1966–1970*	*1971–1975*	*1976–1980*
1984	54–58	49–53	44–48	39–43	34–38	29–33	24–28				
1985	55–59	50–54	45–49	40–44	35–39	30–34	25–29				
1986	56–60	51–55	46–50	41–45	36–40	31–35	26–30				
1987	57–61	52–56	47–51	42–46	37–41	32–36	27–31				
1988	58–62	53–57	48–52	43–47	38–42	33–37	28–32	23–27			
1989	59–63	54–58	49–53	44–48	39–43	34–38	29–33	24–28			
1990	60–64	55–59	50–54	45–49	40–44	35–39	30–34	25–29			
1991	61–65	56–60	51–55	46–50	41–45	36–40	31–35	26–30			
1992	62–66	57–61	52–56	47–51	42–46	37–41	32–36	27–31			
1993	63–67	58–62	53–57	48–52	43–47	38–42	33–37	28–32	23–27		
1994	64–68	59–63	54–58	49–53	44–48	39–43	34–38	29–33	24–28		
1995	65–69	60–64	55–59	50–54	45–49	40–44	35–39	30–34	25–29		
1996	66–70	61–65	56–60	51–55	46–50	41–45	36–40	31–35	26–30		
1997		62–66	57–61	52–56	47–51	42–46	37–41	32–36	27–31		
1998		63–67	58–62	53–57	48–52	43–47	38–42	33–37	28–32	23–27	
1999		64–68	59–63	54–58	49–53	44–48	39–43	34–38	29–33	24–28	
2000		65–69	60–64	55–59	50–54	45–49	40–44	35–39	30–34	25–29	
2001		66–70	61–65	56–60	51–55	46–50	41–45	36–40	31–35	26–30	
2002			62–66	57–61	52–56	47–51	42–46	37–41	32–36	27–31	
2003			63–67	58–62	53–57	48–52	43–47	38–42	33–37	28–32	23–27
2004			64–68	59–63	54–58	49–53	44–48	39–43	34–38	29–33	24–28
2005			65–69	60–64	55–59	50–54	45–49	40–44	35–39	30–34	25–29
2006			66–70	61–65	56–60	51–55	46–50	41–45	36–40	31–35	26–30
2007				62–66	57–61	52–56	47–51	42–46	37–41	32–36	27–31
2008				63–67	58–62	53–57	48–52	43–47	38–42	33–37	28–32
2009				64–68	59–63	54–58	49–53	44–48	39–43	34–38	29–33
2010				65–69	60–64	55–59	50–54	45–49	40–44	35–39	30–34
2011				66–70	61–65	56–60	51–55	46–50	41–45	36–40	31–35
2012					62–66	57–61	52–56	47–51	42–46	37–41	32–36
2013					63–67	58–62	53–57	48–52	43–47	38–42	33–37
2014					64–68	59–63	54–58	49–53	44–48	39–43	34–38

Source: Authors' calculations based on HEIS data files

Table 3.3 Annual observations for cohorts

Table (continued) *Birth-year of household head*	*1926–1930*	*1931–1935*	*1936–1940*	*1941–1945*	*1946–1950*	*1951–1955*	*1956–1960*	*1961–1965*	*1966–1970*	*1971–1975*	*1976–1980*
1984	1427	1558	1443	1394	1592	1936	1612				
1985	994	1383	1257	1331	1621	2122	1948				
1986	202	255	261	249	311	398	365				
1987	194	249	279	282	309	426	368				
1988	289	378	340	347	472	609	588	321			
1989	409	526	524	492	591	848	756	481			
1990	730	784	837	838	985	1309	1335	867			
1991	671	814	836	849	952	1335	1323	938			
1992	443	532	552	495	597	868	904	794			
1993	413	589	574	583	626	956	942	944	430		
1994	782	971	998	1030	1167	1708	1840	1532	959		
1995	1154	1561	1535	1687	2009	2834	3004	2716	1584		
1996	567	826	844	863	1083	1468	1640	1524	1112		
1997		795	779	866	1006	1428	1615	1562	1201		
1998		602	606	639	742	1105	1253	1129	942	404	
1999		846	981	894	1134	1634	1826	1770	1526	727	
2000		688	750	788	1001	1452	1717	1708	1714	1168	
2001		684	744	819	1014	1448	1628	1767	1580	1236	
2002			948	957	1181	1681	1980	2103	2067	1633	
2003			604	644	791	1194	1418	1655	1522	1285	633
2004			554	701	808	1204	1446	1699	1569	1440	888
2005			565	676	825	1386	1546	1772	1806	1664	1139
2006			672	795	1003	1391	1706	1838	2003	1693	1442

(continued)

Table 3.3 (continued)

Table (continued) *Birth-year of household head*	*1926–1930*	*1931–1935*	*1936–1940*	*1941–1945*	*1946–1950*	*1951–1955*	*1956–1960*	*1961–1965*	*1966–1970*	*1971–1975*	*1976–1980*
2007				782	868	1400	1608	1933	1911	1834	1554
2008				984	1236	1834	2205	2538	2677	2388	2125
2009				947	1171	1727	2135	2410	2419	2406	2006
2010				932	1297	1671	2148	2434	2446	2245	1968
2011				971	1286	1861	2144	2461	2456	2198	1784
2012					1262	1842	2165	2386	2456	2122	1767
2013					1018	1499	1798	2041	2212	2415	2369
2014					1043	1553	1916	1966	2281	2358	2274

Source: Authors' calculations based on HEIS data files

Table 3.4 Mean years of education of the cohorts

Birth-year of household head	*1926–1930*	*1931–1935*	*1936–1940*	*1941–1945*	*1946–1950*	*1951–1955*	*1956–1960*	*1961–1965*	*1966–1970*	*1971–1975*	*1976–1980*
1984	5.12	5.44	5.68	5.86	6.08	6.53	6.75				
1985	5.3	5.55	5.71	5.86	6.14	6.45	6.66				
1986	5.5	5.61	6.18	6.12	6.09	6.53	6.25				
1987	4.6	4.75	5.62	5.26	6.5	6.44	6.96				
1988	4.7	4.71	6.21	6.15	6.28	6.68	6.96	7.58			
1989	4.2	4.84	5.41	5.68	5.93	6.47	7.04	7.69			
1990	4.46	4.51	4.94	5.81	5.96	6.36	7.16	7.28			
1991	4.67	4.71	5.11	5.88	6	6.55	7.31	7.43			
1992	4.66	4.69	5.46	6.07	6.41	6.91	7.46	7.81			
1993	4.96	4.87	5.63	6.01	6.38	6.67	7.33	7.99	7.08		
1994	5.11	5.11	5.48	6.23	6.51	6.9	7.45	7.81	7.3		
1995	4.77	5.15	5.39	6.27	6.35	6.91	7.47	7.95	7.47		
1996	5.85	6.3	6.35	7.68	8.01	8.27	8.58	8.52	8.46		
1997		6.46	6.66	7.38	8.05	8.16	8.71	8.73	8.4		
1998		6.06	7.21	7.54	8.06	8.14	8.63	8.65	8.73	8.03	
1999		5.93	6.79	7.24	7.86	8.07	8.57	8.8	8.64	8.08	
2000		6.49	6.76	7.44	7.66	8.22	8.86	8.9	9.01	8.57	
2001		6.33	6.78	7.56	7.95	8.21	8.8	9.06	8.9	8.86	
2002			6.72	7.12	7.69	8.26	8.6	9.1	9.04	8.96	
2003			6.37	6.88	7.47	8.03	8.61	8.99	9.26	9.03	8.8
2004			6.46	7.27	7.8	8.24	8.72	8.97	9.29	9.55	9.44
2005			6.3	6.95	7.66	8.2	8.86	9.04	9.03	9.34	9.17
2006			6.52	6.69	7.35	7.76	8.47	8.69	8.84	9.07	9.22
2007				7.12	7.32	8.14	8.35	8.79	8.96	9.31	9.47
2008				6.67	7.3	8.06	8.59	8.74	8.94	9.25	9.39
2009				6.52	6.81	7.46	8.08	8.38	8.51	8.96	9.28
2010				7.08	7.3	7.68	8.71	8.73	8.9	9.16	9.37
2011				7.02	7.26	7.82	8.56	8.65	8.8	9.14	9.54
2012					7.43	7.71	8.23	8.33	8.55	8.75	9.11
2013					7.13	7.31	8.52	8.07	8.71	8.91	9.33
2014					7.25	7.43	8.43	8.21	8.65	8.7	9.35

Source: Authors' calculations based on HEIS data files

Results

In this section, results of this study are presented in three subsections, namely, poverty and inequality trends, mobility analysis including dynamics of cohort expenditures, and vulnerability.

Poverty and Inequality Trends

Figure 3.1 displays the evolution of headcount index and Gini coefficient during the period 1984–2014 for all cohorts. The interim years of 1984 through 1989 coincide with the Iran-Iraq War in which there is high volatility as well as high incidence of poverty among different cohorts. The highest poverty incidence is recorded for the year 1986, associated with the lowest level of oil revenue in the investigated period. With the initiation of the First Five-Year Economic, Social, and Cultural Plan of the Islamic Republic at the end of the war, increasing oil revenues, and additional receipts of foreign financing, poverty incidence is reduced during 1989–1990. Yet, adverse impacts on both poverty incidence and inequality observed for the years 1991–1992 are likely associated with the removal of subsidies and price liberalization. Then poverty experiences a relatively stable trend until 1999. Subsequently, poverty decreases through 2005, but again experiences an increasing trend until 2014.

Tables 3.5, 3.6, and 3.7 show calculation results for subgroup poverty and inequality indexes in the years 1984, 1989, 1993, 1997, 2001, 2005, and 2009. Table 3.5 indicates that poverty trends across cohorts do not follow specific patterns. Yet, as expected, the proportion of poor people in younger cohorts in any given year is larger than in other cohorts. For instance, a figure of 50.4 percent poverty is associated with the cohort of those born in 1976–1980. Higher levels of poverty for the youngest cohorts can be explained by the fact that most of their members do not participate in the labor market while those who do are likely to receive relatively low wages. For the 1980s, coinciding with the first post-revolutionary decade and the war, the headcount ratio and Gini coefficient increase while average expenditures tend to decrease for all cohorts. During 1989–1993, the incidence of poverty tends to decrease for cohorts born before 1951 (except for 1931–1935 cohort) and to increase for the three consecutive youngest cohorts. In the same period, inequality, as measured by the Gini index,

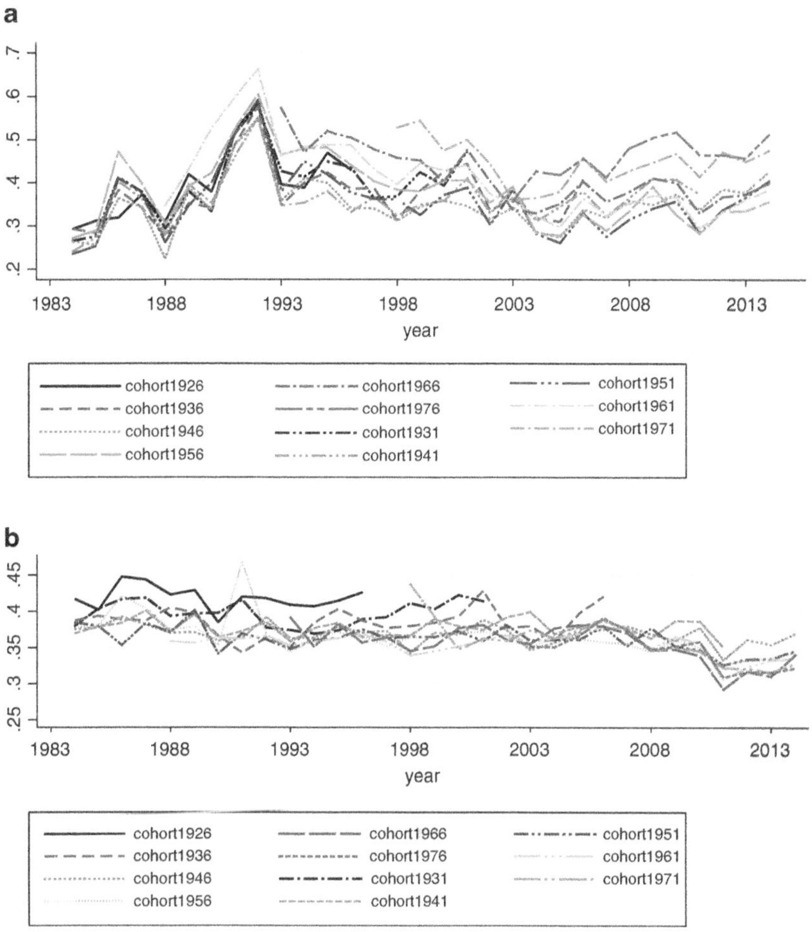

Fig. 3.1 Poverty and inequality indexes by cohort, 1984–2014. *Source*: Authors' calculations based on HEIS data files

decreases and average expenditures of all cohorts increase. Yet, poverty reduction and expenditure and inequality growth are observed for most cohorts during 1993–1997. Between 1997 and 2001, the incidence of poverty increases for every cohort except for the youngest two—whose

Table 3.5 Poverty incidence and inequality by cohort

	Cohort born										
Year	*1926–1930*	*1931–1935*	*1936–1940*	*1941–1945*	*1946–1950*	*1951–1955*	*1956–1960*	*1961–1965*	*1966–1970*	*1971–1975*	*1976–1980*
Per-adult-equivalent expenditures of households (log)											
1984	16.24	16.32	16.37	16.53	16.54	16.61	16.50				
1989	15.78	15.94	15.99	16.03	16.13	16.17	16.08	16.06			
1993	15.97	15.99	16.09	16.17	16.18	16.23	16.15	16.16	15.94		
1997		16.10	16.15	16.16	16.22	16.22	16.22	16.21	16.15		
2001		16.20	16.25	16.24	16.35	16.32	16.37	16.38	16.40	16.30	
2005			16.44	16.39	16.47	16.55	16.53	16.60	16.61	16.56	16.49
2009				16.30	16.36	16.40	16.36	16.44	16.46	16.45	16.39
Absolute changes											
1984–1989	−0.46	−0.38	−0.38	−0.5	−0.41	−0.44	−0.42				
1989–1993	0.19	0.05	0.10	0.14	0.05	0.06	0.07	0.1			
1993–1997		0.11	0.06	−0.01	0.04	−0.01	0.07	0.05	0.21		
1997–2001		0.1	0.1	0.08	0.13	0.1	0.15	0.17	0.25		
2001–2005			0.19	0.15	0.12	0.23	0.16	0.22	0.21	0.26	
2005–2009				−0.09	−0.11	−0.15	−0.17	−0.16	−0.15	−0.11	−0.1
Percentage of people below the poverty line											
1984	29.2	26.5	29.2	24.0	26.3	23.5	27.1				
1989	41.9	37.9	35.2	39.5	38.7	34.7	39.0	43.1			
1993	39.6	42.6	34.7	34.7	35.8	38.0	46.4	46.2	57.3		
1997		36.5	38.6	36.6	34.0	36.2	40.3	43.0	47.7		
2001		47.3	44.3	40.9	34.6	38.8	40.5	44.0	47.6	49.9	
2005			30.9	34.4	27.4	26.1	27.8	29.7	35.2	37.9	41.7
2009				40.9	34.9	34.0	39.0	37.0	41.0	44.7	50.4
Absolute changes											
1984–1989	12.7	11.4	6	15.5	12.4	11.2	11.9				
1989–1993	−2.3	4.7	−0.5	−4.8	−2.9	3.3	7.4	3.1			
1993–1997		−6.1	3.9	1.9	−1.8	−1.8	−6.1	−3.2	−9.6		

1997–2001		10.8	5.7	4.3	0.6	2.6	0.2	1	−0.1		
2001–2005			−13.4	−6.5	−7.2	−12.7	−12.7	−14.3	−12.4	−12	
2005–2009				6.5	7.5	7.9	11.2	7.3	5.8	6.8	8.7
Gini coefficient											
1984	0.41	0.38	0.38	0.36	0.37	0.38	0.37				
1989	0.42	0.39	0.39	0.39	0.37	0.40	0.37	0.35			
1993	0.4	0.37	0.35	0.35	0.36	0.34	0.34	0.35	0.39		
1997		0.39	0.37	0.36	0.37	0.36	0.35	0.35	0.36		
2001		0.41	0.42	0.37	0.38	0.35	0.37	0.35	0.38	0.36	
2005			0.39	0.37	0.37	0.36	0.36	0.36	0.38	0.37	0.36
2009				0.38	0.35	0.35	0.36	0.36	0.34	0.35	0.35
Absolute changes											
1984–1989	0.01	0.01	0.01	0.03	0	0.02	0				
1989–1993	−0.02	−0.02	−0.04	−0.04	−0.01	−0.06	−0.03	0			
1993–1997		0.02	0.02	0.01	0.01	0.02	0.01	0	−0.03		
1997–2001		0.02	0.05	0.01	0.01	−0.01	0.02	0	0.02		
2001–2005			−0.03	0	−0.01	0.01	−0.01	0.01	0	0.01	
2005–2009				0.01	−0.02	−0.01	0	0	−0.04	−0.02	−0.01

Source: Authors' Calculation based on HEIS data

Table 3.6 Per-adult-equivalent expenditures of households, the incidence of poverty, and inequality by cohort and educational level

	Cohort born									
Year	*1926–1930*		*1931–1935*		*1936–1940*		*1941–1945*		*1946–1950*	
	L	*H*	*L*	*H*	*L*	*H*	*L*	*H*	*L*	*H*
Per-adult-equivalent expenditures of households(log)										
1984	16.21	17.08	16.28	17.21	16.31	17.14	16.45	17.28	16.47	17.15
1989	15.74	16.66	15.88	16.67	15.90	16.60	15.92	16.55	16.01	16.52
1993	15.94	16.57	15.95	16.70	16.01	16.58	16.04	16.63	16.00	16.64
1997			16.01	16.99	16.03	16.83	16.01	16.74	16.04	16.69
2001			16.13	16.95	16.14	16.98	16.12	16.76	16.15	16.89
2005					16.37	17.03	16.29	17.00	16.32	17.01
2009							16.21	16.97	16.26	16.89
Absolute changes										
1984–1989	−0.47	−0.42	−0.4	−0.54	−0.41	−0.54	−0.53	−0.73	−0.46	−0.63
1989–1993	0.2	−0.09	0.07	0.03	0.11	−0.02	0.12	0.08	−0.01	0.12
1993–1997			0.06	0.29	0.02	0.25	−0.03	0.11	0.04	0.05
1997–2001			0.12	−0.04	0.11	0.15	0.11	0.02	0.11	0.2
2001–2005					0.23	0.05	0.17	0.24	0.17	0.12
2005–2009							−0.08	−0.03	−0.06	−0.12
Percentage of people below poverty line										
1984	30.8	0	27.0	0	31.1	2.4	25.8	1.8	28.4	2.8
1989	42.6	20.0	39.2	20.3	36.9	22.5	42.1	23.3	42.5	23.6
1993	41.1	10.8	44.8	4.1	38.2	8.7	40.3	10.3	43.0	13.0
1997			39.2	5.0	42.9	5.7	42.4	11.0	40.6	13.7
2001			50.4	10.2	48.8	9.8	46.7	13.4	42.3	8.8
2005					33.7	4.7	37.8	11.2	31.3	10.6
2009							44.9	11.2	39.2	10.26
Absolute changes										
1984–1989	11.8	20	12.2	20.3	5.8	20.1	16.3	21.5	14.1	20.8
1989–1993	−1.5	−9.2	5.6	–	1.3	−13.8	−1.8	−13	0.5	−10.6
1993–1997			−5.6	0.9	4.7	−3	2.1	0.7	−2.4	0.7
1997–2001			11.2	5.2	5.9	4.1	4.3	2.4	1.7	−4.9
2001–2005					−15.1	−5.1	−8.9	−2.2	−11	1.8
2005–2009							7.1	0	7.9	−0.34
Gini coefficient										
1984	0.41	0.32	0.37	0.28	0.37	0.32	0.35	0.33	0.37	0.29
1989	0.42	0.36	0.38	0.38	0.38	0.37	0.38	0.39	0.37	0.34
1993	0.40	0.28	0.36	0.31	0.35	0.26	0.35	0.31	0.33	0.35
1997			0.36	0.39	0.35	0.35	0.33	0.35	0.34	0.36
2001			0.38	0.43	0.40	0.40	0.36	0.34	0.37	0.34
2005					0.39	0.34	0.37	0.29	0.34	0.35
2009							0.36	0.33	0.35	0.30
Absolute changes										
1984–1989	0.01	0.04	0.01	0.1	0.01	0.05	0.03	0.06	0	0.05
1989–1993	−0.02	−0.08	−0.02	−0.07	−0.03	−0.11	−0.03	−0.08	−0.04	0.01
1993–1997			0	0.08	0	0.09	−0.02	0.04	0.01	0.01
1997–2001			0.02	0.04	0.05	0.05	0.03	−0.01	0.03	−0.02
2001–2005					−0.01	−0.06	0.01	−0.05	−0.03	0.01
2005–2009							−0.01	0.04	0.01	−0.05

(*continued*)

Table 3.6 (continued)

	Cohort born											
Year	*1951–1955*		*1956–1960*		*1961–1965*		*1966–1970*		*1971–1975*		*1976–1980*	
	L	*H*	*L*	*H*	*L*	*H*	*L*	*H*	*L*	*H*	*L*	*H*
Per-adult-equivalent expenditures of households(log)												
1984	16.53	17.04	16.44	16.74								
1989	16.03	16.51	15.96	16.29	15.93	16.31						
1993	16.03	16.61	15.96	16.43	16.01	16.33	15.83	16.26				
1997	16.01	16.64	16.00	16.53	16.00	16.49	15.97	16.48				
2001	16.10	16.78	16.08	16.79	16.12	16.72	16.13	16.81	16.08	16.62		
2005	16.34	17.00	16.28	16.93	16.35	16.94	16.36	16.98	16.33	16.86	16.27	16.76
2009	16.28	16.78	16.16	16.77	16.24	16.83	16.25	16.83	16.22	16.78	16.16	16.65
Absolute changes												
1984–1989	−0.5	−0.53	−0.48	−0.45								
1989–1993	0	0.1	0	0.14	0.08	0.02						
1993–1997	−0.02	0.03	0.04	0.1	−0.01	0.16	0.14	0.22				
1997–2001	0.09	0.14	0.08	0.26	0.12	0.23	0.16	0.33				
2001–2005	0.24	0.22	0.2	0.14	0.23	0.22	0.23	0.17	0.25	0.24		
2005–2009	−0.06	−0.22	−0.12	−0.16	−0.11	−0.11	−0.11	−0.15	−0.11	−0.08	−0.11	−0.11
Percentage of people below poverty line												
1984	25.9	6.9	30.1	14.2								
1989	38.2	23.7	43.8	28.1	48.9	29.9						
1993	47.9	14.33	57.2	25.7	56.4	31.95	64.6	34.4				
1997	45.1	14.12	50.0	23.0	55.0	22.4	58.1	25.2				
2001	49.1	13.3	54.6	15.46	58.3	22.13	62.1	19.64	61.2	31.17		
2005	34.4	6.0	38.2	9.2	41.7	12.0	47.3	14.4	52.1	17.27	54.1	23.57
2009	40.0	12.77	50.0	13.67	47.6	14.4	52.3	19.21	57.7	23.67	64.9	31.27
Absolute changes												
1984–1989	12.3	16.8	13.7	13.9								
1989–1993	9.7	−9.37	13.4	−2.4	7.5	2.05						
1993–1997	−2.8	−0.21	−7.2	−2.7	−1.4	−9.55	−6.5	−9.2				
1997–2001	4	−0.82	4.6	−7.54	3.3	−0.27	4	−5.56				
2001–2005	−14.7	−7.3	−16.4	−6.26	−16.6	−10.13	−14.8	−5.24	−9.1	−13.9		
2005–2009	5.6	6.77	11.8	4.47	5.9	2.4	5	4.81	5.6	6.4	10.8	7.7
Gini coefficient												
1984	0.38	0.36	0.37	0.36								
1989	0.39	0.39	0.35	0.39	0.37	0.31						
1993	0.34	0.31	0.32	0.33	0.35	0.34	0.35	0.40				
1997	0.33	0.36	0.33	0.34	0.34	0.35	0.32	0.36				
2001	0.34	0.32	0.34	0.34	0.33	0.33	0.35	0.34	0.35	0.33		
2005	0.34	0.31	0.33	0.32	0.35	0.33	0.35	0.35	0.33	0.36	0.33	0.36
2009	0.35	0.31	0.33	0.34	0.34	0.34	0.33	0.31	0.32	0.32	0.32	0.33
Absolute changes												
1984–1989	0.01	0.03	−0.02	0.03								
1989–1993	−0.05	−0.08	−0.03	−0.06	−0.02	0.03						
1993–1997	−0.01	0.05	0.01	0.01	−0.01	0.01	−0.03	−0.04				
1997–2001	0.01	−0.04	0.01	0	−0.01	−0.02	0.03	−0.02				
2001–2005	0	−0.01	−0.01	−0.02	0.02	0	0	0.01	−0.02	0.03		
2005–2009	0.01	0	0	0.02	−0.01	0.01	−0.02	−0.04	−0.01	−0.04	−0.01	−0.03

Source: Authors' Calculation based on HEIS data

Table 3.7 Per-adult-equivalent expenditures of households, the incidence of poverty, and inequality by cohort and gender

	Cohort born									
Year	*1926–1930*		*1931–1935*		*1936–1940*		*1941–1945*		*1946–1950*	
	M	*W*	*M*	*W*	*M*	*W*	*M*	*W*	*M*	*W*
Per-adult-equivalent expenditures of households(log)										
1984	16.27	16.05	16.33	16.19	16.39	16.12	16.54	16.36	16.57	16.17
1989	15.83	15.54	15.94	15.95	16.01	15.81	16.05	15.76	16.13	16.17
1993	15.98	15.92	15.99	16.05	16.12	15.88	16.19	16.00	16.20	15.87
1997			16.10	16.13	16.12	16.30	16.16	16.18	16.24	16.08
2001			16.20	16.21	16.27	16.16	16.27	16.12	16.36	16.28
2005					16.42	16.51	16.40	16.33	16.48	16.36
2009							16.30	16.29	16.37	16.30
Absolute changes										
1984–1989	−0.44	−0.51	−0.39	−0.24	−0.38	−0.31	−0.49	−0.6	−0.44	0
1989–1993	0.15	0.38	0.05	0.1	0.11	0.07	0.14	0.24	0.07	−0.3
1993–1997			0.11	0.08	0	0.42	−0.03	0.18	0.04	0.21
1997–2001			0.1	0.08	0.15	−0.14	0.11	−0.06	0.12	0.02
2001–2005					0.15	0.35	0.13	0.21	0.12	0.08
2005–2009							−0.1	−0.04	−0.11	−0.06
Percentage of people below the poverty line										
1984	28.0	46.9	26.0	35.5	28.6	40.4	23.6	32.0	25.4	41.4
1989	40.1	63.9	37.5	44.5	34.8	41.4	38.4	63.7	39.5	23.6
1993	39.0	44.5	43.0	38.4	33.5	53.0	33.7	50.0	35.0	54.3
1997			35.9	42.8	39.1	31.8	35.8	47.3	33.2	46.0
2001			47.5	46.0	43.8	50.4	39.9	51.7	33.5	48.6
2005					31.1	30.0	34.1	36.7	27.0	31.5
2009							39.6	49.8	33.3	44.8
Absolute changes										
1984–1989	12.1	17	11.5	9	6.2	1	14.8	31.7	14.1	−17.8
1989–1993	−1.1	−19.4	5.5	−6.1	−1.3	11.6	−4.7	−13.7	−4.5	30.7
1993–1997			−7.1	4.4	5.6	−21.1	2.1	−2.7	−1.8	−8.3
1997–2001			11.6	3.2	4.7	18.6	4.1	4.4	0.3	2.6
2001–2005					−12.7	−20.4	−5.8	−15	−6.5	−17.1
2005–2009							5.5	13.1	6.3	13.3
Gini coefficient										
1984	0.40	0.47	0.37	0.42	0.38	0.39	0.36	0.38	0.37	0.36
1989	0.41	0.51	0.39	0.44	0.39	0.34	0.38	0.47	0.37	0.32
1993	0.39	0.42	0.36	0.42	0.34	0.35	0.35	0.42	0.35	0.54
1997			0.38	0.40	0.37	0.37	0.36	0.39	0.36	0.39
2001			0.39	0.53	0.42	0.40	0.36	0.38	0.38	0.36
2005					0.38	0.42	0.37	0.36	0.36	0.39
2009							0.37	0.41	0.35	0.38
Absolute changes										
1984–1989	0.01	0.04	0.02	0.02	0.01	−0.05	0.02	0.09	0	−0.04
1989–1993	−0.02	−0.09	−0.03	−0.02	−0.05	0.01	−0.03	−0.05	−0.02	0.22
1993–1997			0.02	−0.02	0.03	0.02	0.01	−0.03	0.01	−0.15
1997–2001			0.01	0.13	0.05	0.03	0	−0.01	0.02	−0.03
2001–2005					−0.04	0.02	0.01	−0.02	−0.02	0.03
2005–2009							0	0.05	−0.01	−0.01

(*continued*)

Table 3.7 (continued)

	Cohort born											
Year	*1951–1955*		*1956–1960*		*1961–1965*		*1966–1970*		*1971–1975*		*1976–1980*	
	M	*W*	*M*	*W*	*M*	*W*	*M*	*W*	*M*	*W*	*M*	*W*
Per-adult-equivalent expenditures of households(log)												
1984	16.63	16.30	16.50	16.55								
1989	16.19	15.83	16.08	16.10	16.07	15.80						
1993	16.23	16.20	16.15	16.09	16.16	16.10	15.93	16.30				
1997	16.23	16.14	16.23	15.99	16.22	15.90	16.15	16.02				
2001	16.34	16.10	16.38	16.16	16.40	16.03	16.40	16.25	16.30	16.21		
2005	16.57	16.38	16.55	16.38	16.62	16.29	16.62	16.35	16.57	16.33	16.49	16.42
2009	16.42	16.31	16.37	16.30	16.45	16.40	16.47	16.21	16.46	16.30	16.40	16.24
Absolute changes												
1984–1989	−0.44	−0.47	−0.42	−0.45								
1989–1993	0.04	0.37	0.07	−0.01	0.09	0.3						
1993–1997	0	−0.06	0.08	−0.1	0.06	−0.2	0.22	−0.28				
1997–2001	0.11	−0.04	0.15	0.17	0.18	0.13	0.25	0.23				
2001–2005	0.23	0.28	0.17	0.22	0.22	0.26	0.22	0.1	0.27	0.12		
2005–2009	−0.15	−0.07	−0.18	−0.08	−0.17	0.11	−0.15	−0.14	−0.11	−0.03	−0.09	−0.18
Percentage of people below the poverty line												
1984	22.6	42.0	26.9	32.5								
1989	34.4	41.3	38.8	43.3	42.1	57.8						
1993	37.8	41.4	46.2	50.0	46.0	53.4	57.8	38.6				
1997	35.4	50.9	39.6	60.5	42.8	50.2	47.5	60.6				
2001	37.4	58.9	39.1	65.1	42.9	67.8	47.3	56.0	49.5	69.6		
2005	24.6	42.2	27.2	38.3	29.1	43.5	34.2	57.4	37.2	63.0	41.4	63.2
2009	32.3	49.6	38.1	49.0	36.6	43.2	40.3	54.4	43.9	62.5	49.8	69.9
Absolute changes												
1984–1989	11.8	−0.7	11.9	10.8								
1989–1993	3.4	0.1	7.4	6.7	3.9	−4.4						
1993–1997	−2.4	9.5	−6.6	10.5	−3.2	−3.2	−10.3	22				
1997–2001	2	8	−0.5	4.6	0.1	17.6	−0.2	−4.6				
2001–2005	−12.8	−16.7	−11.9	−26.8	−13.8	−24.3	−13.1	1.4	−12.3	−6.6		
2005–2009	7.7	7.4	10.9	10.7	7.5	−0.3	6.1	−3	6.7	0.5	8.4	6.7
Gini coefficient												
1984	0.38	0.40	0.37	0.41								
1989	0.40	0.37	0.37	0.36	0.35	0.38						
1993	0.34	0.39	0.33	0.42	0.35	0.35	0.39	0.27				
1997	0.36	0.35	0.35	0.34	0.35	0.37	0.36	0.22				
2001	0.35	0.30	0.36	0.38	0.35	0.31	0.38	0.33	0.36	0.32		
2005	0.35	0.35	0.36	0.34	0.36	0.32	0.37	0.35	0.37	0.40	0.36	0.37
2009	0.34	0.37	0.35	0.36	0.36	0.35	0.34	0.32	0.34	0.35	0.34	0.38
Absolute changes												
1984–1989	0.02	−0.03	0	−0.05								
1989–1993	−0.06	0.02	−0.04	0.06	0	−0.03						
1993–1997	0.02	−0.04	0.02	−0.08	0	0.02	−0.03	−0.05				
1997–2001	−0.01	−0.05	0.01	0.04	0	−0.06	0.02	0.11				
2001–2005	0	0.05	0	−0.04	0.01	0.01	−0.01	0.02	0.01	0.08		
2005–2009	−0.01	0.02	−0.01	0.02	0	0.03	−0.03	−0.03	−0.03	−0.05	−0.02	0.01

Source: Authors' Calculation based on HEIS data

Table 3.8 Absolute mobility estimations

Per-adult-equivalent expenditures of households	*All sample*	*Only males*	*Less than a high school education*	*High school & higher education*
Mobility coefficient	0.97	0.96	0.97	0.88
	(0.022)	(0.022)	(0.024)	(0.028)
Cohort fixed effect	NO	NO	NO	NO
R squared	0.92	0.90	0.91	0.92

Source: Authors' calculations based on HEIS data files
Note: Number in parentheses is standard error

Table 3.9 Conditional mobility estimations

Per-adult-equivalent expenditures of households	*All sample*	*Only males*	*Less than a high school education*	*High school & higher education*
Mobility coefficient	0.96	0.95	0.96	0.86
	(0.024)	(0.024)	(0.025)	(0.033)
Cohort fixed effect	YES	YES	YES	YES
R squared	0.94	0.91	0.92	0.92

Source: Authors' calculations based on HEIS data files
Note: Number in parentheses is standard error

members were very young in 1997—while expenditures increase for all cohorts. The Gini coefficient in this period follows no discernable pattern, as inequality increases for some cohorts and decreases for others. The picture changes significantly during 2001–2005, as incidence of poverty is substantially lower for all cohorts. Average expenditures show an increasing pattern for all cohorts but no pattern is found for inequality. At the end of the analyzed period, surprisingly, the level of inequality decreases for most cohorts. However, average expenditures tend to decrease and the incidence of poverty increases for all cohorts. These changes suggest that, during the period under investigation, middle-income groups become poorer and some join the ranks of lower-income groups.

The lower the educational level, the higher is the level of poverty. Furthermore, average per capita household expenditures increase for both educational categories but the increment is greater for those with higher educational achievements. The Gini coefficient also generally associates higher educational attainment with lower inequality. Yet, this relationship is reversed once inequality is measured for the youngest cohort. Perhaps the main explanation for this observation is that cohorts with lower levels of education can find jobs more easily, as compared to the youngest cohort with the highest level of education. This is also reflected in the higher unemployment rate observed for the youngest cohort with higher level of education.

Turing to the gender differences, the average per capita expenditures are generally higher for male-headed households than female-headed households. The incidence of poverty among women is compatible with the

Table 3.10 Mobility over different time intervals

Per-adult-equivalent expenditures of households(log)	*Yearly*	*2-Year*	*5-Year*	*Yearly*	*2-Year*	*5-Year*
Panel A: All sample						
Mobility coefficient	0.97	0.93	0.70	0.96	0.91	0.65
	(0.022)	(0.035)	(0.065)	(0.024)	(0.038)	(0.07)
Cohort fixed effect	NO	NO	NO	YES	YES	YES
R squared	0.92	0.90	0.91	0.94	0.90	0.92
Panel B: Only males						
Mobility coefficient	0.96	0.92	0.69	0.95	0.89	0.62
	(0.022)	(0.035)	(0.065)	(0.024)	(0.038)	(0.07)
Cohort fixed effect	NO	NO	NO	YES	YES	YES
R squared	0.90	0.91	0.87	0.91	0.92	0.90
Panel C: Less than a higher education						
Mobility coefficient	0.97	0.91	0.64	0.96	0.90	0.63
	(0.024)	(0.039)	(0.071)	(0.025)	(0.04)	(0.076)
Cohort fixed effect	NO	NO	NO	YES	YES	YES
R squared	0.91	0.90	0.89	0.92	0.90	0.89
Panel D: High school and higher education						
Mobility coefficient	0.88	0.80	0.52	0.86	0.77	0.45
	(0.028)	(0.039)	(0.061)	(0.033)	(0.045)	(0.072)
Cohort fixed effect	NO	NO	NO	YES	YES	YES
R squared	0.92	0.91	0.85	0.92	0.90	0.89

Source: Authors' calculations based on HEIS data files
Note: Number in parentheses is standard error

average per capita household expenditures. Inequality among most cohorts is higher for women than men.

Mobility Analysis

Table 3.8 provides our results based on the first set of estimations. The fixed effects per cohort are not included, so these are unconditional measures of mobility. In the first column, absolute mobility for all samples is given. The point-estimated value of β is 0.97, suggesting a very low mobility. Column 2 of Table 3.8 gives the reestimated results after restricting the sample to males. They remain nearly the same, suggesting that mobility is not generated by gender differences.

We also consider a different approach, by analyzing the evolution of mobility associated with educational attainment. We construct the pseudo-panels based on the same five-year intervals and two categories of education of the household heads. Column 3 shows that in cohorts with less than a high school education, mobility remains low. On the contrary, for cohorts with secondary school and higher education, the mobility coefficient diminishes to 0.88, suggesting a small degree of mobility. In all the cases, the coefficients are statistically significant at the 95 percent level. This result implies that even though poorer households experience faster income (expenditure) growth than the richer ones, the convergence rate is extremely small. Inequality is thus expected to remain a major problem in

Table 3.11 Mobility measures with control variables

Per-adult-equivalent expenditures of households	*All sample*	*Only males*	*Less than a high school education*	*High school & higher education*
Mobility coefficient	0.849 (0.030)	0.844 (0.029)	0.79 (0.031)	0.709 (0.036)
Cohort fixed effect	NO	NO	NO	NO
Age	0.0087 (0.0042)	0.0085 (0.0041)	0.015 (0.0042)	0.018 (0.0056)
Square age	-0.00009 (0.00004)	-0.00008 (0.00004)	-0.0001 (0.00004)	-0.00014 (0.00005)
Size of the cohort	-0.00002 (0.00001)	-0.00003 (0.00001)	-0.00001 (0.00001)	-0.00009 (0.00005)
R squared	0.90	0.91	0.89	0.88

Source: Authors' calculations based on HEIS data files
Note: Number in parentheses is standard error

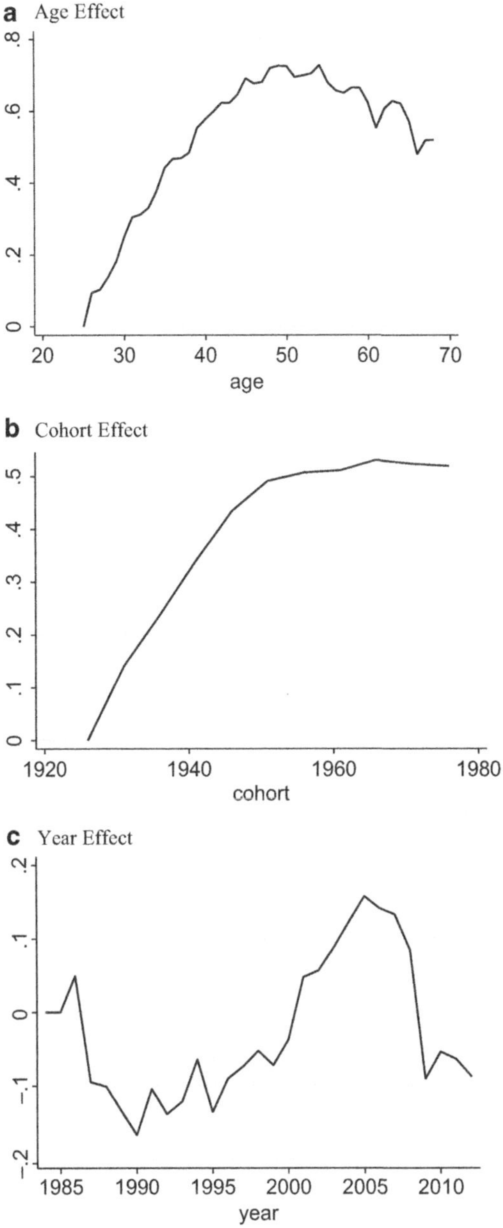

Fig. 3.2 Decomposition of cohort expenditures into year, age, and cohort effects. *Source*: Authors' calculations based on HEIS data files

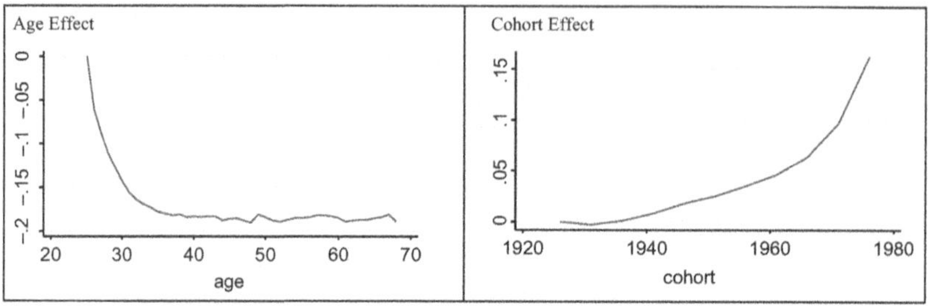

Fig. 3.3 Decomposition of cohort unemployment rate by age and cohort effects. *Source*: Authors' calculation based on HEIS data files

Iran as it cannot be overcome through personal effort. The $R^2$of the estimations are also relatively high, supporting the idea that equal opportunity is absent.

Next, we allow the presence of individual effects through cohort-specific intercepts to probe conditional mobility. Column 1 in Table 3.9 shows estimation results of the original model for all households in the sample. In column 2, only males are considered, while columns 3 and 4 show the results in terms of educational attainment. Estimation results for the mobility coefficient indicate low mobility across all scenarios, suggesting that shocks to household incomes (expenditures) are likely to have amplifying effects on income inequality. For instance, a 10 percent difference in income (expenditure) between two households with the same fixed effects is reduced to a 9.6 percent difference after one year. Households experiencing adverse income (expenditure) shocks, which take them below the level of income (expenditure) determined by their individual attributes, are faced with serious challenges to recover the resulting gap after one year. We can see that there is a very strong positive correlation between both measures of mobility. Table 3.10 provides estimates of the mobility coefficient over one-, two-, and five-year time periods. Columns 1 through 3 of the table provide the estimates of absolute mobility, while columns 4 through 6 include cohort fixed effects and therefore give measures of conditional mobility.

In Panel A of Table 3.10, the estimate of β is 0.93 for the two-year interval and 0.7 for the five-year interval. Thus, poorer households experience slightly faster income (expenditure) growth than the richer ones. In

Table 3.12 Estimations for being poor—1971–1975 and 1946–1950 cohorts

Explanatory variables	*2005*				*2010*			
	Cohort born 1971–1975		*Cohort born 1946–1950*		*Cohort born 1971–1975*		*Cohort born 1946–1950*	
	Coefficient	p-*value*	*Coefficient*	p-*value*	*Coefficient*	p-*value*	*Coefficient*	p-*value*
Household head characteristics								
Gender	-0.14	0.00	-0.16	0.00	-0.38	0.00	-0.27	0.00
Employed	-0.46	0.00	-0.23	0.00	-0.5	0.00	-0.25	0.00
Education	-0.53	0.03	-0.21	0.00	-0.72	0.00	-0.38	0.00
Household characteristics								
Dependency ratio	0.57	0.00	0.54	0.00	0.42	0.00	0.36	0.00
Number of children	0.2	0.00	0.1	0.00	0.3	0.00	0.2	0.00
Geographic characteristics								
Region 5 (Tehran)	0.13	0.00	0.14	0.00	0.32	0.00	0.38	0.00
Region 2	-0.08	0.00	-0.1	0.00	-0.01	0.00	-0.02	0.00
Region 3	0.25	0.00	0.28	0.00	0.34	0.01	0.36	0.00
Region 4	0.25	0.02	0.31	0.00	0.37	0.00	0.49	0.00
Region 6	0.1	0.00	0.9	0.00	0.25	0.04	0.24	0.00
Region 7	-0.002	0.00	-0.9	0.00	-0.01	0.00	-0.03	0.00
Region 8	0.44	0.01	0.44	0.00	0.59	0.00	0.58	0.00
Region 9	0.42	0.00	0.35	0.00	0.43	0.00	0.57	0.00
Pseudo R squared	0.28		0.25		0.27		0.3	

Source: Authors' calculations based on HEIS data files

other words, a household that enjoys 10 percent higher income (expenditure) than another one today will continue to enjoy 9.3 percent higher income (expenditure) two years later. The conditional mobility results are similar to absolute mobility. A 10 percent difference in income (expenditure) between two households today, with the same fixed effects, will be reduced to a 9.1 percent after two years and to 6.5 percent after five years. The results after including two control variables—age and age squared—and the size of the cohort are shown in Table 3.11. After adding the control variables in Model 3, the mobility coefficients remain low and almost similar to the original model of absolute mobility. The coefficients of age and their squares have the expected sign, positive and negative, respectively. But none of them is found to be significant in statistical or economic terms. The marginal effect corresponding to the size of the cohort is negative but statistically insignificant. The sign is as expected—belonging to bigger cohorts would affect the expenditures of households negatively.

Decomposition of Expenditures and Unemployment Rate

In Fig. 3.2, mean log consumption expenditures of various generations between 1984 and 2012 are decomposed to the age, cohort, and year effects. The following points of high importance should be made for the figure. The first graph displays the age effect and fluctuation in consumption expenditures related to age. Concerning the age effect, the age of 25 is taken as reference for all ages. That is, the age effect for age 25 is zero. Consumption expenditures increase up to age 50, remain constant between ages 50 and 60, and are then reduced with a very moderate slope. The latter effect is likely due to the life-cycle income changes, as most consumption expenditures are based on labor income rather than saving and transfer payment. Predictable changes in life-cycle income, especially as associated with the retirement age, thus affect people's purchasing power and decrease levels of consumption and consumption expenditures.

The middle graph shows the cohort effect with the 1926 generation as reference. As indicated, consumption expenditures of new generations have increased in comparison with the same ages in previous generations. Although the cohort effect is increasing, this graph shows a decreasing trend for new generations where there is a negative growth for generations after 1971.

The third graph concerns the year effect, showing macroeconomic fluctuations in detail. Between 1984 and 1990, there are significant decreases in consumption expenditures associated with the war. Subsequently, even though another negative shock is observed for 1995—attributable to price controls, a fixed exchange rate, and high rate of inflation—the overall trend is of an increasing nature through 2005. Despite the substantial growth in oil revenues, a decreasing trend is observed from 2008 onward.

Generational positions in the labor market affect consumption expenditures and should therefore be taken into account. This is particularly important for the case of Iran with its very young and increasingly educated population. The results of our unemployment rate analysis are displayed in Fig. 3.3. They show the year effect to be insignificant. This suggests that the unemployment rate has been under the effect of the cohort and age effects. Results for the age effect indicate that the unemployment rate decreases from age 25 to age 37 and remains stable thereafter. Furthermore, the unemployment rate of age 37 is approximately nine percent less than that of age 27—hence, the importance attached to this period of life in determining income and consumption rate. Based on the results for the cohort effects, there is no noticeable difference in unemployment rate among those born between 1926 and 1970 at identical ages. Yet, there exists an increasing effect for those born in 1971 or later. Unemployment rates for people born between 1971 and 1975 and between 1976 and 1980 are, respectively, around three and ten percent higher than those born between 1966 and 1970. Younger generations thus face higher unemployment rates.

Vulnerability

Our estimation results concerning the probability of being poor for cohort 1971–1975 and cohort 1946–1950 in the years 2005 and 2010 are reported in Table 3.12. Being unemployed increases the probability of being poor for both cohorts in both years. This effect is higher for cohort 1971–1975 in comparison with cohort 1946–1950. This finding confirms that government policies aimed at enhancing the labor market are important in reducing poverty observed among younger cohorts. The education of household heads is another key variable explaining reduction of poverty. The level of education has a positive impact on "moving out of poverty," suggesting that better educated heads of household are associated with higher chances of "upward mobility." Female-headed households have a higher probability of being poor in comparison to male-headed households. As expected, the dependency ratio and number of children increases the probability of being poor for both cohorts. The regional variable indicates that people who live in regions 8 and 9 have a highest probability of being poor than those who live in region 1 (omitted variable).

Conclusion

In this chapter, poverty, inequality, income mobility, and vulnerability were probed in Iran across different generations. For this purpose, a pseudo-panel was constructed that combined 31 years of cross-sectional household surveys from 1984 to 2014. The pseudo-panel was constructed with cohorts of those born between 1926 and 1980. In light of Iran's low employment rate especially among the youth, the unemployment rate was also considered as a factor affecting people's expenditures.

Our results show that consumption expenditures of the younger cohorts relative to their predecessors at the same age have increased, but the increasing rate is decreasing. Findings on the age effects indicate that expenditures rise until age 50, remain relatively flat between the ages 50 and 60, and then slowly decline. The year effects show that life-cycle expenditure is consistent with economic changes across the years in Iran.

Furthermore, the unemployment rate falls between age 25 and age 37 to remain nearly constant afterward. Also, results for the cohort effects suggest that in similar ages, there is no significant differences in the unemployment rate of those born between 1926 and 1970 but the cohort effects have risen for those born after 1971. Younger generations are thus facing a serious unemployment problem, which translates into inadequate income for a decent living (these two interact with each other). Low rate of job creation and high unemployment rates hint at the reasons behind wage repression in Iran. Yet, repressed wages can also positively influence the labor force participation rate. The high unemployed figures, particularly among the youth, are a serious source of concern and require appropriate government policy measures. Public policy should aim at inclusive growth toward full employment to guarantee economic growth consistent with the country's capacities.

Poverty and inequality are associated in greater ways with female-headed households as well as low levels of educational attainment. Lack of adequate employment opportunities for women is a main culprit behind the former observation, which must be addressed through appropriate public policy measures. Thus, public policy should further focus on the promotion of quality educational services accessible to all.

As revealed by our study of inequality and income mobility, income trend is not convergent with the total mean. This suggests inflexibility of the social system and unequal distribution of life opportunities that can in turn create economic, social, and political instability. Since poverty is greatest among the young and the old generations, public sector policies should also focus on job creation for the youth and social safety nets for the elderly.

Notes

1. Moffitt (1993), Collado (1997), Girma (2000), McKenzie (2004), Antman and McKenzie (2005), Verbeek and Vella (2005) discuss the conditions required to obtain consistent estimates in a variety of dynamic linear models by using the pseudo-panels. Our study is based on Antman and McKenzie's (2005) work.
2. They are as follows: *Region 1* Ardabil, East Azerbaijan, and West Azerbaijan (omitted variable); *Region 2* Gilan, and Mazandaran; *Region 3* Golestan, Razavi Khorasan, Semnan, and North Khorasan; *Region 4* South Khorasan, Hormozgan, Sistan-Baluchestan, and Kerman; *Region 5* Tehran; *Region 6* Qom, Markazi, and Qazvin; *Region 7* Esfahan, Yazd, and Fars; *Region 8* Bushehr, Khuzestan, Chaharmahaal-Bakhtiari and Kohgiluyeh-Boyrahmad; *Region 9* llam, Hamadan, Kermanshah, Kordestan, Zanjan, and Lorestan.
3. Various methods for estimating per-adult-equivalent expenditures of households have by proposed. Out study is based on Haughton and Khandker (2009).

References

Assadzadeh, A., & Paul, S. (2001). *Poverty, growth and redistribution: A case study of Iran.* WIDER Working Paper 124. UNU-WIDER, Helsinki.

Antman, F., & McKenzie, D. J. (2005). *Earnings mobility and measurement error: A pseudo-panel approach.* World Bank Policy Research Working Paper No. 3745. Washington, DC: The World Bank Group.

Antman, F., & McKenzie, D. J. (2007). Earnings mobility and measurement error: A pseudo-panel approach. *Economic Development and Cultural Change, 56*(1), 125–161.

Browning, M., Deaton, A., & Irish, M. (1985). A profitable approach to labor supply and commodity demand over the life-cycle. *Econometrica, 53*(3), 503–544.

Chen, S., & Ravallion, M. (2007). *Absolute poverty measures for the developing world, 1981–2004.* World Bank Policy Research Working Paper No. 4211, Washington, DC: The World Bank Group.

Collado, M. D. (1997). Estimating dynamic models from time series of independent cross-sections. *Journal of Econometrics, 82*, 37–62.

Cuesta, J., Nopo, H., & Pizzolitto, G. (2007). Using pseudo- panels to measure income mobility in latin america, research department publications 4557, Inter-American Development Bank, Research Department.

Deaton, A. (1985). Panel data from times series of cross-sections. *Journal of Econometrics, 30*, 109–126.

Deaton, A. (1997). *The analysis of household surveys. A microeconometric approach to development policy.* Baltimore, MD: Johns Hopkins University Press.

Deaton, A., & Paxson, C. (1994). Intertemporal choice and inequality. *The Journal of Political Economy, 102*(3), 437–467.

Fields, G. S. (2006). The many facets of economic mobility. ILR School Articles & Chapters, Paper 230, Cornell University, Ithaca, NY. Retrieved March 21, 2016, from http://digitalcommons.ilr.cornell.edu/articles/230/

Foster, J., Greer, J., & Thorbecke, E. (1984). A class of decomposable poverty measures. *Econometrica, 52*(3), 761–766.

Girma, S. (2000). A quasi-differencing approach to dynamic modeling from a time series of independent cross-sections. *Journal of Econometrics, 98*, 365–383.

Haughton, J., & Khandker, S. R. (2009). *Handbook on poverty and inequality. International bank for reconstruction and development.* Washington, DC: The World Bank Group.

Kakwani, N., & Son, H. (2008). Poverty equivalent growth rate. *Review of Income and Wealth, 54*(4), 643–655.

McKenzie, D. J. (2004). Asymptotic theory for heterogeneous dynamic pseudo-panels. *Journal of Econometrics, 120*(2), 235–262.

Moffitt, R. (1993). Identification and estimation of dynamic models with a time series of repeated cross-sections. *Journal of Econometrics, 59*(1), 99–124.

Pritchett, L., Suryahadi, A., & Sumarto, S. (2000). Quantifying vulnerability to poverty: A proposed measure applied to indonesia. World Bank Policy Research Working Paper No. 2437, Washington, DC: The World Bank Group.

Raghfar, H., & Sanei, L. (2010). Measuring household vulnerability to poverty in city of Tehran. *Social Welfare, 38*, 389–427. (in Persian).

Raghfar, H., Khoshdast, F., & Yazdanpanah, M. (2012). Measurement of income inequality in Iran, 1984–2010. *Social Welfare, 45*, 275–305. (in Persian).

Raghfar, H., & Babapour, M. (2014). The intergenerational analysis of urban household expenditure by using the Pseudo-panel. *Quarterly Journal of Applied Economics Studies, 10*, 177–199. (in Persian).

Raghfar, H., Babapour, M., & Yazdanpanah, M. (2015). Survey on the relationship between economic growth, poverty, and inequality in Iran during five-year development plan. *Quarterly Journal of Applied Economic Studies, 16*, 59–80. (in Persian).

Raghfar, H., Yazdanpanah, M., & Babapour, M. (2016). Three decades of poverty in Iran. To be published (in Persian).

Salehi-Isfahani, D., & Majbouri, M. (2013). Mobility and the dynamics of poverty in Iran: Evidence from the 1992–1995 panel survey. *The Quarterly Review of Economics and Finance, 53*(3), 257–267.

SCI [Statistical Center of Iran]. (1984 through 2014). Household expenditure and income surveys.

Scott, C., & Litchfield, J. A. (1994). *Inequality, mobility and the determinants of income among the rural poor in chile, 1968–1986*. STICERD Working Paper No. 53, London School of Economics, London.

Verbeek, M., & Vella, F. (2005). Estimating dynamic models from repeated cross-sections. *Journal of Econometrics, 127*, 83–102.

CHAPTER 4

Oil Rents, Political Institutions, and Income Inequality in Iran

Sajjad Faraji Dizaji

Introduction

In this chapter, I investigate the moderating influence of political institutions on the income inequality effect of oil rents in Iran. At least since the first oil shock in 1973, economic performance in Iran has been under the heavy influence of oil exports and direct government expenditures derived from oil revenues. Indeed, a rentier state argument has been advanced to describe Iran's political economy (see Mahdavy 1970: 466). Oil exports gave impetus to rapid economic growth in the 1960s and the earlier part of the 1970s, but they may have also facilitated the unfolding of revolutionary events in 1979. Furthermore, by all accounts, Iran's economy has underperformed in terms of per capita GDP growth since the Revolution. These observations may thus support the hypothesis that natural resources have been more of a curse than a blessing for Iran.

Poverty and income inequality have been a central theme in Iran's post-revolutionary discourse (Salehi-Isfahani 2009). Yet, on the basis of available income distribution statistics, inequality has remained relatively high in the country. The latest Human Development Report (UNDP 2015) gives a figure of 33.6 (on the scale of 0 to 100) for Iran's average Gini coefficient between 2005 and 2013—ranking it 46th among 142 countries. The

S.F. Dizaji (✉)
Tarbiat Modares University, Tehran, Iran

M.R. Farzanegan, P. Alaedini (eds.), *Economic Welfare and Inequality in Iran*, DOI 10.1057/978-1-349-95025-6_4

average Gini figure available from the Central Bank of Iran (CBI 2015) for 1970–2012 is 41.8 percent (and around 38 percent in the last few years of the period). Furthermore, based on the same figures, between 1970 and 1975, the Gini coefficient experienced a rising trend, which may be attributed to sudden increases in oil prices. The Gini coefficient then decreased slightly until 1978, due most likely to rising imports and subsidies. In 1979, income inequality was aggravated due to the initial effects of the Revolution. Yet, from 1980 to 1988, coinciding with the Iran-Iraq War, public-sector monetary transfers to the poor and significant subsidies on products and services kept the inflation rate and income inequality under control. The fall in income inequality in the initial post-revolutionary years should also be associated with other pro-poor policy initiatives adopted by the government, including significant investments in rural areas, provision of infrastructure, and literacy campaigns. Furthermore, a number of important para-statal charity organizations, such as the Imam Khomeini Relief Foundation, were created to address the plight of the poor after the Revolution and rapidly expanded their operations in ensuing decades (Esfahani 2005; Salehi-Isfahani 2006).

Despite a steady fall in poverty since the end of the Iran-Iraq War in 1988, inequality has remained relatively stable over the years. The income gap between the poor and the rich widened in 1991–1992 as a set of market liberalization and privatization programs were carried out by the Rafsanjani administration (Salehi-Isfahani 2009; Tabibian 2000). The Gini coefficient increased slightly—from 39.9 percent in 1997 to 40.16 percent in 2005 (CBI 2015)—during the reformist administration of Khatami as well. Some analysts suggest that increasing income inequality during the administration of Rafsanjani and Khatami was one of the reasons behind the success of Ahmadinejad's presidential campaign in 2005, which ran on a populist platform (Salehi-Isfahani 2007; Farzanegan 2009). One of his famous campaign promises in 2005 was to bring the oil wealth to the people's dinner table by, among other things, combating the country's oil mafia. His tenure in office did coincide with some improvements in the Gini coefficient. The Gini coefficient decreased to 37.6 percent in 2011 and was 38.1 percent in 2012 (CBI 2015).

A negative relationship between natural resource rents and income inequality has been highlighted in the literature (e.g., Leamer et al. 1999; Torvik 2002; Gylfason and Zoega 2003; Lopez-Feldman et al. 2006; Ross 2007; Goderis and Malone 2009; Fum and Hodler 2009). The question is whether the effects of natural resource rents on inequality are unconditional or are further shaped by the quality of political institutions? If political institutions matter, the resource curse can be avoided by aiming to enhance the quality of political institutions.

My main task in this chapter is thus to probe the link between political institutions, resource rents, and inequality in Iran. The political history of Iran allows one to examine the mechanisms of rent-seeking and resource curse, as the country has experienced different political regimes over the last four decades—in particular, autocracy during the Pahlavi era and factionalized semi-democratic politics in the post-revolutionary period (see Bjorvatn et al. 2013; Dizaji et al. 2015; Habibi 2013). The chapter first examines the moderating effect of political institutions on Iran's oil-inequality nexus. It then investigates the effects of different categories of government expenditures—namely, military and non-military spending—on income inequality. In the next section, a brief literature review is provided on the relationships among resource rents, political institutions, and income inequality. This is followed by a discussion of the study's data and econometric model. Empirical results and robustness checks are presented in the fourth section. The final section provides the study's conclusions.

Resource Rents, Political Institutions, and Inequality

A number of studies have examined the relationship between resource rents and inequality, with mixed findings. Some suggest that an abundance of natural resources is likely to lead to high levels of inequality (e.g., Stevens 2003; Auty 1994; Fields 1989; Sarraf and Jiwanji 2001). Leamer et al. (1999) argue that resource exploitation does not require significant human capital and therefore the labor force in resource-rich countries is unprepared for the transition to human capital-intensive manufacturing and a knowledge-based economy. As a result, these countries may experience higher income inequality for longer periods than resource-scarce economies. Goderis and Malone's (2009) study suggests that income inequality falls in the short run immediately after a resource boom and then increases steadily over time. Sokoloff and Engerman (2000) associate inequality with unequal land ownership stemming from scale economies as well as the effect of institutions. Nikoloski (2009) also emphasizes the impact of institutions and resource wealth on inequality. Yet, Ross (2007) does not find any significant association between mineral dependence of an economy and its level of inequality, but acknowledges potential bias in his results due to the possible under-reporting of income inequality in mineral-rich countries.

In another study, Ross (1999) explains how resource rents lead to abuse of political power for private benefits. The challenge of pervasive corruption in resource-rich countries is also emphasized by Kolstad et al. (2008) and Karl (2004), while Aresky and Gylfason (2011) provide empirical evidence in the African context for a positive association between resource rents and corruption. Fors and Olsson (2007) highlight the reluctance of the elites in resource-rich countries to create institutions that could deal with rent-seeking behavior.

The effects of democracy on income inequality have also received a great deal of attention in the literature. Democracy is theoretically conducive to the reduction of income gap between the rich and the poor. Adoption of redistributive policies—such as a higher budget levels for social welfare, education, and healthcare as well as more progressive tax systems—are more likely in democracies (Reuveny and Li 2003). Democracies are also more likely to facilitate the participation of the poor and reflection of their demands for income redistribution in the decision-making process (Lenski 1966; Boix 1998; Chan 1997). Additionally, unions and nongovernmental organizations, representing the lower and middle classes, are more active in democracies and can pressing for better distribution of income and opportunities.

Empirical studies on the relationship between democracy and inequality have yielded mixed results. Some suggest that democracy reduces inequality (Muller 1988; Moon 1991; Rodrik 1998). In contrast, Huber et al. (2006) argue that the democratic traditions are positively associated with income inequality. Others find no statistically significant relationship between democracy and income distribution (Bollen and Jackman 1985; Deininger and Squire 1998; Gasiorowski 1997). Yet, Simpson (1990) finds an inverted U-shaped relationship between democracy and income inequality—income inequality rises with democracy up to some level of democracy and then declines.[1]

Mahdavy (1970) is credited with the elaboration of the rentier state concept for the case of Iran (in the 1960s). According to him, "oil revenues received by the governments of the oil exporting countries have very little to do with the production processes of their domestic economies" (Mahdavy 1970: 429). Yet, the "problems of income distribution are more serious in Rentier States because of the concentration of vast external rents in few hands. The temptations for a government bureaucracy to turn into a rentier class with its own independent source of income are considerable" (Ibid.:467). Thus, the government increasingly plays an "allocative" role in oil-rich economies (Luciani 1987: 70). As oil revenues are external to the domestic economy and a very small minority has a role in their generation, "the rest of the society is only engaged in the distribution and utilization of this wealth" (Beblawi 1987: 51). Bjorvatn and Farzanegan (2013) argue that governments in resource-rich countries tend to maximize their patronage benefits by expanding public-sector employment.[2]

Tabibian's (2000) examination of Iran's 1997 household survey underscores the significant consequences of the rentier economic structure in terms of inherent functional inequalities. It shows that rises in the oil price benefit the highest income decile more than any other income group. Furthermore, oil rents in the form of government's extensive subsidies on fuel, basic foodstuffs, and utilities, while helping to reduce poverty, are likely to worsen income inequality. Asadzadeh and Jalili (2015) examine the relationship between income inequality and the shadow economy in Iran over the period 1971–2010. They find that the shadow economy has an increasing effect on income inequality. They argue that the shadow economy has a direct effect on income inequality by shaping the employment environment. Moreover, its indirect effects on inequality are through affecting the government budget and economic growth.[3]

The above-reviewed studies as well as others that investigate the effects of resource rents and political institutions on inequality mostly do so using separate models. In particular, to the best of knowledge, no attempt has been made so far to probe the simultaneous and interactive effects of these two variables on income distribution in Iran. In the following section, I set up a model that includes both oil rents and political institutions in a simple framework to study how a higher level of democracy mitigates the increasing effect of oil rents on income inequality in Iran.

Research Design, Data, and Empirical Specification

To estimate whether the relationship between oil/gas rents and income distribution varies systematically with the level of democracy, I employ the following model:

$$Gini_t = \alpha_1.Gini_{t-1} + \alpha_2.X_t^{'} + \beta_1.oil_t + \beta_2.democ_t + \beta_3.(oil_t \times democ_t) + \varepsilon_t$$

In the above equation, *Gini* is the Gini coefficient representing income distribution. Its lagged value on the right-hand side is included to control for the dynamic path of the Gini coefficient. The main proxy for oil dependence (oil) is real oil and gas exports per capita. The *democ* variable refers to the level of democracy as measured by Vanhanen index of democratization (Vanhanen 2011). It is defined as the product of two underlying indices for political competition and political participation. *oilt*× *democt* is an interaction term of the oil dependence variable with an index of democracy, and ε is the error term which is assumed to be independent of other regressors. X is a vector of control variables—including money and quasi money per capita (M2) as a proxy for monetary policy; per capita real government expenditures on military (mil); education (edu), social affairs (social), and housing (housing) as proxies for government fiscal policies; and real GDP per capita as a proxy for economic development. Moreover, in order to test the possible nonlinear relationship between income inequality and GDP per capita, I also use the squared form of GDP per capita. Finally, to capture the effects of the (1973–1974) oil crisis, Iranian Islamic revolution (1979), and the Iran-Iraq war (1980–1988) I employ three dummy variables—DUM74, DUM 79, and DUM80, respectively.

The initial estimation method is dynamic OLS (Ordinary Least Squares). The marginal impact of a unit increase in oil and gas exports on Gini coefficient is β1 + β3.*democ*. I expect the sign of β3 to be negative. This means that increasing oil rents in a situation of weak political institutions have negative effects on income distribution ceteris paribus. Thus, the final effect of oil and gas rents on income distribution is conditional on the level of democracy.

The anticipated effects of the control variables are straightforward. I expect the lagged values of inequality used in the econometric simulations to be associated with higher contemporaneous levels of Gini. As indicated by Reuveny and Li (2003), inclusion of the lagged values of inequality helps to control for some excluded but potentially important variables in the model. Gupta et al. (2002) also include lagged values of the Gini coefficient in their model.

A higher level of natural resource revenues may increase income inequality. The production of and the overall reliance on natural resources are likely to create rents easily captured by the ruling elite, which in turn can result in exacerbation of the income gap between the ruling minority and the poor majority. Moreover, the high levels of inequality in resource-rich countries may also be associated with the reluctance of the elites to allow redistribution (Nikoloski 2009).

One would expect economic development to decrease inequality as the income of the poor rises due to increases in the average income (Anderson et al. 2003: 8). However, according to Kuznets (1963), in the early stages of development, economic growth is associated with increasing inequality, but as countries grow and develop, their income gap between the rich and the poor decreases (hence, an inverted U-shaped relationship between real GDP per capita and inequality).

As discussed in the literature review, democracy may decrease income inequality (Muller 1988; Moon 1991; Rodrik 1998) or aggravate it up to some level (Simpson 1990).

I control for government's spending in order to capture its involvement in the economy (also as a wider proxy for the effect of redistribution). I divide government spending into two categories—military and non-military—and expect (as indicated below) these two variables to work in opposite directions. That is, military spending is likely to divert resources from the regular redistributive processes and increase the level of inequality, whereas the effect of non-military government spending on income distribution should be positive.

Finally, broad money (M2) in this study is used to represent financial deepening. Earlier studies (e.g., Dizaji 2011) suggest that monetary factors have been important determinants of inflation in Iran. Government spending associated with oil receipts increases liquidity injections, leading to higher inflation rates and therefore income inequality.

It is also possible that the quality of political institutions and oil-rent-related variables are affected by income distribution. Such an endogeneity problem in the specification may be due to omitted variable bias or simultaneity (see Bjorvatn et al. 2013). I use the Ramsey's RESET (regression specification error test) test (Ramsey 1969) to investigate the possibility of omitted variable bias in the OLS models. The null hypothesis under the RESET test is that the estimated OLS model has no omitted variable (Baum 2006, p. 123; Block 2001; QMS 2010). However, OLS estimations, to be elaborated in the results section, do not show a specific problem due to omitted variable or other forms of misspecification bias, as the linear (but not the quadratic) form of the GDP per capita is employed.

Yet, simultaneity may also play a role and deserves addressing. According to Alexeev and Conrad (2010), natural resource endowments and resource revenues of a country are largely exogenous. Furthermore, the possibility of reverse feedback in the case of Iran is low since it must maintain crude oil production quotas as a member of the Organization of Oil-Producing Countries (Farzanegan 2011). Nonetheless, to address simultaneity concerns, some instrumental variables are used that meet the following two conditions—being correlated with the suspected explanatory variables such as oil revenues and democracy and be uncorrelated with the error term (Bjorvatn et al. 2013).

For the diagnostic tests, I use 1–4 year lags and 1–3 year lags of independent variables as instruments in 2SLS (Two-Stage Least Squares) and GMM (Generalized Method of Moments) estimations, respectively.[4] The lagged explanatory variables are correlated with the current values of independent variables, while there is no significant correlation between lagged variables and the disturbance term (see Barro 1996 and Barro and Sala-i-Martin 2004 and Bjorvatn et al. 2013 for the similar approach). The second condition can be examined by using an over-identifying restriction test such as that of Sargan (1958). The null hypothesis under the Sargan test is that the instruments are uncorrelated with the error term (Gundlach and Paldam 2009). According to Murray (2006), the Sargan test inquires about the invalidity of any of the instruments, but assumes the validity of enough instruments to identify the equation exactly—as in the intuitive two-stage least squares over-identification test. More details on variables and sources are presented in Table 4.1. The summary statistics of the variables are shown in Appendix A.

Results

The first step before running regressions is checking the time-series properties of the variables in the model. I use the ADF (Augmented Dicky-Fuller) (Dickey and Fuller 1981) and Phillips-Perron tests to establish the order of integration of the variables. These tests include a constant but not a time trend, as recommended by Dickey and Fuller (1979).

As reported in Table 4.2, the Phillips-Perron unit root test indicates that all variables are integrated of order 1. The ADF test shows similar results although housing expenditure is stationary in its level at five percent.

Table 4.3 shows the direct and indirect effects of oil dependency on the Gini coefficient. A few important results emerge from the analysis. There is a strong support for a dynamic effect of inequality in the models (as expressed by the lagged value of inequality). Inequality is characterized by a certain degree of inertia, which does not allow for a rapid and dramatic change.

Table 4.1 Data description and sources

Variable	*Description*	*Source*
Gin	Logarithmic form of Gini coefficient	CBI (2015)
Expoilgas	Logarithmic form of real exports of oil and gas per capita	CBI (2015)
Van	Vanhanen index of democratization	Vanhanen (2011)
GDP	Logarithmic form of real GDP per capita	CBI (2015)
M2	Logarithmic form of real money and quasi money per capita	CBI (2015)
Education	Logarithmic form of real education expenditure per capita	CBI (2015)
Military	Logarithmic form of real defense expenditure per capita	CBI (2015)
Social	Logarithmic form of real government expenditure on social affairs per capita	CBI (2015)
Housing	Logarithmic form of real government expenditure on housing per capita	CBI (2015)
ungin (for robustness check)	Unbounded Gini coefficient	Author's calculation
ratio-rp (for robustness check)	Logarithmic form of ratio of richest 10 % to poorest 10 %	CBI (2015)
valoilgas (for robustness check)	Logarithmic form of real value added of oil and gas per capita	CBI (2015)
Polity (for robustness check)	Modified version of the polity variable	Marshall et al. (2012)

Indeed, higher past levels of inequality are associated with higher current levels of inequality. Only Model 5 in Table 4.3 does not confirm the significance of this dynamic relationship.

Lagged levels of Gini are significant at five percent in Models 2 and 4, while they are significant at one percent in Models 1, 3, and 6, as shown in Table 4.3. Research on inequality has come to this conclusion numerous times. The dynamic link in the inequality equation has been used by Calderon and Chong (2001), Li and Zou (1998), Ranjan (2001), and Nikoloski (2009). They find a strong positive correlation between past and present values of the Gini coefficient. As shown in Table 4.3, in all six models, the relationship between oil and gas exports and income inequality is positive and significant (at one percent level of significance), which suggests that higher reliance on oil and gas revenues increases inequality. Findings from other studies, such as Auty (1994), Fields (1989), Sarraf and

Table 4.2 ADF and Phillips-Perron unit root tests

Variable	*ADF*	*Phillips-Perron*		
	Level	*First difference*	*Level*	*First difference*
gin	−1.16	−4.80**	−1.02	−8.47**
ungin	−1.17	−4.74**	−1.10	−7.95**
ratio-rp	−0.89	−4.65**	−0.71	−8.12**
expoilgas	−2.04	−5.09**	−1.34	−3.80**
valoilgas	−1.58	−5.08**	−1.23	−4.30**
van	−2.7	−8.91**	−2.60	−9.04**
polity	−2.11	−7.31**	−2.11	−7.35**
GDP	−2.65	−5.09***	−1.34	−3.80***
M2	−2.38	−5.23**	−2.38	−5.27**
education	−2.01	−5.75**	−1.93	−5.89**
military	−2.53	−5.16**	−2.21	−4.92**
social	−2.74	−5.49**	−2.65	−5.48**
housing	−3.28*	−5.86**	−2.68	−5.40**

Source: Author's calculations
*Rejection of null hypothesis at 5 % level
**Rejection of null hypothesis at 1 % level
Notes: Null hypothesis: variable has a unit root

Jiwanji (2001), and Anderson et al. (2003), also indicate the aggravating effects of resource wealth on inequality. Yet, the final effect of oil revenues on inequality depends on the quality of political institutions. The negative and significant sign of the interaction term (β_3) in all specifications shows that increasing oil rents under more democratic circumstances reduces income inequality. A more democratic regime is more likely to shift resources toward public goods such as education, social affairs, and housing that increase the well-being of the population and decrease income inequality, whereas an autocratic state may direct oil rents toward national defense to protect its own vested interests (Dizaji et al. 2015).[5] The coefficient for the introduced interaction term is negative and highly significant (at one percent for Models 2–6 and at five percent for Model 1). The negative effect of interaction of the index of democracy and oil and gas exports remains robust in all models. These results show that democracy is a moderator in the inequality-oil nexus in the Iranian economy.

Models 1, 2 and 3 are testing the linear effects of GDP per capita on income distributions. All of these models show that economic development has a decreasing and significant effect on the Gini coefficient. Economic

Table 4.3 OLS, 2SLS, and GMM results using Gini coefficient, oil and gas exports per capita, and Vanhanen index

Variable	*OLS(1)*	*2SLS(2)*	*GMM(3)*	*OLS(4)*	*2SLS(5)*	*GMM(6)*
Constant	0.63(2.53)**	0.56(2.18)**	0.62(5.87)***	0.26(0.65)	−0.07(−0.15)	0.10(0.45)
gin_{t-1}	0.42(2.81)***	0.43(2.72)**	0.44(8.41)***	0.36(2.19)**	0.26(1.45)	0.31(6.67)***
expoilgas	0.11(3.09)***	0.12(3.30)***	0.11(11.54)***	0.13(3.28)***	0.15(3.8)***	0.13(9.1)***
van	0.02(2.64)**	0.03(2.87)***	0.03(9.1)***	0.03(2.83)***	0.03(3.29)***	0.03(9.59)***
expoilgas ×van	−0.04(−2.61)**	−0.04(−2.87)***	−0.04(−8.5)***	−0.04(−2.82)***	−0.05(−3.35)***	−0.04(−9.36)***
GDP	−0.07(−2.28)**	−0.035(−0.89)	−0.064(−6.53)***	0.65(0.99)	1.32(1.63)*	1.02(2.81)***
GDP^2					−0.51(−1.67)*	−0.41(−2.94)***
M2	0.03(2.39)**	0.03(2.19)**	0.03(5.01)***	0.03(2.35)**	0.03(2.02)**	0.03(4.44)***
education	−0.03(−2.25)**	−0.05(−2.57)**	−0.035(−6.65)***	−0.03(−2.09)**	−0.05(−2.75)***	−0.03(−6.14)***
military	0.006(0.31)	−0.01(−0.49)	0.001(0.19)	0.016(0.73)	0.007(0.29)	0.02(2.02)**
social	−0.006(−0.3)	−0.029(−0.96)	−0.005(−0.52)	−0.007(−0.35)	−0.05(−1.59)	−0.018(−1.75)*
housing	−0.01(−1.37)	−0.019(−1.63)*	−0.015(−4.81)***	−0.015(−1.38)	−0.02(−2.06)**	−0.019(−6.33)***
Dum74	0.02(1.79)*	0.005(0.26)	0.022(6.05)***	0.02(1.75)*	−0.005(−0.27)	0.017(3.89)***
Dum79	0.07(2.84)***	0.08(3.14)***	0.073(9.03)***	0.07(2.98)***	0.09(3.52)***	0.077(9.88)***
Dum80	0.005(0.45)	0.008(0.72)	0.005(1.33)	0.003(0.33)	0.004(0.31)	0.001(0.31)
R^2	0.94	0.93	0.94	0.94	0.94	0.94
LM	0.14	0.12		0.14	0.24	
Jarque-Bera (*p* value)	0.45	0.52	0.21	0.81	0.84	0.78
Reset	0.1	0.17		0.009	0.12	
Sargan (*p* value)		0.46	0.99		0.52	0.98

*Statistical significance at 1 %

**Statistical significance at 5 %

***Statistical significance at 10 %

Notes: Dependent variable is Gini coefficient. Sample period is 1970–2012. *t* statistics shown in parentheses are based on Newey-West HAC standard errors and covariance. LM is Breusch-Godfrey Serial Correlation LM Test (*F* form, *p* value for OLS & Obs*R^2, *p* value for 2SLS) which shows the probability of null hypothesis (no autocorrelation in residuals) acceptance (*p* values larger than 0.05 means acceptance of null hypothesis); Jarque-Bera *p* value shows the acceptance probability of null hypothesis of residual normality; RESET is Ramsey test (using powers of the independent variables) for omitted variables. The *p* value of RESET tests the H0: model has no omitted variables (*p* values larger than 0.05 means acceptance of null hypothesis—model has no omitted variables). Instruments consist of 1–4 (1–3) year lagged values of oil abundance, political variable, GDP per capita, M2, interactions terms, education expenditure, housing and social affairs expenditures, military expenditure as well as 2–4 (3) year lagged values for "lagged dependent variable" in 2SLS (GMM) method. Sargan *p* value test shows the probability of acceptance of over-identification restriction (instruments are uncorrelated with the error term and hence validity of instruments) growth may decrease income inequality since economic development is often positively associated with higher investments and higher employment. In addition, there is evidence for the existence of Kuznets curve using 2SLS and GMM methods. However, the dynamic OLS model for testing the quadric effect of GDP per capita (Model 4) does not pass the Ramsey's RESET test for regression specification error. In Models 5 and 6, GDP per capita and the squared term of the GDP per capita enter the equations with the expected signs (GDP per capita is positive, while the square term is negative). In Model 5, both variables are significant at the ten percent level of significance, while in Model 6 they are significant at one percent. In order to analyze the effect of government spending, I use disaggregated values for the government military spending and non-military spending (such as education expenditure, social affairs expenditure, and housing expenditure). While the coefficient of military spending is positive in all models, it is only significant in Model 6. As indicated in Table 4.3 government's non-military expenditures have decreasing effects on income inequality, indicating that government's social expenditures improve income distribution. The negative coefficient of education expenditure is statistically significant in all models (at one percent or five percent levels of significance), while spending on social affairs has a significant coefficient only in Model 6. Also the coefficients for housing expenditure are significant in 2SLS and GMM methods (Models 2, 3, 5 and 6).

For all models, there is strong statistical evidence that money and quasi money (M2) increase inequality significantly (at one and five percent statistical significance). Development of the financial sector may increase inequality due to the emergence of a well-paid "financial nomenklatura" that augments the gap between them and the rest of the population. Cox and Jimenez (1990) argue that financial sector development may be initially responsible for the breakdown of the informal private transfers and borrowing, which may in turn increase inequality. Moreover, the evidence shows that increasing money supply has caused higher inflation rates in Iran over the period of this study (Dizaji 2011). Al-Marhubi (1997), using data on income inequality, finds that countries with greater inequality have higher inflation. These findings are robust controlling for the possible endogeneity of the determinants of income inequality.

The Sargan test confirms the validity of instruments in the 2SLS and GMM models. In other words, the *lagged explanatory variables as instruments* are appropriately uncorrelated with the disturbance process. To check the relevancy of the instruments, I have regressed each of the endogenous regressors on a full set of instruments. The first stage *R* squares show a high explanatory power of employed instruments for the endogenous variables.

The dummy variable used for capturing the effects of the Islamic Revolution (D79) has its positive and strong significant effect on Gini (at one percent level of significance) in all specifications. The dummy variable used for capturing the 1973–1974 oil crises shows increasing and significant effects on inequality using OLS and GMM methods. There is no evidence that the Iran-Iraq war has any significant impact on inequality using 2SLS method. The Ramsey test indicates no serious problem of omitted variable bias in the models (one exception is Model 4, which does not pass the test). Also based on the LM test, in all specifications, the main findings are immune to the possible autocorrelation of residuals. The normality assumption is required in order to conduct single or joint hypothesis tests about the model parameters. The Jarque-Bera tests in all specifications cannot reject the null hypothesis of residual normality, increasing the confidence in the inferences that we make about the coefficient estimates. The *R*-squared criteria show that a considerable portion of changes in the Gini coefficient can be explained by the included explanatory variables in the specifications.

Robustness Checks

Alternative Definition for the Oil Dependency Variable (Value Added of Oil and Gas Rents per Capita)

In order to check the robustness of the results, I use the logarithmic form of real oil and gas rents per capita as an alternative to the oil and gas exports per capita. The corresponding data are value added of the oil and gas sector in the Iranian National Accounts. Rent is the difference between the output value of non-renewable resources (oil and gas in this case) and intermediary consumption (or intermediary costs). The net value indicates a value added amount of the respective resources (Farzanegan 2011). Following Bolt et al. (2002), the formula for calculating oil and gas rents is:

Rent = (production volume) × (international market price-average unit production cost)

Taking into account exploration and development costs, this formula provides a precise measure of the oil and gas rents, which are transferred to the Iranian government budgets. The estimation results are presented in Table 4.4. There is strong evidence that oil and gas rents per capita are associated with increases in inequality—significant at the one percent level

Table 4.4 OLS, 2SLS, and GMM results using Gini coefficient, oil and gas rents per capita, and Vanhanen index

Variable	*OLS(1)*	*2SLS(2)*	*GMM(3)*	*OLS(4)*	*2SLS(5)*	*GMM(6)*
Constant	0.55(2.24)**	0.49(1.89)*	0.49(2.86)***	0.19(0.44)	−0.19(−0.39)	0.34(1.18)
gin_{t-1}	0.45(3.03)***	0.44(2.86)***	0.5(5.51)***	0.39(2.49)**	0.29(1.67)*	0.44(3.46)***
valoilgas	0.09(2.78)***	0.1 (2.94)***	0.07(3.85)***	0.11(2.94)***	0.14(3.44)***	0.09(3.38)***
van	0.02(1.84)*	0.02(2.04)**	0.017(3.18)***	0.022(2.06)**	0.03(2.54)**	0.021(4.07)***
valoilgas×van	−0.025(−1.81)*	−0.03(−2.04)**	−0.02(−2.98)***	−0.03(−2.04)**	−0.04(−2.59)**	−0.03(−3.85)***
GDP	−0.06(−2.2)**	−0.03 (−0.76)	−0.05(−2.71)***	0.62(0.91)	1.34(1.59)	0.33(0.58)
GDP^2				−0.26(−1.01)	−0.52(−1.63)*	−0.14(−0.67)
M2	0.04(2.66)**	0.04(2.48)**	0.03(3.78)***	0.04(2.62)**	0.03(2.32)**	0.03(3.87)***
education	−0.03(−1.97)**	−0.05(−2.29)**	−0.025(−3.15)***	−0.03(−1.84)*	−0.05(−2.53)**	−0.03(−3.66)***
military	0.01(0.49)	−0.00(−0.28)	0.012(0.85)	0.018(0.84)	0.01(0.4)	0.011(0.8)
social	−0.017(−0.9)	−0.04(−1.36)	−0.02(−1.56)	−0.018(−0.95)	−0.06(−1.97)*	−0.018(−1.46)
housing	−0.01(−1.46)	−0.02(−1.7)*	−0.015(−2.92)***	−0.017(−1.47)	−0.03(−2.12)**	−0.016(−3.34)***
Dum74	0.02(1.52)	0.001(0.08)	0.021(3.32)***	0.02(1.49)	−0.01(−0.47)	0.021(3.46)***
Dum79	0.054(2.13)**	0.06(2.4)**	0.05(3.45)***	0.06(2.3)**	0.08(2.86)***	0.06(5.68)***
Dum80	0.001(0.13	0.004(0.41)	−0.00(−0.51)	−0.000(−0.03)	−0.001(−0.11)	−0.000(−0.04)
R^2	0.93	0.93	0.93	0.94	0.94	0.93
LM	0.14	0.15		0.14	0.43	
Jarque-Bera (*p* value)	0.55	0.84	0.39	0.75	0.84	0.45
Reset	0.044	0.12		0.004	0.15	
Sargan (*p* value)		0.52	0.86		0.52	0.92

Notes: See notes for Table 3.3

for all models. The interaction term between democracy and oil and gas rents per capita is negative and significant in all models. This reconfirms the initial finding that an increasing and statistically significant effect of oil revenues on the Gini coefficient is reduced by a higher degree of democracy in Iran.

Alternative Definition for the Quality of Political Institutions Variable (Polity IV Index)

An alternative institutional quality indicator, called Polity IV index, may be used that describes combinations of autocratic and democratic characteristics of the institutions of government (Marshall et al. 2012). Subtracting the autocracy score from the democracy score yields a summary measure Polity. This variable detects shifts in the autocracy-democracy dimension caused by changes in the qualitative aspects of institutions: A shift toward more democracy can be caused by a lower score for the sub-characteristic autocracy, a higher score for the sub-characteristic democracy, or by any combination where the increase (decrease) of democracy is larger (smaller) than the increase (decrease) of autocracy (Dizaji and Van Bergeijk 2013). Polity IV and Vanhanen indexes not only differ conceptually, but have different measurements—Polity scores are subjective/judgmental, whereas Vanhanen deploys numerical voting records. Consequently, they show different patterns of variation.

Results obtained with the Polity measure of democracy are presented in Table 4.5. They reconfirm the earlier findings from the first set of models. First, there is evidence of a dynamic model (except for Model 5). Although exports of oil and gas per capita do not show a significant effect on the Gini coefficient in this case, the interaction term still has its negative and significant coefficient (except for Model 1).

Alternative Definitions for Income Inequality

To finalize the robustness check, two other variables for income inequality are introduced. In Table 4.6, a secondary transformation of the Gini data (*ungin*) has been made, as described by Reuveny and Li (2003). According to them, since the Gini coefficient is bounded between 0 and 100, using ordinary least squares (OLS) regression could be problematic (OLS assumes that the dependent variable is unbounded). The usual practice is to transform a bounded variable (such as the Gini coefficient) into an unbounded

Table 4.5 OLS, 2SLS, and GMM results using Gini coefficient, oil and gas exports per capita, and polity IV index

Variable	*OLS(1)*	*2SLS(2)*	*GMM(3)*	*OLS(4)*	*2SLS(5)*	*GMM(6)*
Constant	0.78(2.84)***	0.79(2.74)***	0.81(8.08)***	0.53(1.3)	0.25(0.57)	0.41(2.3)**
gin_{t-1}	0.35(2.16)**	0.35(1.87)*	0.35(8.76)***	0.3 (1.66)*	0.13(0.63)	0.21(4.47)***
expoilgas	−0.003(−0.07)	−0.02 (−0.43)	−0.007(−0.50)	−0.01(−0.21)	−0.05(−0.82)	−0.02(−1.18)
Polity	0.006(1.5)	0.008(1.87)*	0.006(4.92)***	0.007(1.7)*	0.013(2.48)**	0.009(6.39)***
expoilgas ×polity	−0.008(−1.23)	−0.01(−1.62)*	−0.008(−4.17)***	−0.01(−1.45)	−0.018(−2.26)**	−0.013(−5.82)***
GDP	−0.04(−1.3)	−0.007 (−0.18)	−0.035(−4.47)***	0.51(0.76)	1.35(1.63)*	0.94(4.03)***
GDP^2				−0.21(−0.82)	−0.51(−1.64)*	−0.37(−4.11)***
M2	0.03(2.44)**	0.03(2.13)**	0.03(5.04)***	0.03(2.35)**	0.03(1.82)*	0.03(4.04)***
education	−0.025(−1.68)*	−0.04(−2.15)**	−0.03(−6.4)***	−0.02(−1.52)	−0.044(−2.29)**	−0.025(−4.79)***
military	0.035(1.7)*	0.02(0.82)	0.03(9.77)***	0.04(1.88)*	0.04(1.51)	0.05(6.48)***
Social	−0.03(−1.48)	−0.06(−1.87)*	−0.03(−8.57)***	−0.03(−1.45)	−0.07(−2.39)**	−0.04(−6.38)***
housing	−0.01(−1.05)	−0.016(−1.38)	−0.012(−4.31)***	−0.01(−1.00)	−0.019(−1.69)*	−0.01 (−4.6)***
Dum74	0.01(0.83)	−0.009(−0.49)	0.008(3.7)***	0.009(0.74)	−0.02(−1.08)	0.003(0.87)
Dum79	0.03(1.45)	0.044(1.84)*	0.033(6.12)***	0.03(1.55)	0.052(2.22)**	0.04(6.88)***
Dum80	−0.001(−0.15)	0.00(0.05)	−0.003(−1.27)	−0.000(−0.25)	−0.004(−0.35)	−0.006(−3.42)***
R^2	0.94	0.93	0.93	0.94	0.94	0.93
LM	0.13	0.19		0.16	0.54	
Jarque-Bera (*p* value)	0.68	0.91	0.47	0.87	0.98	0.48
Reset	0.03	0.17		0.003	0.15	
Sargan (*p* value)		0.46	0.99		0.46	0.98

Notes: See notes for Table 3.3

Table 4.6 OLS, 2SLS, and GMM results using transformed Gini coefficient, oil and gas exports per capita, and Vanhanen index

Variable	*OLS(1)*	*2SLS(2)*	*GMM(3)*	*OLS(4)*	*2SLS(5)*	*GMM(6)*
Constant	−0.59(−2.69)***	−0.71(−2.98)***	−0.56(−6.69)***	−1.37(−1.73)*	−2.23(−2.3)**	−1.78(−3.65)***
$ungin_{t-1}$	0.42(2.69)***	0.42(2.57)**	0.44(8.39)***	0.36(2.17)**	0.26(1.41)	0.32(6.7)***
expoilgas	0.19(2.95) ***	0.21 (3.18)***	0.19(10.88)***	0.22(3.12)**	0.27(3.67)***	0.23(8.37)***
van	0.044(2.54)**	0.051(2.78)***	0.05(8.97)***	0.049(2.7)***	0.058(3.18)***	0.05(9.41)***
expoilgas ×van	−0.06(−2.51)**	−0.07(−2.78)***	−0.07(−8.34)***	−0.07(−2.69)***	−0.09(−3.24)**	−0.075(−9.08)***
GDP	−0.11(−2.13)**	−0.05(−0.74)	−0.11(−5.97)***	1.06(0.92)	2.25(1.59)	1.69(2.54)**
GDP^2				−0.45(−1.02)	−0.87(−1.63)*	−0.68(−2.65)**
M2	0.055(2.24)**	0.051(2.04)**	0.05(4.53)***	0.054(2.19)**	0.046(1.86)*	0.05(3.9)***
education	−0.056(−2.14)**	−0.088(−2.52)**	−0.06(−6.53)***	−0.05(−1.98)**	−0.091(−2.69)**	−0.06(−6.4)***
military	0.012(0.34)	−0.02(−0.47)	0.004(0.27)	0.03(0.71)	0.012(0.27)	0.03(1.95)*
social	−0.012(−0.34)	−0.055(−1.02)	−0.011(−0.69)	−0.013(−0.37)	−0.09(−1.62)*	−0.033(−1.89)*
housing	−0.026(−1.32)	−0.03(−1.6)	−0.026(−5.02)***	−0.025(−1.32)	−0.04(−2.01)**	−0.033 (−7.28)***
Dum74	0.04(1.89)*	0.009(0.29	0.04(6.39)***	0.04(1.84)*	−0.008(−0.24)	0.03(4.19)***
Dum79	0.12(2.75)***	0.14 (3.07)***	0.13 (8.86)***	0.12(2.86)***	0.15(3.42)***	0.13(9.8)***
Dum80	0.008(0.41)	0.015(0.69)	0.008(1.12)	0.006(0.3)	0.006(0.29)	0.001(0.19)
R^2	0.94	0.93	0.93	0.94	0.94	0.94
LM	0.15	0.13		0.15	0.22	
Jarque-Bera (*p* value)	0.39	0.5	0.16	0.76	0.89	0.71
Reset	0.072	0.13		0.004	0.08	
Sargan (*p* value)		0.46	0.99		0.46	0.98

Notes: See Notes for Table 3.3 (dependent variable is transformed unbounded Gini coefficient)

Table 4.7 OLS, 2SLS, and GMM results using ratio of richest 10 % to poorest 10 %, oil and gas exports per capita, and Vanhanen index

Variable	*OLS(1)*	*2SLS(2)*	*GMM(3)*	*OLS(4)*	*2SLS(5)*	*GMM(6)*
Constant	0.03(0.06)	−0.25(−0.52)	0.004(0.03)	−0.89(−0.63)	−2.54(−1.54)	−1.78(−4.86)***
ratio−rp	0.41(2.22)**	0.4(2.16)**	0.44(8.05)***	0.36(1.79)*	0.23(1.04)	0.3(5.47)***
expoilgas	0.34(2.77) ***	0.39 (3.14)***	0.33(9.13)***	0.38(2.79)**	0.49(3.51)***	0.41(11.62)***
van	0.07(2.19)**	0.085(2.58)**	0.07(8.77)***	0.079(2.27)**	0.09(2.91)***	0.08(9.89)***
expoilgas×van	−0.1(−2.13)**	−0.12(−2.57)**	−0.1(−8.77)***	−0.11(−2.22)**	−0.15(−2.96)**	−0.12(−10.36)***
GDP	−0.22(−2.21)**	−0.08(−0.61)	−0.2(−9.13)***	1.3(0.59)	3.78(1.42)	2.79(4.55)***
GDP^2				−0.58(−0.69)	−1.46(−1.45)	−1.14(−4.99)***
M2	0.087(1.86)*	0.075(1.64)*	0.08(6.38)***	0.084(1.78)*	0.06(1.33)	0.075(6.69)***
education	−0.02(−0.41)	−0.1(−1.5)	−0.035(−2.88)***	−0.013(−0.23)	−0.091(−1.38)	−0.017(−1.24)
military	0.06(0.85)	−0.012(−0.15)	0.046(3.01)***	0.08(1.06)	0.058(0.61)	0.11(4.37)***
social	−0.04(−0.59)	−0.15(−1.5)	−0.04(−3.21)***	−0.04(−0.63)	−0.22(−2.04)**	−0.09(−4.00)***
housing	−0.009(−0.25)	−0.03(−0.79)	−0.013(−1.46)	−0.007(−0.2)	−0.038(−0.99)	−0.017 (−1.89)*
Dum74	0.027(0.61)	−0.05(−0.81)	0.025(2.45)**	0.023(0.52)	−0.09(−1.34)	0.002(0.23)
Dum79	0.21(2.55)**	0.26 (3.11)***	0.21(14.12)***	0.21(2.6)***	0.28(3.38)***	0.22(14.92)***
Dum80	0.03(0.9)	0.05(1.21)	0.032(2.31)**	0.03 (0.84)	0.037(0.93)	0.023(1.53)
R^2	0.93	0.94	0.94	0.94	0.94	0.94
LM	0.21	0.27		0.21	0.35	
Jarque-Bera (*p* value)	0.36	0.55	0.19	0.24	0.39	0.13
Reset	0.076	0.23		0.003	0.07	
Sargan(*p* value)		0.57	0.99		0.58	0.98

Notes: See notes for Table 3.3 (dependent variable is the ratio of richest 10 % to poorest 10 %)

one. The Gini coefficient is transformed into an unbounded measure using the formula log [Gini/(100-Gini)]. Also, in Table 4.7, logarithm of the ratio of richest ten percent to poorest ten percent (*ratio-rp*) is used as a proxy for income inequality.

In both cases (Tables 4.6 and 4.7), the evidence remains strong for a dynamic relationship in the inequality equations. Results further indicated that natural resource abundance is associated with higher income inequality, as the coefficient for exports of oil and gas is positive and significant in Tables 4.6 and 4.7 using all methods. The tables suggest that interactions of democracy with oil and gas exports have decreasing and significant effects on income inequality. This supports the previous findings regarding the moderating effect of democracy on the oil-inequality nexus. Furthermore, economic growth has a decreasing and significant effect on income inequality. The existence of a Kuznets curve is confirmed only when using the GMM method, as indicated in Tables 4.6 and 4.8. Finally, financial deepening (M2) shows an increasing and significant effect on the Gini coefficient.

Conclusion

This chapter has examined the moderating role of political institutions in the income inequality-oil rents nexus in Iran. Regression analysis with annual data from 1970 to 2012 provides strong evidence for the increasing effects of oil rents on income inequality in Iran. However, the results also suggest that improving the quality of democratic institutions can reduce the negative externality of oil rents affecting income distribution in Iran. Furthermore, financial development in the country aggravates income inequality. Increasing financial development and liquidity in the economy fuel inflation and thus worsen the income gap between the rich and the poor. Finally, there is evidence that government spending on education, housing, and social affairs reduces income inequality in Iran, whereas military spending is likely to increase it.

Appendix A

Table 4.8 Summary statistics

Variable	*Mean*	*SD*	*Min*	*Max*
Logarithmic form of Gini coefficient (gin)	1.62	0.03	1.60	1.70
Logarithmic form of real exports of oil and gas per capita (expoil gas)	0.77	0.23	0.3	1.25
Vanhanen index of democratization (van)	1.92	1.7	0	6.1
Logarithmic form of real GDP per capita (GDP)	1.3	0.12	1.01	1.55
Logarithmic form of real money and quasi money per capita (M2)	7.63	0.31	6.9	8.02
Logarithmic form of real education expenditure per capita (education)	−0.86	0.3	−1.46	−0.48
Logarithmic form of real defense expenditure per capita (military)	−0.18	0.31	−0.78	0.43
Logarithmic form of real government expenditure on social affairs per capita (social)	−0.93	0.54	−2.29	−0.39
Logarithmic form of real government expenditure on housing per capita (housing)	−0.95	0.37	−1.6	0.19
Unbounded Gini coefficient (ungin)	−0.14	0.05	−0.21	0.00
Logarithmic form of ratio of richest 10 % to poorest 10 % (ratio-rp)	1.25	0.10	1.09	1.51
Logarithmic form of real value added of oil and gas per capita (valoil gas)	0.82	0.22	0.43	1.3
Modified version of the polity variable (polity)	−6.09	4.23	−10	3

Source: Author's calculations

Notes

1. In their literature survey, Sirowy and Inkeles (1991) report that six studies find the effect of democracy on income inequality to be negative, whereas another six studies find the effect to be positive or statistically insignificant.
2. For further discussions concerning the effects of oil rents on the political economy of Iran, see Farzanegan (2013), Farzanegan and Markwardt (2009), and Farzanegan (2011); Bjorvatn and Selvik (2008); Bjorvatn et al. (2013).
3. Biswas et al. (2012) also show that environmental costs of the shadow economy are larger in countries with higher corruption.

4. In 2SLS and GMM estimations, all explanatory variables are treated as endogenous except for the different dummy variables.
5. Under the Shah, when oil prices rose sharply in the 1970s, the defense expenditure increased several fold. The defense budget between 1970 and 1976 increased from 8.2 percent to 14.2 percent of the GNP, growing from $1.160 billion to $9.503 billion. Of the $8.3 billion in revenues from foreign military sales, which the United States received during the fiscal year 1974, $3 billion were associated with Iran's purchases (Banuazizi 1976: 495). Despite these huge military expenses, half of the personnel of the armed forces were unable to read or write in 1977.

References

Alexeev, M., & Conrad, R. (2010). The natural resource curse and economic transition. *Economic Systems, 35*(4), 445–461.

Al-Marhubi, F. (1997). A note on the link between income inequality and inflation. *Economic Letters, 55*(3), 317–319.

Anderson, E., Convey, T., McKay, A., Moncrieffe, J., O'Neil, T., & Piron, L. H. (2003). Inequality in middle income countries: Key conceptual issues. Overseas development institute occasional paper. Poverty and Public Policy Group, Overseas Development Institute, London.

Arezki, R., & Gylfason, T. (2011). Resource rents, democracy and corruption: Evidence from sub-saharan Africa. *CESifo Working Paper No. 3575.* CESifo Group, Munich.

Asadzadeh, A., & Jalili, Z. (2015). Shadow economy and income inequality in Iran. *Faslnameh-ye Modelsazi-ye Eqtesadi, 30*, 91–109. (in Persian).

Auty, R. (1994). The resource curse thesis: Minerals in bolivian development, 1970–1990. *Singapore Journal of Tropical Geography, 15*(2), 95–111.

Banuazizi, A. (1976). Iran: The making of a regional power. In A. L. Udovitch (Ed.), *The middle east: Oil, conflict and hopes* (pp. 463–505). Lanham, MD: Lexington Books.

Barro, R. J. (1996). Democracy and growth. *Journal of Economic Growth, 1*(1), 1–27.

Barro, R. J., & Sala-i-Martin, X. (2004). *Economic growth* (2nd ed.). Cambridge, MA: MIT Press.

Baum, C. F. (2006). *An introduction to modern econometrics using stata.* College Station, TX: Stata Press.

Beblawi, H. (1987). The rentier state in the Arab world. In H. Beblawi & G. Luciani (Eds.), *Nation, state, and integration in the arab world: Volume 2* (pp. 49–62). London: Croom Helm.

Biswas, A., Farzanegan, M. R., & Thum, M. (2012). Pollution, shadow economy and corruption: Theory and evidence. *Ecological Economics, 75*, 114–125.

Bjorvatn, K., Farzanegan, M. R., & Schneider, F. (2013). Resource curse and power balance: Evidence from Iran. *Review of Middle East Economics and Finance, 9*(2), 133–158.

Bjorvatn, K., & Selvik, K. (2008). Destructive competition: Factionalism and rent-seeking in Iran. *World Development, 36*(11), 2314–2324.

Block, S. A. (2001). Does Africa grow differently? *Journal of Development Economics, 56*, 443–467.

Boix, C. (1998). *Political parties, growth and equality: Conservative and social democratic economic strategies in the world economy*. Cambridge, UK: Cambridge University Press.

Bollen, K. A., & Jackman, R. W. (1985). Political democracy and the size distribution of income. *American Sociological Review, 50*, 438–457.

Bolt, K., Matete, M., & Clemens, M. (2002). *Manual for calculating adjusted net savings*. Washington, DC: The World Bank Group.

Calderon, C., & Chong, A. (2001). External sector and income inequality in interdependent economies using a dynamic panel data approach. *Economic Letters, 71*(2), 225–231.

CBI [Central Bank of Iran]. (2015). Time series data tables. Retrieved December 13, 2015, from www.tsd.cbi.ir

Chan, S. (1997). Democracy and inequality: Tracking welfare spending in Singapore, Taiwan, and South Korea. In M. Midlarski (Ed.), *Inequality, democracy and economic development* (pp. 227–243). Cambridge, UK: Cambridge University Press.

Cox, D., & Jimenez, E. (1990). Achieving social objectives through private transfers: A review. *The World Bank Research Observer, 2*, 205–218.

Deininger, K., & Squire, L. (1998). New ways of looking at old issues: Inequality and growth. *Journal of Development Economics, 57*(2), 259–288.

Dickey, D. A., & Fuller, W. A. (1979). Distribution of the estimators for autoregressive time series with a Unit Root. *Journal of the American Statistical Association, 74*(366), 427–431.

Dickey, D. A., & Fuller, W. A. (1981). Likelihood ratio statistics for autoregressive time series with a unit root. *Econometrica, 49*(4), 1057–1072.

Dizaji, S. F. (2011). Analysis of domestic price and inflation determinants in Iran (as a developing oil-export based economy). ISS Working Paper No. 530. International Institute of Social Studies (ISS), The Hague.

Dizaji, S. F., & Van Bergeijk, P. A. G. (2013). Potential early phase success and ultimate failure of economic sanctions: A VAR approach with an application to Iran. *Journal of Peace Research, 50*(6), 721–736.

Dizaji, S. F., Farzanegan, M. R., & Naghavi, A. (2015). Political institutions and government spending behavior: Theory and evidence from Iran. *International Tax and Public Finance*. doi:10.1007/s10797-015-9378-8.

Esfahani, H. S. (2005). Alternative public service delivery mechanisms in Iran. *The Quarterly Review of Economics and Finance, 45*, 497–525.

Farzanegan, M. R. (2009). Macroeconomic of populism in Iran. MPRA Paper No. 15546. Munich.

Farzanegan, M. R. (2011). Oil revenue shocks and government spending behavior in Iran. *Energy Economics, 33*(6), 1055–1069.

Farzanegan, M. R. (2013). Oil and the future of Iran: A blessing or a curse? legatum institute, London.

Farzanegan, M. R., & Markwardt, G. (2009). The effects of oil price shocks on the Iranian economy. *Energy Economics, 31*(1), 134–151.

Fields, G. S. (1989). Changes in poverty and inequality in the developing countries. *World Bank Research Observer, 4*(2), 167–185.

Fors, H. C., & Olsson, O. (2007). Endogenous institutional change after independence. *European Economic Review, 51*(8), 1896–1921.

Fum, R. M., & Hodler, R. (2009). Natural resources and income inequality: The role of ethnic divisions. *OxCarre Research Paper*, Oxford Centre for the Analysis of Resource Rich Economies, Oxford.

Gasiorowski, M. J. (1997). Political regimes and industrial wages: A cross-national analysis. In M. Midlarski (Ed.), *Inequality, democracy and economic development* (pp. 244–267). Cambridge, UK: Cambridge University Press.

Goderis, B., & Malone, S. W. (2009). Natural Resource Booms and Inequality: Theory and Evidence. OxCarre Research Paper, Oxford Centre for the Analysis of Resource Rich Economies, Oxford.

Gundlach, E., & Paldam, M. (2009). A farewell to critical junctures: Sorting out long-run causality of income and democracy. *European Journal of Political Economy, 25*, 340–354.

Gupta, S., Davoodi, H., & Alonso, T. R. (2002). Does corruption affect income inequality and poverty? *Economics of Governance, 3*(1), 23–45.

Gylfason, T., & Zoega, G. (2003). Inequality and economic growth: Do natural resources matter? In T. S. Eicher & S. J. Turnovsky (Eds.), *Inequality and growth: Theory and policy implications* (pp. 255–292). Cambridge, MA: MIT Press.

Habibi, N. (2013). The economic legacy of mahmoud Ahmadinejad. Middle East Brief No. 74. Crown Center for Middle East Studies, Brandeis University, Waltham, MA.

Huber, E., Nielsen, F., Pribble, J., & Stephens, J. D. (2006). Politics and inequality in Latin America and the Caribbean. *American Sociological Review, 71*, 943–963.

Karl, T., (2004). The oil trap. *Transparency International Quarterly Newsletter 1* (Transparency International—Berlin).

Kolstad, I., Wiig, A., & Williams, D. A., (2008). Tackling corruption in oil rich countries: The Role of transparency. U4Brief No. 3. Anti-Corruption Resource Centre, Bergen.

Kuznets, S. (1963). *Quantitative aspects of the economic growth of nations, economic development and cultural change*. Chicago: University of Chicago Press.

Leamer, E. E., Maul, H., Rodriguez, S., & Schott, P. K. (1999). Does natural resource abundance increase Latin American income inequality? *Journal of Development Economics, 59*, 3–42.

Lenski, G. E. (1966). *Power and privilege: A theory of social stratification*. New York: McGraw-Hill.

Li, H., & Zou, H. F. (1998). Income inequality is not harmful for growth: Theory and evidence. *Review of Development Economics, 2*(3), 318–334.

Lopez-Feldman, A., Mora, J., & Taylor, J. E. (2006). Does natural resource extraction mitigate poverty and inequality? Evidence from rural Mexico. Paper presented at the International Association of Agricultural Economists Conference, Gold Coast, Australia.

Luciani, G. (1987). Allocation vs. production states: A theoretical framework. In H. Beblawi & G. Luciani (Eds.), *Nation, state, and integration in the arab world: volume 2* (pp. 63–82). London: Croom Helm.

Mahdavy, H. (1970). The patterns and problems of economic development in rentier states: The case of Iran. In M. A. Cook (Ed.), *Studies in economic history of the Middle East* (pp. 428–467). London: Oxford University Press.

Marshall, M. G., Gurr, T. R., & Jaggers, K. T. (2012). *Polity IV project: Dataset users' manual*. Vienna, VA: Center for Systemic Peace.

Moon, B. (1991). *The political economy of basic human needs*. Ithaca, NY: Cornell University Press.

Muller, E. N. (1988). Democracy, economic development, and income inequality. *American Sociological Review, 53*, 50–68.

Murray, M. P. (2006). Avoiding invalid instruments and coping with weak instruments. *Journal of Economic Perspectives, 20*(4), 111–132.

Nikoloski, Z. (2009). *Economic and political determinants of income inequality*. Research Paper. University College London (UCL), London.

QMS [Quantitative Micro Software]. (2010). EViews 7 user's Guide II. Retrieved February 3, 2015, from http://schwert.ssb.rochester.edu/a425/ev72.pdf

Ramsey, J. B. (1969). Tests for specification errors in classical linear Least-Squares regression analysis. *Journal of the Royal Statistical Society, 31*(2), 350–371.

Ranjan, P. (2001). Dynamic evolution of income distribution and credit-constrained human capital investment in open economies. *Journal of International Economics, 55*, 329–358.

Reuveny, R., & Li, Q. (2003). Economic openness, democracy and income inequality: An empirical analysis. *Comparative Political Studies, 36*(5), 575–601.

Rodrik, D. (1998). Symposium on globalization in perspective: An introduction. *Journal of Economic Perspectives, 12*(4), 3–8.

Ross, M. L. (1999). The political economy of resource curse. *World Politics, 51*(2), 297–322.

Ross, M. L. (2007). How mineral rich states can reduce inequality? In J. D. Sachs, J. E. Stiglitz, & M. Humphreys (Eds.), *Escaping the resource curse* (pp. 237–255). New York: Columbia University Press.

Salehi-Isfahani, D. (2006). Iran's third development plan: A reappraisal. Virginia Polytechnic Institute and State University, Department of Economics, Blacksburg, VA.

Salehi-Isfahani, D. (2007). Class and labor in Iran: Did the revolution matter? *Middle East Journal, 61*, 162–163.

Salehi-Isfahani, D. (2009). Poverty, inequality, and populist politics in Iran. *Journal of Economic Inequality, 7*(1), 5–28.

Sargan, J. D. (1958). The estimation of economic relationships using instrumental variables. *Econometrica, 26*(3), 393–415.

Sarraf, M., & Jiwanji, M, (2001). Beating the resource curse: The case of Botswana. Environment Department Paper No. 83. The World Bank Group, Washington, DC.

Simpson, M. (1990). Political rights and income inequality: A cross-national test. *American Sociological Review, 55*(5), 682–693.

Sirowy, L., & Inkeles, A. (1991). The effects of democracy on economic growth and inequality: A review. In A. Inkeles (Ed.), *On measuring democracy* (pp. 125–156). New Brunswick, NJ: Transaction Publishing.

Sokoloff, K. L., & Engerman, S. L. (2000). History lessons: Institutions, factor endowments, and paths of development in the New World. *Journal of Economic Perspectives, 14*(3), 217–232.

Stevens, P. (2003). Resource impact: Curse or blessing? A Literature survey. University of Dundee, Centre for Energy, Petroleum, and Mineral Law and Policy.

Tabibian, M. (2000). *Faghr va towzi'-e daramad dar Iran [Poverty and income distribution in Iran]*, Institute for Research in Planning and Development, Tehran, Iran (in Persian).

Torvik, R. (2002). Natural resources, rent seeking and welfare. *Journal of Development Economics, 67*, 455–470.

UNDP [United Nations Development Programme]. (2015). *Human development report 2015*. Retrieved January 9, 2016, from http://hdr.undp.org/en/2015-report

Vanhanen, T. (2011). Measures of democracy 1810–2010. FSD1289, version 5.0. Tampere: Finnish Social Science Data Archive.

CHAPTER 5

Housing Costs and Inequality in Post-revolutionary Iran

Mohammad Reza Farzanegan, Hassan F. Gholipour, and Jeremy Nguyen

Introduction

In this chapter, we investigate the association between housing prices and income inequality in Iran over the last three decades. In the recent period, Iran has had the highest average Gini coefficient in the Middle East (see Table 5.1), a region where inequality has triggered social tension, political instability, and armed conflict (Azeng and Yogo 2013). Moreover, debates on inequality and poverty have featured prominently in Iran's domestic politics since the 1979 Revolution. For example, popular dissatisfaction with inequality is believed to have contributed to an electoral victory in 2005 for the populist presidential candidate Mahmoud Ahmadinejad (Farzanegan 2009)—whose subsequent management of the national economy nonetheless resulted in negative economic growth as well as double-digit inflation and unemployment rates.

M.R. Farzanegan (✉)
Center for Near and Middle Eastern Studies, School of Business & Economics, Philipps-Universität Marburg, Marbug, Germany

H.F. Gholipour • J. Nguyen
Swinburne University of Technology, Melbourne, Australia

M.R. Farzanegan, P. Alaedini (eds.), *Economic Welfare and Inequality in Iran*, DOI 10.1057/978-1-349-95025-6_5

Table 5.1 Gini coefficients for selected Middle Eastern countries

Country	*GINI index (1984–2013)*
Algeria	35.33
Egypt	30.75
Iran	42.26
Iraq	29.54
Israel	39.30
Jordan	36.13
Morocco	39.84
Syria	35.77
Tunisia	39.95
West Bank and Gaza	34.54
Yemen	35.89

Source: World Bank (2016)
Note: Gini index measures the extent to which the distribution of income (or, in some cases, consumption expenditure) among individuals or households within an economy deviates from a perfectly equal distribution. A Gini index of 0 represents perfect equality, while an index of 100 implies perfect inequality

It has been demonstrated that pro-poor policies of the Iranian government (mainly in the provision of basic infrastructure such as safe drinking water, electricity, and health) have not been effective in reducing inequality (Salehi-Isfahani 2009). Furthermore, available studies on drivers of income distribution in Iran (e.g. Ahmadi and Mehregan 2006; Khodadad and Heydari 2009; Salehi-Isfahani 2009) have highlighted the role of economic growth, government expenditures, oil revenues, government policies, economic openness, education, and household characteristics. Yet, an issue that has received little attention in the literature concerned with Iran's economy is the effect of housing prices on income inequality.

Housing prices and rents in Iran have risen at a rapid pace over the last three decades: in 1982, the rental housing index (RH) in all urban areas was 1; after an annual average growth rate of 17 percent, the RH was 112.60 in 2012 (base year 2011 = 100).[1] This housing boom has been blamed for an array of socioeconomic problems, including low levels of household formation (Gholipour and Farzanegan 2015), high divorce rates (Farzanegan and Gholipour 2015), illegal land takeovers (Sodaei 2015; Gholipour 2012), and poor housing affordability together with the expansion of urban slums (Alaedini and Fardanesh 2014).

Income inequality has also been suspected of being influenced by rising home prices in Iran (Majles Research Center 2009), as increases in housing costs have gone hand in hand with relatively high levels of inequality. Rising housing prices may aggravate inequality through a number of channels. If rising prices make homeownership prohibitively expensive for lower-income families, then these families lose access to the financial benefits of housing as an investment vehicle. Furthermore, with rising home prices, capital becomes concentrated in the hands of a smaller proportion of the population. Unaffordable housing additionally restricts labor migration to regions with greater opportunities. In the long term, there may also be increased intergenerational effects of rising housing prices. In addition, persistent increases in housing prices, along with low returns to agricultural activities in rural areas and smaller cities, are likely to have given impetus to illegal land takeovers in Iran. Land takeovers in rural areas and smaller cities decreases the incomes of poorer households (who are reliant on access to land and natural resources), with negative consequences for the overall income distribution. Finally, sizable capital gains on property investments due to continued increases in real estate prices and the absence of effective capital gains tax (Gholipour 2012)—as well as an ineffective taxation system in general[2]—are also likely to have increased income inequality in Iran.

To investigate causality from housing prices to inequality in this study, we control for other important economic, political, and social determinants of inequality. Our main task is to probe the effect of RH (which we use as a proxy for housing prices) on income inequality in Iran after controlling for other important determinants. We use annual time series data from 1982 to 2012 and apply fully modified ordinary least squares (FMOLS) to estimate the long-run impact of housing prices on income inequality. We show that increases in housing prices lead to higher inequality, ceteris paribus. We further suggest that, to reduce income inequality, the Iranian government should consider policies that increase the supply of affordable housing and redefine capital gains tax on investment properties.

The chapter is structured as follows: the next section describes potential theoretical mechanisms whereby housing prices increase income inequality. The third section provides some stylized facts for income distribution and housing markets in Iran. This is followed by a section that describes our variables and data. The fifth section discusses our empirical methodology and results, and the last section concludes the chapter.

Housing Prices and Its Impact on Income Inequality

Several studies are available that examine the effects of housing prices on inequality in open developed countries. For example, Muellbauer and Murphy (2008) argue that increases in housing prices change the distribution of welfare toward home owners, and away from non-homeowners in the UK. Furthermore, Abeysinghe and Wong (2014) find a significant positive effect of increasing private residential property prices on income inequality in Singapore. A similar suggestion is made for Singapore by Phang (2015) as well. Yet, to our knowledge, no empirical study has analyzed this link between housing prices and inequality in a developing country with limited integration to the world economy. This is the task we take up in this chapter. In the rest of this section, we summarize the primary mechanisms through which rising housing prices may contribute to increased inequality.

1. *Housing is a major financial asset class with income advantages; unaffordable housing restricts low-income households' access to the associated financial benefits.*

Homeownership makes up a significant proportion of the household sector's wealth; this is even more pronounced for lower- and moderate-income households (Oliver and Shapiro 1990). Frick and Grabka (2003) note that homeowner-occupancy confers a number of income advantages—capital return when house prices are rising, as well as imputed rent. Homeownership is also subject to favorable tax treatment. Further, the greater tax concessions associated with homeownership are typically granted to households with higher wealth (Cho and Francis 2011). Whereas a positive real capital return associated with homeownership is disputed elsewhere—for example, in the US—Iran's housing market has seen a clearly positive rate of return on this type of investment in the previous decade (Masron and Gholipour 2010). In addition, mortgages can be viewed as a form of forced saving for households—with their associated benefits (Tachibanaki 1994: 183). Mortgages also provide incentives to save for the needed down payments, particularly in liquidity constrained markets (Jappelli and Pagano 1994).

If low-income households are prevented from homeownership as a result of rising prices, they will not benefit from forced savings and saving incentives, capital returns, imputed rents, or tax concessions either. Those who are excluded from homeownership will then see their incomes fall behind. Drudy and Punch (2002) find rising home prices and rents to be a major source of wealth generation for landowners, speculators, and landlords, in opposition to the effects on tenants and those in public housing. Frick and Grabka (2003) also find evidence of increasing inequality between owner-occupiers and renters. Oliver and Shapiro (1990) show that limited access to home ownership due to rising prices has clear implications for inequality. Even in situations where decreasing affordability of housing does not preclude all lower income earners from purchasing homes, there are still implications for inequality. Filandri and Olagnero (2014) find significant inequality between homeowners, depending on income and social class. Larsen and Sommervoll (2004) shows that there are considerable differences in return for different housing submarkets: markets characterized by investors and speculators outperform property in other submarkets.

2. *There are intergenerational effects on inequality: decreases in affordable housing increase the segregation of wealthy families from lower-income families, leading to greater differences in education and human capital formation for the children of poor and rich families.*

Parents affect the likelihood of their children growing up to be high-income-earning adults via influence on the education and peers that their children will be exposed to: human and non-human capital passed to children (Becker and Tomes 1979). The quality of schooling a child receives has significant effects on his/her adult earnings (Card and Krueger 1992). Wealthy adults thus have an incentive to cluster into neighborhoods with other wealthy families, to decrease the cost of providing high-quality education for their children and for other socio-logical and human capital positive externalities (Durlauf 1996). Decrease in affordable housing makes it easier for this segregation to occur, leading to persistent and likely increasing inequality.

3. *Rising house prices impede the migration of unskilled labor to more productive regions, thus slowing regional income convergence.*

Regional income convergences can reduce income inequalities, as poorer geographic regions experience faster economic growth (Barro and Sala-i-Martin 1992). One driver of regional income convergence is mobility of labor: low-income workers migrating to more productive regions. Ganong and Shoag (2013) find that rising house prices relative to incomes reduce the mobility of labor and income convergence, and have been a contributor to rising inequality.

4. *More generally, rising house prices may lead to increasing concentration of capital, and increasing returns to owners of capital.*
Piketty's (2014) well-known argument is that income inequality increases when long-run returns to capital are greater than the rate of economic growth, such that the share of national income accruing to owners of capital will rise at the expense of income share accruing to labor. Yet, Rognlie's (2015) examination of the share of national income paid to net capital for G7 countries shows that growth in the income share of net capital is primarily driven by increasing returns to housing.

Income Distribution and Housing Market in Iran: Stylized Facts

Real estate, particularly residential property, has been a very important asset class for Iranian households and investors (Gholipour and Bazrafshan 2012). Over the last three decades, the sector has represented approximately 40 percent of the national capital stock (CBI 2015); 81 percent of Iranian urban households were homeowners (Statistical Centre of Iran 2015). Several interrelated economic and political factors have increased the desirability of real estate as an investment vehicle: high inflation rates, low real interest rates, underdeveloped financial markets and institutions, limited access to international financial and property markets, international sanctions, a weak national currency, and the absence of an effective taxation system on property. 40–60 percent of the demand for Iranian housing has been attributed to investment motives (Alaedini and Fardanesh 2014: 43).

As a result of high demand and insufficient supply (Ibid.:43–47), the last three decades have witnessed strong growth in housing prices and rents in Iran's urban areas (see Fig. 5.1). Housing has become less affordable for Iranian households (Gholipour and Farzanegan 2015). During the 1980s, the RH grew at the relatively slow pace of approximately ten percent per annum. The slow growth was primarily due to the effects of the Iraq-Iran War (September 1980 to August 1988). In the last two decades, growth in the housing market has accelerated (22.6 percent per annum over 1990–2000 and at 16.2 percent per annum over 2001–2012), experiencing at least four cycles of boom and recession (Mohammadpour 2015). The first boom and recession cycle occurred from 1993 to 1999. The RH rose to a peak in 1996 and slumped to a low point in 1999. The second cycle ran

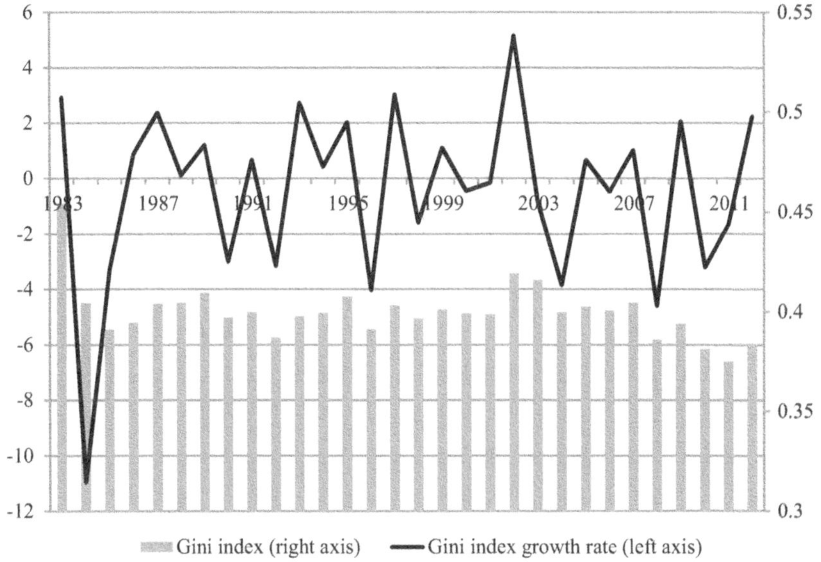

Fig. 5.1 Gini index (level and growth rate) in Iran. Higher scores represent higher income inequality. *Source*: CBI (2015)

from 1999 to 2005 with a peak in 2002 and a trough in 2005. The third cycle began in 2005, peaked in 2008, and ended in 2010. Finally, the fourth cycle occurred between 2010 and 2014, peaking in 2013.

Data Description

To examine the impact of housing prices on inequality in Iran, we utilize annual data for the period 1982–2012. Our empirical specification is as follows:

$$\text{Gini}_t = \text{cons.} + \beta_1.\text{RH}_t + \beta_2.\text{Controls}_t + \varepsilon_t \quad (1)$$

where *Gini* is the Gini index, *RH* represents the rental housing index, and *Controls* represents the control variables detailed below. Appendix A explains notations, measures, and data sources for all variables in the empirical analyses.

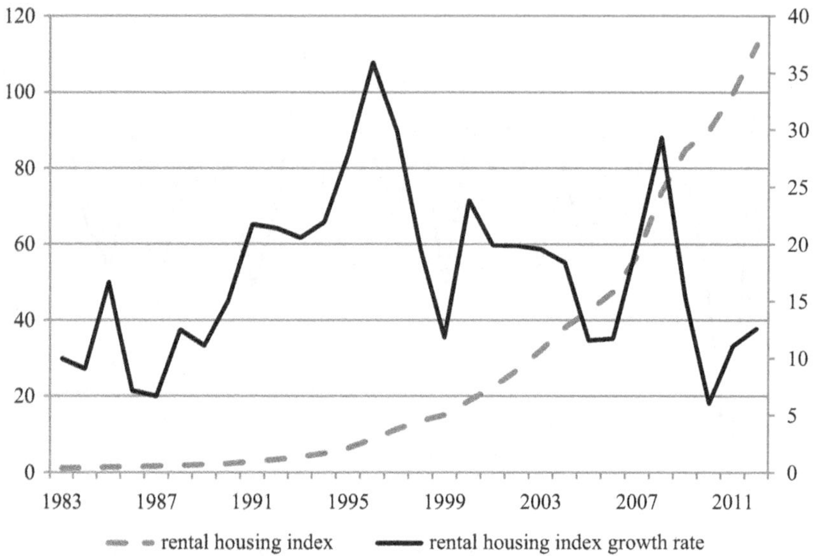

Fig. 5.2 Rental housing index (level and growth rate) in Iran. *Source*: CBI (2015)

Dependent Variable: Income Inequality

Our primary measure of inequality is Gini coefficient data from the Central Bank of Iran (CBI 2015). The Gini coefficient, which takes values between zero and one, is the most widely used measure of inequality in the empirical literature (see, e.g. Dollar and Kraay 2002; Delis et al. 2014). A Gini coefficient of zero describes a society where all individuals earn equal income (complete equality); a Gini coefficient equals to unity describes a society where a single individual earns all of the economy's income (complete inequality). Figure 5.2 depicts the Gini coefficient and its growth rate in Iran from 1982 through 2012.

We also employ another standard measure of inequality: the ratio of tenth decile expenditures (highest expenditure) to first decile expenditures (lowest expenditure). This ratio is provided by the Central Bank of Iran as a measure of income distribution (CBI 2015). The higher this ratio, the greater the inequality of expenditure.

Primary Independent Variable: Housing Prices (RH)

We use the rental housing index (RH) in all urban areas as a measure of housing prices in Iran. The RH is available for the period 1982–2012. We use the RH in preference over raw housing prices for two reasons. First, the RH is available beginning in 1982. Second, RH is a suitable proxy for housing prices: housing prices and rents are highly correlated in Iran (Farzanegan and Gholipour 2015). Figure 5.2 illustrates the variation in growth rates of the RH in post-revolutionary Iran.

Control Variables

We control for drivers of income inequality that are standard in the literature, taking into account their availability for Iran (see Delis et al. 2014). We include the logarithm of real gross domestic product (GDP) per capita. To investigate the possibility of a Kuznets curve, that is, a hypothesized inverted U-shaped relationship between income per capita and inequality (Kuznets 1955), we also include the logarithm of real GDP as a squared term. Data for GDP (at base prices and in billion rials) are from the Central Bank of Iran (CBI 2015).

We control for trade openness, measured as the sum of imports and exports, as a proportion of GDP. Whereas globalization is likely to reduce inequality *between* countries, it is also likely to *increase* income inequality *within* countries: international firms in developing countries tend to and pay higher wage premiums and hire the more highly skilled workers, widening the gap between skilled and unskilled labor. Data on trade are from the Central Bank of Iran (CBI 2015). We also include a financial openness index (Chinn and Ito 2006).

As a proxy for the degree of government intervention in the economy, we include government spending (as a share of GDP) as a control variable. Income inequality may be reduced by government policies such as: government spending, transfers, subsidies, and public sector employment. However, if the quality of political institutions is weak, government spending may be more patronage based, and thus unlikely to reduce inequality. We include the share of public consumption expenditures (billion rials) in constant prices as a ratio of GDP. We also control for the quality of political institutions by using the Polity2 index, which ranges from −10, representing full autocracy, to 10, representing full democracy (Marshall et al. 2014). Dizaji et al. (2015) show that, in the case of Iran, positive shocks to the quality of political institutions are reflected in positive responses of government spending on public education and negative responses of military spending.

Inflation is also an important driver of income inequality which we control for; inflation generally has a negative effect on the relative income share of the poor (Easterly and Fischer 2001).

Empirical Methodology and Results

To estimate the long-run relationships between variables, we employ the FMOLS estimator (Phillips and Hansen 1990). This method is most efficient in testing the long-run relationships between variables, and has been employed by several researchers to test the long-run relationship between income inequality and its determinants (e.g. Cavusoglu and Dincer 2015; Herzer and Nunnenkamp 2012).

Our primary reason for utilizing FMOLS is to account for endogeneity in the model. We also face the issue of simultaneity: we assume that increases in housing prices increase income inequality; however, research has shown that increased income inequality also has a negative impact on housing prices (e.g. Määttänen and Terviö 2014). In such cases, ordinary least squares (OLS) produces biased and inconsistent estimates. We employ FMOLS to correct for endogeneity in the regressors and serial correlation in the errors in cointegrating regressions, thereby providing unbiased estimates of the coefficients.

We perform Augmented Dickey-Fuller (ADF) unit root tests to determine the order of integration of the series, testing for the presence of a unit root in both the log levels and log levels of the first differences of each. Results of the unit root tests are presented in Appendix B; the results suggest that all series, except log (Gini index) and Inflation/100, are integrated at order one (I (1)). Given that all variables are I (1), we test for the presence of a long-run equilibrium relationship among the variables using Johansen's Trace and Max-Eigen statistics. The Trace and Max-Eigen statistics indicate that there is at least one cointegrating relationship between the dependent variable (income inequality) and its determinants. Having established that a long-run cointegrating relationship exists, equations are estimated using the FMOLS estimator.

Table 5.2 shows the main results. Models 1–10 (M.1 to M.10) in Table 5.2 use the logarithm of the Gini coefficient as a dependent variable. In Model 11 (M.11), we use the ratio of tenth decile expenditures to first

Table 5.2 FMOLS results of the long-run effect of housing prices on income inequality in Iran, 1982–2012

	Dependent variable: Logarithm of Gini index (Models 2.1–2.10)										*R10/P10 (c)*
	M3.1	M3.2	M3.3	M3.4	M3.5	M3.6	M3.7	M3.8	M3.9	M3.10	M3.11
log(RH)	0.124***	0.098***	0.159***	0.176***	0.112***	0.150***	0.143***	0.130***	0.119***	0.125***	0.248***
	(3.35)	(2.94)	(4.11)	(5.26)	(3.35)	(4.73)	(4.47)	(4.03)	(4.50)	(4.79)	(3.44)
log(GDPPC)		4.03	−0.187	−6.213	5.234	5.33	5.59	10.09**	3.22	−0.34	−4.28
		(1.01)	(−0.04)	(−1.47)	(1.09)	(1.26)	(1.37)	(2.23)	(0.81)	(−0.08)	(−0.37)
log(GDPPC)^2		−0.118	0.006	0.184	−0.162	−0.165	−0.173	−0.307**	−0.099	0.006	0.123
		(−1.00)	(0.05)	(1.48)	(−1.13)	(−1.30)	(−1.42)	(−2.28)	(−0.84)	(0.05)	(0.36)
log(Trade)			0.093***	0.089***	0.178***	0.199***	0.206***	0.193***	0.185***	0.177***	0.435***
			(2.81)	(3.19)	(5.38)	(6.39(	(6.63)	(6.21)	(6.15)	(6.02)	(5.33)
log(OIL)				0.033**	0.011	0.003	0.002	0.006	0.007	0.006	−0.010
				(2.20)	(0.77)	(0.28)	(0.20)	(0.55)	(0.63)	(0.51)	(−0.32)
log(POP)						−1.372***	−1.392***	−1.489***	−1.06***	−1.056***	−2.834***
						(−4.11)	(−4.37)	(−4.75)	(−4.98)	(−5.09)	(−4.93)
Inflation/100							0.100***	0.116***	0.146***	0.119***	0.304***
							(3.10)	(3.61)	(4.10)	(3.23)	(2.98)
GOVEX								−0.001	0.000	−0.015	−0.060**
								(−0.39)	(0.22)	(−1.65)	(−2.36)
FINOPEN								0.058**	0.057**	0.010	0.037
								(2.29)	(2.18)	(0.31)	(0.39)
POLITY									0.002*	0.039**	0.125**
									(2.08)	(2.19)	(2.53)
GOVEX×POLITY										−0.002*	−0.009**
										(−2.03)	(−2.38)
C &Time Trend	C&T	C&T	C&T	C&T	C&T(a)	C&T(a)	C&T(a)	C&T(b)	C(b)	C(b)	C(b)
Adj. R2	0.30	0.24	0.36	0.39	0.48	0.52	0.50	0.51	0.54	0.55	0.80
Obs.	30	30	30	30	30	30	30	30	30	30	30

***Statistical significance at 99 %
**Statistical significance at 95 %
*Statistical significance at 90 %
Note: Method of estimation is the Fully Modified OLS (FMOLS); *t statistics* are reported in (): a, no constant/trend is statistically significant; b, only intercept is included in the cointegrating equation; c, dependent variable is the ratio of tenth decile expenditures (the richest) to first decile expenditures (the poorest). The higher the ratio, the more inequality in the society. In all models, the long-run variances are computed using a nonparametric method with the Bartlett kernel and a real-valued bandwidth chosen by Newey-West fixed bandwidth selection method

decile expenditures. In line with theoretical expectations, we find a robust positive association between income inequality and the rental housing index (log (RH)). The sign and the size of the effect are stable across multiple specifications and are not sensitive to the inclusion of control variables. Since both the rental housing index and our dependent variable are in logarithmic form, the coefficients can be interpreted as elasticities: a 1 percent increase in the rental housing index increases income inequality by 0.125 percent (as measured by the Gini coefficient) in our general model (M.10). The magnitude of effect is even greater when considering the ratio of the richest 10 percent to the poorest 10 percent's expenditure: a 1 percent increase in the rental housing index increases this ratio by 0.248 percent, controlling for other drivers of inequality. Our results underscore the importance of housing policies: the provision of affordable accommodation is an important channel for reducing the concentration of wealth and improving income distribution. A taxation structure favorable to low-income, first-time homeowners would enhance public access to more stable housing and would additionally provide the beneficiaries with longer-term financial benefits.

The effects of some control variables are also interesting. First, there is no robust evidence for a Kuznets-type inverted U-shaped relationship between income per capita and inequality. The coefficients of log (GDPPC) and log (GDPPC)^2 are not significant (except in M.8).

Second, there is a robust and highly significant effect of trade openness (log (Trade)) on income inequality in post-revolutionary Iran. The effect of trade and economic globalization on inequality is positive (i.e. inequality increases with trade). This finding is in line with the literature focusing on mechanisms through which trade liberalization and globalization lead to increased inequality within developing countries. In our general model (M.10), a one percent increase in trade openness increases inequality by 0.177 percent, ceteris paribus. Also, there is some evidence for the impact of financial liberalization (FINOPEN) on income inequality. Our results suggest that higher economic and financial globalization in Iran is unlikely to lead to increasing demand for unskilled labor and a corresponding closing of the wage gap between skilled and unskilled labor force.

Third, inflation (Inflation/100) is another robust driver of income inequality in Iran. Inflation, which acts as an additional tax on the poor, is widening the income gap between the poor and the rich. Low-income earners often lack indexation of their wages and access to financial investment. In contrast, the value of real estate and fixed capital, typically held by high-income, high-wealth individuals, increases in an inflationary economy like Iran's. The average inflation rate in Iran between 1982 and 2012 was 19 percent, ranging from a minimum of 6.9 percent and a peak of 49 percent.

Fourth, the size of government spending as a share of GDP has (GOVEX) a mostly negative effect on income inequality and the ratio of the richest ten percent to the poorest ten percent's expenditure. However, this negative effect is only statistically significant when we use the ratio of richest to the poorest as the dependent variable. As we expect, the final effect of government spending on income inequality and the gap between the rich and the poor is dependent on the quality of political institutions, as can be seen from the negative and significant interaction term (GOVEX ×POLITY). In other words, when the quality of political institutions is low, government spending is unlikely to be an effective tool for dealing with the income gap between the rich and the poor.

Our general model (M.10) explains about 55 percent of the variation in income inequality from 1982 to 2012. M.11, which uses the ratio of tenth decile expenditures (the richest) to first decile expenditures (the poorest), is more powerful and explains about 80 percent of the variation in the dependent variable.

Conclusion

The housing industry and its related activities and services have become increasingly influential in the Iranian economy. Based on information from the Central Bank of Iran (CBI 2016), the average share of the construction industry from 1982 to 2012 was approximately seven percent of Iran's GDP, while the average share of real-estate-related professional services to GDP for the same period was 11.5 percent. The latter ratio shows a significant increase over the period, rising from 6.6 percent in 1982 to 17 percent in 2012.

In this chapter, we examined the effect of housing prices on income inequality in Iran. Probing the association between housing prices and income inequality, we employed FMOLS on data from 1982 to 2012 to investigate the long-run relationship. The analysis controlled for drivers of inequality such as income per capita, inflation, trade and financial openness, government spending, population size, and the quality of political institutions. Our main results show a robust positive, and highly significant, association between housing prices and income inequality in Iran—that is, higher housing prices are associated with increased income inequality. One potential policy to reduce the relatively high income gap between the poor and the rich in Iran would thus be the provision of affordable housing, involving both supply- and demand-side initiatives. In addition, policymakers should redefine capital gains taxes on investment properties to reduce income disparities between owners and tenants.

Appendix A

Table 5.3 Variable definitions and sources

Variable	*Definition*	*Source*
Gini Index	Gini coefficient, which is a number between zero and one, is an important measure of inequality in distribution of income. Zero indicates a society with absolute equality in distribution of income and one indicates a society with inequality in income distribution. Logarithmic transformation is used.	CBI (2015)
R10/P10	Ratio of tenth decile expenditures (the richest) to first decile expenditures (the poorest). Logarithmic transformation is used.	CBI (2015)
RH	Logarithm of rental housing index. Rent Index is part of the CPI group of consumer goods and services basket. This index is available for urban areas including Tehran as well as other large, medium, and small cities.	CBI (2015)
GDPPC	Logarithm of gross domestic product in billion Iranian rials (base year: 2004).	CBI (2015)
POP	Logarithm of the population	CBI (2015)
INF/100	The CPI inflation rate (%)/100	CBI (2015)
TRADE	The ratio of the sum of exports and imports over GDP (%)	CBI (2015)
GOVEX	The ratio of government expenditures over GDP (%)	CBI (2015)
OIL	Logarithm of oil revenues in total government revenues	CBI (2015)
FINOPEN	Financial openness index. The Chinn-Ito index is normalized between zero and one. Higher values of this index indicate that a country is more open to cross-border capital transactions.	Chinn and Ito (2006)
POLITY	Quality of political institutions (−10: full autocracy, +10: full democracy)	Marshall, et al. (2014)

Appendix B

Table 5.4 Augmented Dickey-Fuller (ADF) unit root test results

Level	t-*Statistic*	*First difference*	t-*Statistic*
log(Gini Index)	−3.36**	Δlog(Gini Index)	−6.53***
log(R10/P10)	−2.48	Δlog(R10/P10)	−7.32***
log(RH)	−0.34	Δlog(RH)	−2.99**
log(GDPPC)	−0.15	Δlog(GDPPC)	−3.71***
log(Trade)	−1.78	Δlog(Trade)	−4.86***
log(OIL)	−0.30	Δlog(OIL)	−5.26***
log(POP)	−1.56	Δlog(POP)	−2.32**
Inflation/100	−2.94*	ΔInflation/100	−5.52***
GOVEX	−1.44	ΔGOVEX	−5.97***
FINOPEN	−1.69	ΔFINOPEN	−3.56**
POLITY	−1.61	ΔPOLITY	−5.19***

***refers to statistical significance at 99 % confidence intervals
**refers to statistical significance at 95 % confidence intervals
*refers to statistical significance at 90 % confidence intervals
Notes: Lag length is based on SIC

Notes

1. Economists and other observers have identified several factors that pushed housing prices and rents upward in Iran: excess demand in the housing market (particularly investment demand); speculation of real estate agents; high inflation; Dutch disease; increases in costs of construction (due to reduction of subsidies during the Ahmadinejad presidency, as well as sanctions imposed on the economy of Iran by the United Nations (UN), the United States (U.S.) and European Union); increases in land prices; and currency crisis (for a review see Farzanegan and Gholipour 2015).
2. Iran was ranked 139 out of 189 economies surveyed in 2013 in terms of paying taxes (World Bank 2013).

References

Abeysinghe, T., & Wong, Y. H. (2014). Income inequality in Singapore: Do housing prices play a role? SCAPE Working Paper No. 2014/01. Department of Economics, National University of Singapore (NUS), Singapore.

Ahmadi, A. M., & Mehregan, N. (2006). The effect of economic adjustment policies on income distribution in Iran. *[University of Tehran] Journal of Economic Research, 40*(3), 209–232. (in Persian).

Alaedini, P., & Fardanesh, F. (2014). *From shelter to regeneration: Slum upgrading and housing policies in islamic republic of Iran*. Tehran: Urban Development and Revitalisation Organisation.

Azeng, T. F., & Yogo, T. U. (2013). Youth unemployment and political instability in selected developing countries. *Working Paper No. 171*. African Development Bank Group, Abidjan.

Barro, R. J., & Sala-i-Martin, X. (1992). Convergence. *Journal of Political Economy, 100*, 223–251.

Becker, G. S., & Tomes, N. (1979). An equilibrium theory of the distribution of income and intergenerational mobility. *Journal of Political Economy, 87*, 1153–1189.

Card, D., & Krueger, A. B. (1992). Does school quality matter? Returns to education and the characteristics of public schools in the United States. *Journal of Political Economy, 100*, 1–40.

Cavusoglu, T., & Dincer, O. (2015). Does decentralization reduce income inequality? Only in rich states. *Southern Economic Journal, 82*(1), 285–306.

CBI [Central Bank of Iran]. (2015). Time series database. Retrieved November 8, 2015, from http://tsd.cbi.ir

CBI [Central Bank of Iran]. (2016). Annual national accounts, national product at constant prices. Retrieved April 22, 2016, from http://www.cbi.ir/simplelist/5796.aspx

Chinn, M. D., & Ito, H. (2006). What matters for financial development? Capital controls, institutions, and interactions. *Journal of Development Economics, 81*, 163–192.

Cho, S. W., & Francis, J. L. (2011). Tax treatment of owner occupied housing and wealth inequality. *Journal of Macroeconomics, SI: Macroeconomics with Frictions, 33*, 42–60.

Delis, M. D., Hasan, I., & Kazakis, P. (2014). Bank regulations and income inequality: Empirical evidence. *Review of Finance, 18*, 1811–1846.

Dizaji, S. F., Farzanegan, M. R., & Naghavi, A. (2015). Political institutions and government spending behavior: Theory and evidence from Iran. *International Tax and Public Finance*. doi:10.1007/s10797-015-9378-8.

Dollar, D., & Kraay, A. (2002). Growth is good for the poor. *Journal of Economic Growth, 7*, 195–225.

Drudy, P. J., & Punch, M. (2002). Housing models and inequality: Perspectives on recent Irish experience. *Housing Studies, 17*, 657–672.

Durlauf, S. N. (1996). A theory of persistent income inequality. *Journal of Economic Growth, 1*, 75–93.

Easterly, W., & Fischer, S. (2001). Inflation and the poor. *Journal of Money, Credit and Banking, 33*, 160–178.

Farzanegan, M. R. (2009). Illegal trade in the Iranian economy: Evidence from structural equation model. *European Journal of Political Economy, 25*, 489–507.

Farzanegan, M. R., & Gholipour, F. H. (2015). Divorce and the cost of housing: Evidence from Iran. *Review of Economics of the Household*. doi:10.1007/s11150-014-9279-0.

Filandri, M., & Olagnero, M. (2014). Housing inequality and social class in Europe. *Housing Studies, 29*, 977–993.

Frick, J. R., & Grabka, M. M. (2003). Imputed rent and income inequality: A decomposition analysis for Great Britain, West Germany and the US. *Review of Income and Wealth, 49*, 513–537.

Ganong, P., & Shoag, D. (2013). Why has regional income convergence in the U.S. declined? SSRN Scholarly Paper No. ID 2081216. Social Science Research Network, Rochester, NY.

Gholipour, F. H. (2012). The role of real estate agents on housing prices and rents: The Iranian experience. *International Journal of Housing Markets and Analysis, 5*, 134–144.

Gholipour, F. H., & Bazrafshan, E. (2012). Determinants of returns on housing: The Iranian case. *International Journal of Housing Markets and Analysis, 5*, 351–360.

Gholipour, F. H., & Farzanegan, M. R. (2015). Marriage crisis and housing costs: Empirical evidence from provinces of Iran. *Journal of Policy Modeling, 37*, 107–123.

Herzer, D., & Nunnenkamp, P. (2012). The effect of foreign aid on income inequality: Evidence from panel cointegration. *Structural Change and Economic Dynamics, 23*, 245–255.

Jappelli, T., & Pagano, M. (1994). Saving, growth, and liquidity constraints. *The Quarterly Journal of Economics, 109*, 83–109.

Khodadad, K. F., & Heydari, K. (2009). Income distribution in Iran's economy, application of gini coefficient, theil and atkinson indices. *Economic Research Review, 4*, 151–179.

Kuznets, S. (1955). Economic growth and income inequality. *American Economic Review, 45*, 1–28.

Larsen, E. R., & Sommervoll, D. E. (2004). Rising inequality of housing: Evidence from segmented house price indices. *Housing Theory and Society, 21*, 77–88.

Määttänen, N., & Terviö, M. (2014). Income distribution and housing prices: An assignment model approach. *Journal of Economic Theory, 151*, 381–410.

Majles [Islamic Consultative Assembly] Research Center (2009). Tashrih va tabyin-e hobab-e qeymat-e zamin va maskan dar Tehran [Explaining the issue of land and housing price bubble in Tehran]. Retrieved March 22, 2016, from http://rc.majlis.ir/fa/report/show/738961 (in Persian).

Marshall, M. G., Gurr, T. R., & Jaggers, K. (2014). Polity IV project: Dataset users' manual. http://www.systemicpeace.org/inscr/p4manualv2013.pdf

Masron, T. A., & Gholipour, F. H. (2010). Performance and diversification benefits of housing investment in Iran. *International Journal of Economics and Finance, 2*, 7–11.

Mohammadpour, S. (2015). Siklha-ye rownaq va rokud dar bazar-e maskan [Boom-recession cycles in housing market]. *Tejarat-e Farda*. Retrieved March 22, 2016, from http://tejarat.donya-e-eqtesad.com/fa/packagestories/details?story=e8bc6910-8fca-4332-90bc-5115ebccf937 (in Persian).

Muellbauer, J., & Murphy, A. (2008). Housing markets and the economy: The assessment. *Oxford Review of Economic Policy, 24*, 1–33.

Oliver, M. L., & Shapiro, T. M. (1990). Wealth of a nation. *American Journal of Economics and Sociology, 49*, 129–151.

Phang, S. Y. (2015). Home prices and inequality: Singapore versus other global superstar cities. *The Straits Times*. Retrieved March 22, 2016, from http://works.bepress.com/sockyong_phang/79

Phillips, P. C. B., & Hansen, B. E. (1990). Statistical inference in instrumental variable regression with I(1)processes. *Review of Economic Studies, 57*(1), 99–125.

Piketty, T. (2014). *Capital in the 21st century*. Cambridge: Harvard University Press.

Rognlie, M. (2015). Deciphering the fall and rise in the net capital share. *Brookings Papers on Economic Activity*, BPEA Conference Draft.

Salehi-Isfahani, D. (2009). Poverty, inequality, and populist politics in Iran. *Journal of Economic Inequality, 7*(1), 5–28.

Sodaei, A. (2015). Che kasani zaminha-ye Iran ra mikorand? [Who grabs land in Iran?]. BBC (in Persian). Retrieved March 22, 2016, from http://www.bbc.com/persian/business/2015/10/151010_l45_iran_land_grabbing

Statistical Centre of Iran. (2015). Statistics by topic, Retrieved November 8, 2015, from http://www.amar.org.ir/english/Statistics-by-Topic/Construction-and-Housing#287176-statistical-survey

Tachibanaki, T. (1994). Housing and saving in Japan. In Y. Noguchi & J. M. Poterba (Eds.), *Housing markets in the United States and Japan* (pp. 161–190). Chicago, IL: University of Chicago Press.

World Bank. (2016). World development indicators. Retrieved March 23, 2016, from http://databank.worldbank.org/data/reports.aspx?source=world-development-indicators

World Bank. (2013). *Doing business 2014: Understanding regulations for small and medium-size enterprises*. Washington, DC: World Bank Group.

CHAPTER 6

Gender Inequality and Income Inequality in Iran

Nadereh Chamlou

Introduction

In his monumental and seminal book *Capital in the Twenty-first Century*, Thomas Piketty (2014) meticulously analyzes and presents the cross-country dynamics of income inequality over the past two centuries. He offers a myriad of underlying factors and trends that have over time led to vast wealth and power accumulation of a few and limited upward mobility for the rest. His main argument is that in order to gain wealth and opportunity, birth matters more than effort or talent.

Despite the impressive volume of data and careful analysis, however, Piketty disregards gender inequality as a possible contributing factor to income inequality. This failure of coverage comes despite the evidence from the social science literature about the nexus between gender and marginalization, gender-based lack of access to external and intra-household resources, or the "feminization of poverty" (Cagatay 1998) as women comprise 60 percent of the poor. It has been widely documented that upward economic mobility for women has been far more challenging, and quite often impossible, throughout the ages and across nearly every society. Over centuries, women's biology has served as justification in the construction of social and cultural roles, which have resulted in biases that exacerbate the effects of

N. Chamlou (✉)
International Development Advisor, Wasington, DC, USA

M.R. Farzanegan, P. Alaedini (eds.), *Economic Welfare and Inequality in Iran*, DOI 10.1057/978-1-349-95025-6_6

poverty, dependency, and income inequality. The persistence of deep-rooted discriminatory views and institutions has impeded women from all socioeconomic classes, race, or ethnicity to develop their full economic potential.

To bridge the income inequality gap, Piketty does not shy away from proposing a bold solution—a global wealth tax—that is unlikely to gain broad support. However, he falls short of making any recommendations that target the elimination of the many legal and institutional barriers that invariably hold back more than half of the world's population by sex, race, and ethnicity—hence, purely due to the incidence of birth rather than capabilities—among whom women account for the largest share.

Unfortunately, Piketty has not been alone in omitting the linkage between gender-based inequalities and income inequalities. In fact, many prominent economists and policy-makers have shied away from the gender debate by compartmentalizing it into the social, cultural, or religious realms. This disconnect may have also resulted from broader ambiguity in economic literature about the effect of income inequality on growth and vice versa (Aghion et al. 1999; Carvalho and Rezai 2014; Barro 2000). Fortunately, there is a consensus that the distribution of income matters on its own right, even if not for growth purposes. And, the evidence from US data, which are the most widely available and studied, shows that income inequality reduces the potential of the poor to participate in growth-generating activities (Van der Weide and Milanovic 2014). Furthermore, it reduces an individual's lifetime upward mobility and often affects inter-generational mobility due to lower investments in physical and human capital for children. More and more economists are beginning to understand, or venture into, the nature of equality between the sexes and its implication for economic growth.

For the conclusion of the 2015 Millennium Development Goals (MDGs) and in preparation for the 2030 Sustainable Development Goals (SDGs), there is a rapidly expanding body of economic literature between varying dimensions of gender inequality and income inequality across time, across groups, and across countries (World Bank 2012a, 2012b). The empirical evidence suggests that reducing gender inequality, by leveling the playing field for men and women, can impact the overall inequality of opportunity within a society and will over time reduce income inequality in a more sustainable manner than traditional policies used to improve income redistribution, such as taxation, subsidies, or populist policies (Gonzales et al. 2015a).

This chapter first reviews recent literature on the global evidence for the linkages between gender inequality and income inequality. The drivers for sex and income inequality can vary among countries and even within countries by different groups or regions. In the second section, the chapter will discuss some of the specificities of Iran. Income inequality, and certainly the perception of unjust income distribution, has plagued the Iranian society for decades. Oil revenues have been lavishly spent on implicit and explicit subsidies, as well as populist policies implemented in hopes to achieve the equitable society that was promised since the dawn of the 1979 Islamic Revolution. But more needs to be done. An important policy lever for the Iranian Government could, in fact, be the removal of sex- and gender-based barriers that could free up the earnings potential of Iranian families, particularly those in lower- to middle-income strata, to build a stronger household financial security. Only 17 percent of working age women are in the labor force in Iran (ILO 2015). This rate is among the lowest in the world. It suggests that around 80 percent of Iranian families could be traditional one-earner families. In the United States, only 7 percent of households are one-earner families. Thus, Iranian families are more exposed to economic shocks. Since the purpose of this chapter is to present a synthesis of recent empirical literature, given data constraints, it draws on existing empirical analyses rather than engage in new analytical work.

Recent Evidence

The concepts and consequences of gender inequality and income inequality have been considered as separate topics in economics. However, gender inequality persists as a major barrier to human development. Women and girls face multiple disadvantages and differential treatment in most social and economic activities; this impedes their capabilities and freedom of choice. As such, evidence is gradually emerging that a host of gender-based inequalities influences macro-economic outcomes (Elborgh-Woytek et al. 2013). One of the most commonly used indicators is United Nations Development Programme's (UNDP) Gender Inequality Index (GII), which is available for 188 countries. The GII uses the same framework as UNDP's human development index to expose the differences between men and women.[1] The GII ranges from 0 to 1—the higher, the more inequality. For instance, Norway ranks number 1 with the lowest GII value (0.067), while Niger ranks last (0.713). Iran is ranked 69th with a value of 0.515 (UNDP 2016).

Since the 1990s, most middle- to upper-income countries have overcome "access" disparities to education and health (see Stotsky et al. 2016). Indeed, in most countries, the younger generations of men and women—those under the age of 30—have almost equal education. Women are also increasingly outnumbering men in tertiary education in more and more countries. Across the Middle East and North Africa, for instance, among university students, women outnumber men in 13 (out of 18) countries including Iran (UNESCO 2016). Despite this progress, nearly every country experiences persistent gender disparities of one type or another in economic and social empowerment terms.

Economists use two main economic indicators, per capita income and GDP growth, for cross-country comparisons. When exploring the relationship between GII and per capita income, one discovers a strong negative association (Fig. 6.1). One can observe a similar relation when regressing GDP growth against gender inequality (Fig. 6.2). The data suggest that countries with greater gender equality have experienced higher per capita growth.

The evidence from recent studies indicates that gender equality affects macro-economic indicators through the three channels of economic growth, macro-stability, and long-term development. Reducing gender inequalities can deepen and broaden the talent pool, which leads to greater efficiency, higher productivity, and innovation—all of which boost economic growth

Fig. 6.1 Gender inequality and GDP per capita. *Source*: Gonzales et al. (2015a: 5), based on UNDP Human Development Report, World Bank's World Development Indicators, and IMF Staff estimates

Fig. 6.2 Gender inequality and GDP per capita growth. *Source*: Gonzales et al. (2015a: 6) based on UNDP Human Development Report, World Bank's World Development Indicators, and IMF Staff estimates. *Note*: 1/GDP per capita growth was regressed on initial income to control for convergence

(Cuberes and Teignier 2014; Esteve-Volart 2004; Klasen 1999). Removing gender-based barriers results ultimately in women's greater participation in the labor force. For countries that face stagnant or declining birth rates, increased economic participation rates of women mitigate the risk of a shrinking workforce for the productive sectors and alleviate pressures on pension systems, which are essential for long-term macro-economic stability (Steinberg and Nankane 2012). Finally, there is confirmation that women's income is used toward higher expenditures for school enrollment and children's health (Aguirre et al. 2012)—hence, investment in the future generation improves a country's long-run competitiveness and development (Duflo 2012; WEF 2015).

We now look at the association between gender inequality, income inequality, and poverty. The Gini index is frequently used as a measure of income distribution. It ranges from 0 percent which indicates perfect equality to 100 percent meaning maximum inequality. Though there is some debate about the interpretation of the Gini coefficient and its limitation for comparison across populations, it is routinely used in cross-country regressions. Figure 6.3 demonstrates the relationship between GII to (a) Gini index,

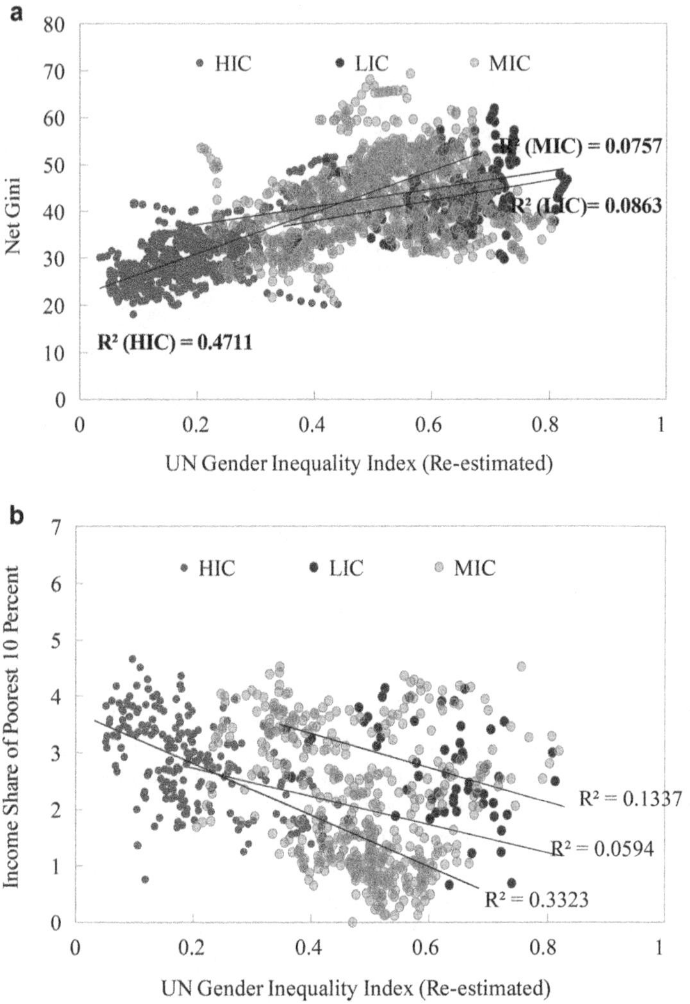

Fig. 6.3 Gender inequality, income inequality, and poverty. (a) Income inequality and gender inequality. *Source*: Gonzales et al. (2015a: 13) based on Standardized World Income Inequality Database (SWIID), United Nations; and further estimates. (b) Income inequality and gender inequality. *Source*: Gonzales et al. (2015a: 13) based World Bank's World Development Indicators; United Nations, and further estimates. (c) Poverty ($2) and Gender Inequality. *Source*: Gonzales et al. (2015a: 13) based World Bank's World Development Indicators; United Nations, and further estimates. (d) Poverty ($1.25) and Gender Inequality. Source: Gonzales et al. (2015a: 13) based World Bank's World Development Indicators; United Nations, and further estimates. *Note*: HIC = High-income countries; LIC = Low-income countries; MIC = Middle-income countries

c

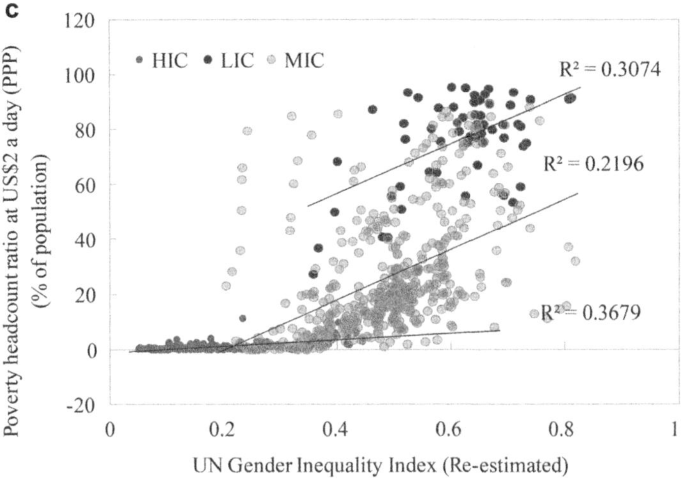

d

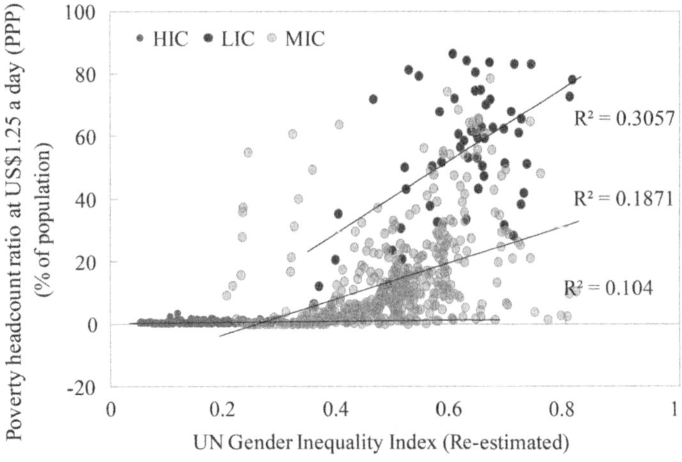

Fig. 6.3 (continued)

(b) income of the poorest decile, (c) poverty at $1.25 PPP, and (d) poverty headcount at $2 PPP thresholds (Gonzales et al. 2015a).

Countries with higher gender inequality seem to have wider income inequality. Different components of gender inequality affect countries differently. Gender gaps in education and health affect income inequality in emerging markets or low-income countries where such disparities persist (Ibid.:24). The gender gap in labor force participation matters more for income equality in high-income countries as well as those that have narrowed the gap in human capital.

The slope of the relationship is steeper for middle-income countries, which means that in these countries reducing gender barriers has a greater overall impact than in low- or high-income economies. In high-income countries, the lowest 10 percent income groups would respond more rapidly to improved gender equality (per steeper slope), with those below the \$1.25 and \$2 PPP international poverty lines registering an even stronger impact from the removal of gender-based barriers. In short, the analyses are conclusive that income inequality responds to gender inequality. It does so better for the relatively poorer economic strata within high-income countries—hence, removal of gender-based barriers is (or could definitely be) a tool for upward economic mobility. In low- and middle-income countries, greater gender equality has a higher impact on the absolute poor, thus promising to be a strong poverty alleviation tool (Gonzales et al. 2015a).

Gender gaps in labor force participation rates, wages, and political participation are also strongly related to income inequality, particularly in countries where education and health disparities appear to have been bridged. As men and women possess nearly equal human capital in these countries, differences in earnings are a direct result of discrimination or persistent institutional barriers and translate into economic inequality. For instance, in OECD countries, with greater homogeneity in terms of women's access to education and health, countries with larger pay gaps also have the widest male–female employment gaps and higher overall income inequality (see OECD 2015). Thus, to address income inequality, it is necessary to educate and improve the health of women. Yet, these will not be sufficient, if there are other barriers that prevent women from equal access to opportunities.

> A higher proportion of working women has been associated with lower income in equality in the OECD. In particular, an increase in the proportion of households with working women increases from 52 percent in the mid-1980s/early 1990s to 61 percent in the late 2000s, on average decreased income inequality by 1 Gini point. The increasing work intensity of women was also associated with lower income inequality, having more households with women in paid work, especially full-time work, means less income inequality by about 2 Gini points. (Gonzales et al. 2015a)

Table 6.1 Distribution of male and female workers by type of employment (000), 2014

	M	*F*	*Total*	*Share of total workers*		*Share of women workers*
				M (percent)	*F (percent)*	*F (percent)*
Total workers	17,746	2477	20,223	87.8	12.2	100
Unemployment rate	8.6 %	19.3 %	10.6 %			
Wage & salaried workers (employees) ('000)	10,159	1750	11,909	50.2	8.7	71
Total self-employed workers ('000)	7587	727	8314	37.5	3.6	29
of which:						0
Employers ('000)	745	36	781	3.7	0.2	1
Own-account workers ('000)	6842	691	7533	33.8	3.4	28
Contributing family workers ('000)	449	605	1054	2.2	3.0	24

Source: KILM 2016 (http://www.ilo.org/global/publications/books/WCMS_409035/lang--en/index.htm)

Economic literature identifies several key drivers of income equality in emerging economies. Among them are trade openness, technological progress, skills premium, access to finance, fiscal spending, financial deepening, labor market institutions, and, at times, female mortality rates. Indeed, Dabla-Norris et al. (2015: 25) find a statistically significant association between these variables and various measures of income distribution at the global level (see Table 6.2 in Appendix A). When a similar analysis is carried out with the additional gender equality index (see Table 6.3 in Appendix A), the latter variable has a high economic value and is statistically significant, while some variables in the earlier regression are no longer significant, such as trade openness (Gonzales et al. 2015a). Hence, the association between gender inequality and the actual income distribution is strong. According to Gonzales et al. (2015a: 22):

> An increase in the GII from 0 (perfect gender equality) to 1 (perfect gender inequality) is associated with an increase in net inequality by almost 10 points. Alternatively, if the GII falls from the highest level of 0.7 (highest level in the sample, seen in Yemen) to the median level of 0.4 (seen in Peru), the net Gini decreases by 3.4 points, which is similar to the difference in net Gini between

Mali and Switzerland. Higher gender inequality is strongly associated with higher income shares in the top 10 percent income group. If the GII index increases from the median to the highest levels, the income share of the top 10 percent increases by 5.8 percentage points, which is the difference between Norway and Greece. Gender inequality also goes hand in hand with lower income shares at the bottom of the income distribution. As before, if the GII index increases from median to highest levels, the income share of the bottom 20 percent declines by 2 percentage points (which is similar to the difference between Estonia and Uganda).

While the regression shows robust results, questions could be raised about the direction of causality between gender and income inequality. Could gender inequality be the result of, or be influenced by, income inequality rather than income inequality be impacted by gender inequality? To address this, Gonzales et al. (2015a: 27) use a set of legal restrictions on women's economic participation as an instrument to carry out the following two-stage analysis and find that the direction of causality is in fact one way, from gender inequality to income inequality[2]:

Legal rights appear as valid instruments since they are not expected to affect income inequality directly but only indirectly through the labor force participation gap. The legal restrictions related to guaranteed equality under the law and a daughter's inheritance rights are the strongest instruments as seen in the first stage regression. The statistical tests support the validity of the instruments. Using these instruments for the gender gap in labor force participation, the second stage regression highlights that a widening of the gender gap in labor force participation leads to greater income inequality. In addition to the legal restrictions, we use other instruments to test the robustness of the results. Our results also hold when the labor force participation gap is instrumented by other instruments used in the literature. For instance, we include the lag of the share of female tertiary teachers as an instrument for the LFP gap.

To further explore the effect of policy interventions on gender equality (specifically), female labor force participation, and income inequality, we employ the Synthetic Control Method, a methodology to formalize a case-study approach to examine the effect of policy interventions on the variable of interest. This data-driven procedure is used to construct a counterfactual, and the effect of the policy intervention can be discerned by comparing the actual outcome and outcome for the constructed "synthetic" country. Using Chile as an illustrative case, the finding is that changes to the law to guarantee legal equality for women led to a fall in the gender gap in labor force participation, which in turn lowered income inequality. These effects were not seen in the synthetic control group.

Why does gender inequality of opportunity and outcome matter? Inequality of opportunity of any kind significantly undermines individuals' life choices. It leads to misallocation of resources and high social costs when the privileged group advances through favored treatment, patronage, or nepotism. Inequality of any kind often goes hand in hand with weak rule of law, poor governance, biased institutions in favor of the powerful, and corruption (Dabla-Norris et al. 2015). Gender inequality exacerbates these circumstances even further and hurts the welfare of the society (see Jain-Chandra 2015).

According to the late Gary Becker (1992), when the share of the discriminated is small compared to discriminators, for instance a religious or ethnic minority, then discrimination does not have much of a negative effect on the discriminator and would not lower overall social well-being. However, when the share of the discriminated is large in comparison to the total population, as is the case with women who constitute half of the population, discrimination injures the discriminator as well.

Aguirre et al. (2012) estimate that some 865 million women worldwide (of whom over 800 million live in emerging markets) have the potential to contribute more fully to their family's well-being and national economies. No pay, low pay, low participation, or insecure employment, which affect women more than men, may drag down the global economy as a whole. According to ActionAid (2015), the global cost of gender inequality is in the order of $9 trillion per year (see also Watson 2015). The above discussion indicates that the income equality benefits to an economy can be significant if women can develop their full economic potential.

The Case of Iran

Iran's Gini index, which stood at 0.56 in the late 1970s, fell to about 0.46 following the Revolution and the Iran-Iraq War, and has hovered around 0.37 in the recent period (Salehi-Isfahani 2009). Iran's Gini index is below Turkey's but above Egypt's—the latter two countries being comparable to Iran in terms of population and region. Factors likely to have influenced Iran's Gini include the age structure of the population over the last 3–4 decades, the near reversal of the share of the rural/urban population, and the considerable populist policies of the government for income redistribution through government transfers from oil revenues. Despite the decline in the share of the country's population below the international poverty line to below 2 percent (Salehi-Isfahani 2009), relatively high inequality, particularly in urban areas, is a cause of resentment among Iranians.

A formidable accomplishment over the last four decades has been the expansion of educational opportunities, particularly for rural women. Average years of schooling for rural women born in the 1960s were 40 percent of their male counterparts; it has risen to 90 percent for those born in the late 1980s. The availability of free education from primary to university level has also improved tertiary educational opportunities for women. "The education Gini of years of schooling for adults born in the 1950s was more than 0.60. It declined to 0.35 for cohorts born 20 years later, which is a substantial increase in access to education inequality in just one generation (Salehi-Isfahani 2009)." Beginning in the mid-1990s, women began to outnumber men 2:1 in universities by receiving higher scores in entrance exams. This ratio led the Iran's Majles (the Iranian parliament, also known as the Islamic Consultative Assembly) to implement a 60:40 affirmative quota for men, and quite a few schools even began rejecting women in certain disciplines—some in science and engineering. Despite these actions, according to UNESCO (2016) data, females outnumber males by a significant margin at institutions of higher education in science, technology, engineering, and mathematics (STEM) fields. In fact, Iran posts one of the highest absolute numbers of female STEM students globally. And, women also account for a considerable share of students in medicine.

A further factor in reducing inequality has been the improvement in health, particularly in rural areas, due to the provision of good-quality basic services as well as electricity and potable water. Iran's maternal mortality was reduced drastically and stands now at similar levels as in high-income countries. Fertility rates, especially in rural areas, have been lowered drastically due to better maternal education and provision of one of the world's best family planning schemes. For instance, the average number of births per woman dropped from eight in the mid-1980s to about two by 2006 (Salehi-Isfahani 2009; see Table 6.4 in Appendix B).

Despite these impressive gains, Iran continues to show a disappointing record on the utilization of its female economic potential. Overall, Iran's rank among the World Economic Forum's Gender equality index in 2015 was 141 out of 146 (WEF 2015). This is mainly due to women's low economic participation rate and even lower rates of political representation. Iranian women's rate of labor force participation is only 17 percent with no improvement or even some decline over the last 15 years (Fig. 6.4). Among those women who are included in the active workforce, unemployment is as high as 20 percent—nearly double the male unemployment rate (Table 6.1). Among employed women, one in five is a family worker (compared with only

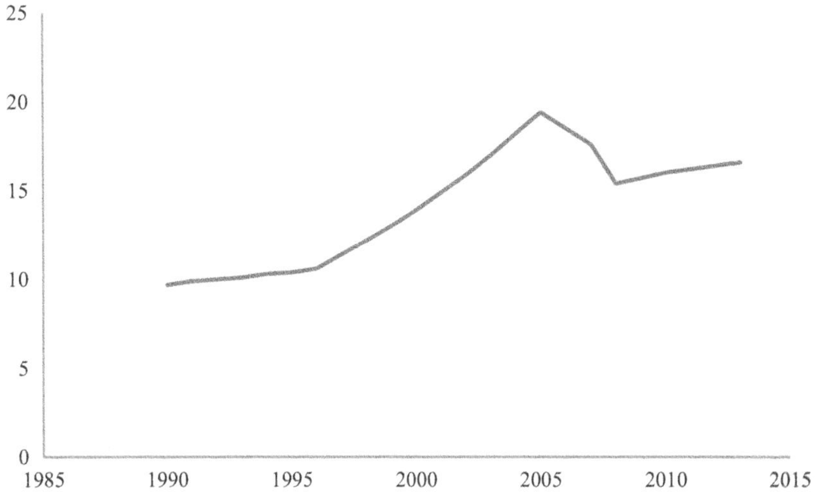

Fig. 6.4 Female labor force participation in Iran (percent of total labor force). *Source*: ILO (2015); author's illustration

2.5 percent of men); about 24 percent are self-employed and only 56 percent are wage and salary workers (ILO 2016). The male-female participation gap (Fig. 6.5), which is a measure of level playing field, is wide in absolute terms and in comparison with many other countries.

Iran's low female labor force participation rates result from (a) overall economic policies generate private-sector employment and (b) legal barriers or social norms that in effect impede women's access to jobs and entrepreneurial opportunities (Gonzales et al. 2015a; World Bank 2004; Chamlou 2008).

With highly inflexible labor market regulations, Iran ranks 118 out of 189 countries in the *Doing Business* (World Bank 2016a) report. Globally, difficult business climates and cumbersome labor regulation reduce the agility of the private sector to grow and create jobs. High levels of unemployment affect women and youth more significantly, because men are seen as the main breadwinners and more deserving of jobs. Moreover, the *Women, Business and the Law 2016* (World Bank Group 2015), which monitors the number and kind of gender-based legal barriers globally, reports that the Iranian legal framework imposes an additional 23 specific and significant gender-based legal differences that disadvantage women over and above the considerable difficulties men already face on a day-to-day basis. In fact, it places Iran as

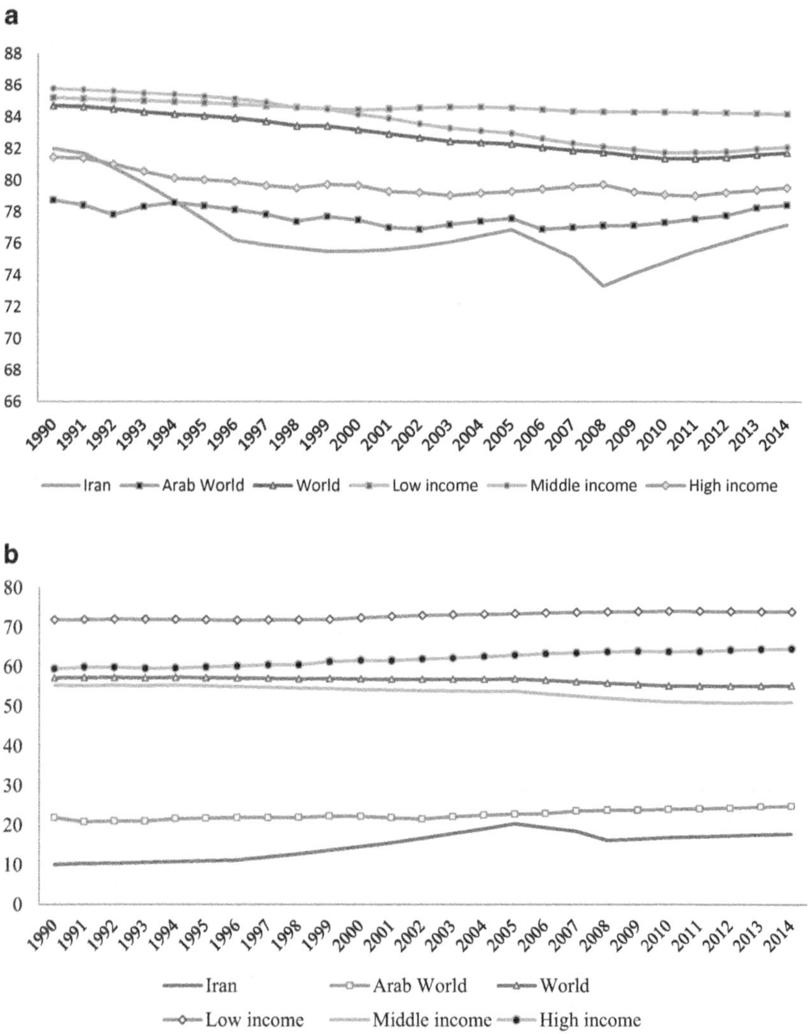

Fig. 6.5 Gender gaps in labor force participation. *Source*: World Bank (2016b); author's illustration. (a) Labor force participation rate, male (percent of male population ages 15–64) (modeled ILO estimate). (b) Labor force participation rate, female (percent of female population ages 15–64) (modeled ILO estimate)

having the third highest number of economic barriers for women, even among Muslim-majority countries (Fig. 6.6). More equal laws, according to the IMF, boost female labor force participation, while empowering women economically is an important tool for tackling income inequality (Gonzales et al. 2015b).

Over the last three decades, some government policies readily reduced female participation in Iran's formal and informal sectors. For instance, women or their husbands received cash incentives if women were to quit their jobs; working conditions were made difficult for married women; and employers were overburdened with female-protective laws that discouraged hiring women (Moghadam 2001). In 2015, the government announced that between 2009 and 2014, the actual number of women in the workforce declined from 3.7 million to 3.145 million—a yearly decline of 100,000 women who left the job market and were not replaced (Taghato 2015). This translates into 400 women becoming economically inactive every day.[3] The decline was also partly due to the dearth of job creation for women; during said period, the economy created 871,000 male jobs and destroyed 568,000 female jobs (Salehi Esfahani 2015). The decrease in the absolute number of female workers in relation to a rising share of 15–64 age cohort in the total population (as Iran has a young population structure) is one explanation of a declining female labor force participation in Iran, which is among the lowest in the world (World Bank 2016b). For those still economically active, unemployment rate jumped from 16.8 to 19.8 percent between 2009 and 2013 when male unemployment declined from 19.8 to 8.6 percent (ILO 2015).

International experience suggests that for female labor force participation (FLFP) to go beyond the 30 percent threshold, married women with children need integration into the workforce. This increase entails removing hurdles and inconveniences that married women face in balancing work and family, such as explicit legal restrictions limiting married women's choice of work, availability of an infrastructure for various types of care (not just childcare but also elderly care), and work environments that value diversity and meritocracy.

Several studies have attempted to estimate the effects of women's under-utilization in the economy. Chamlou and Karshenas (2016) estimate that Iran's GDP could have been between 22 (net) and 35 (gross) percent higher than it is today.[4] Cuberes and Teignier (2014) estimate the gender shortfall slightly differently. For Iran, based on a cross-country regression, they estimate that the short-run (i.e. when capital stock is fixed) total income loss due to gender gap to be 38 percent, and the long-run income loss to be 41 percent (i.e. when capital stock takes a steady-state value). The

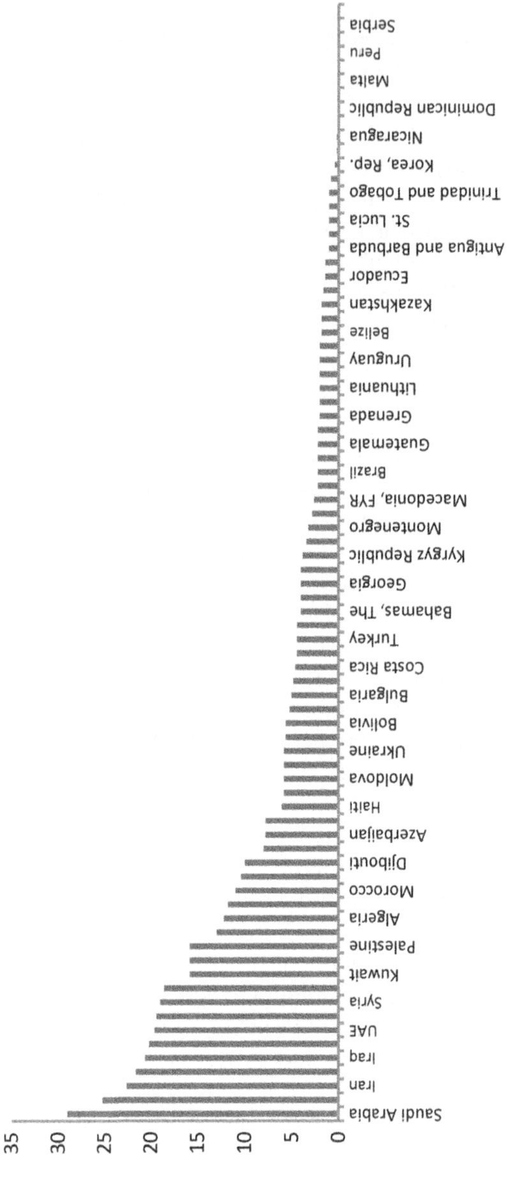

Fig. 6.6 Gender-based legal barriers. *Source:* IBRD (2016); author's illustration

long-term versus the short-term value takes into account female entrepreneurship as well. Comparing countries of similar population size, Cuberes and Teignier's results for Turkey are 30 and 33 percent, for Germany 13 and 15 percent, and for Egypt 36 and 39 percent, respectively. The losses for Iran are the highest, given its large population and the size of its economy (Fig. 6.7).

To put the above figures in perspective, Iran's nominal GDP in 2014 was $416 billion, which made the country the 29th largest economy in the world; a 40 percent larger GDP would have meant an economy of $150–170 billion more (roughly the size of Bangladesh or Kuwait) and could push Iran at least 8–9 ranks up. Iran cannot afford to exclude women and still realize its ambitions with respect to domestic welfare and its aspiration of being a regional power, if not a major global driver.

At a time when Iranian policy-makers are considering deep-rooted economic reforms within the next five-year plan under the slogan "resilience economy," it is critical that—at various stages of the reform process—specific attention be given to updating laws and institutions that have held back women's economic empowerment. Iran can benefit from specific examples and actions taken by advanced and emerging economies that promoted growth through better engagement of the female workforce. Countries with high per capita income, less poverty, and better income distribution, such as Norway, or leading world economies like Japan, realized that their long-term economic health depends on a meaningful integration of women into the economy, politics, decision-making, and leadership.

Conclusion

The purpose of this chapter has been to demonstrate the association between gender inequality and income inequality. Recent studies show that equality of opportunities for women and removing the obstacles that prevent them from reaching their full economic participation have a considerable impact on the distribution of income and upward mobility of families. The economic power of women remains untapped. Equal law boosts female labor force participation, which in turn reduces income inequality (Gonzales et al. 2015b).

Particularly in Iran, and in spite of the relatively low Gini coefficient, the perception of income inequality is high and heavy emphasis has been placed on social justice in political rhetoric (Salehi-Isfahani 2009). The economy and society have suffered from years of sanctions and economic mismanagement; removing gender-based barriers can give a considerable

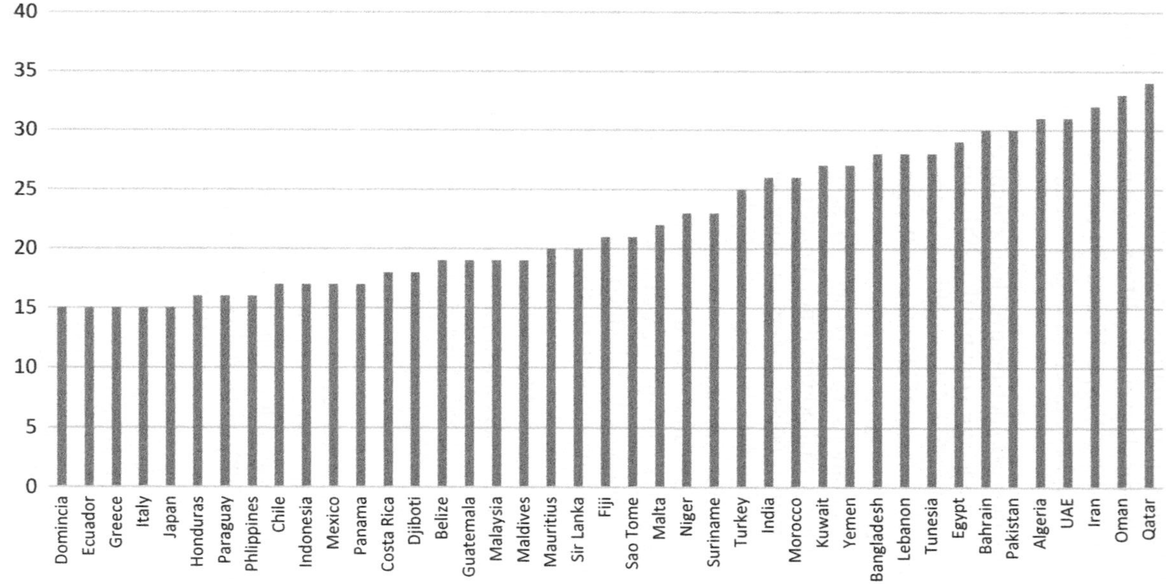

Fig. 6.7 GDP losses due to economic gender gaps in selected countries (percent of GDP). *Source*: Gonzales et al. (2015b: 5), based on estimates by Cuberes and Teignier (2014). *Note*: Losses are estimated for a particular year for each country and can thus be interpreted as a one-off increase in GDP if gender gaps were to be removed

boost to growth and income distribution. While Iran has successfully bridged education and health disparities, it has failed to make sufficient progress on women's economic opportunities. Iran's gender-based barriers are among the highest in the world. And, these obstacles, like any other obstacles in an economy, translate themselves into a very high cost. Iran's GDP would have been around 40 percent higher if Iranian women could have made a similar contribution as their peers in other countries, commensurate with their acquired skills. This gain could then be spent on much needed social protection, infrastructure, or investments that could boost the welfare of the entire population and narrowed income disparities.

Different components of gender inequality affect countries differently. The cross-country empirical evidence provided in this chapter suggests that the gender gap in labor force participation matters more with respect to reducing income inequality in middle-income countries, which have bridged the gap in education and health. This would be the case for Iran as well. The impact of removing gender barriers could particularly impact urban areas where income inequalities are more glaring. Continuing to bridge remaining gender gaps in education and health could further improve income inequality distribution in marginalized and low-income regions where disparities are high.

Beyond income gains, removing barriers to women's empowerment has non-monetary benefits that are not easily quantifiable. Countries with greater inclusion of women in decision-making tend to have better rule of law, stronger governance, and lower corruption. In this context, consider a passage from the memoir of a nineteenth-century Princess Taj Al-Saltaneh (2003: 288), daughter of Qajar monarch Nassereddin Shah, who expresses in simple language how she imagines women's empowerment could benefit her society:

> A Persian wage-earner makes two *qerans* a day. He has to support his mother, his sister, his niece, his wife, and his daughter. If we divide two *qerans* by five, we get seven *shahis* a day. With these seven *shahis*, how can one person provide for clothing and food as well as have a savings? Thus it is that necessity corrupts people. In order to gain comfort and ease, they will submit to any gross indignity, prepare to perform any wicked deed. Now if these five women and children were not forced into a veil, they would have to be educated. After education, each of these five could take a job in a store, a tea-house, a shop, a school, or an office. Then every person would have an income of two *qerans* a day. Six people making twelve *qerans* a day could feed and clothe themselves comfortably, without the need to degrade themselves or change their lifestyle. And they could preserve their conscience, their honor, their chastity, and

their family and national pride. In addition, there would be spiritual unity within this group, and many great benefits would accrue from unity.

Appendix A

Table 6.2 Economic drivers of inequality, 1980–2012

Variables	*Market Gini (1)*	*Net Gini (2)*	*Top10 % (3)*	*Fifth Income Decile (4)*	*Bottom10 % (5)*
Trade openness	−0.025	−0.008	−0.011	0.002	0.005
	(0.017)	(0.014)	(0.014)	(0.003)	(0.005)
Financial openness	0.098***	0.047**	0.026**	−0.002	−0.008*
	(0.016)	(0.019)	(0.011)	(0.002)	(0.004)
Technology	56.85*	15.03	31.11*	−3.775	−11.51***
	(31.01)	(30.01)	(15.81)	(3.572)	(3.587)
Financial deepening	0.050**	0.026**	0.022***	−0.004	−0.002
	(0.021)	(0.011)	(0.007)	(0.001)	(0.002)
Aes × Financial deepening	−0.049**	−0.033**	−0.03***	0.007***	0.004*
	(0.021)	(0.014)	(0.008)	(0.002)	(0.002)
Skill Premium	−0.413	−1.351	−0.475	0.063	−0.083
	(0.726)	(0.859)	(0.670)	(0.110)	(0.139)
Aes × Skill premium	1.165**	0.555	1.184***	−0.131**	0.024
	(0.521)	(0.556)	(0.346)	(0.064)	(0.057)
Education Gini	6.085	−3.245	12.52	−1.906	−3.370*
	(10.94)	(11.39)	(8.104)	(1.364)	(1.721)
Labor market institutions	0.803***	0.497	0.338*	−0.045	−0.140**
	(0.291)	(0.320)	(0.195)	(0.036)	(0.063)
Female mortality	0.021**	0.015*	0.026	−0.005***	0.001
	(0.009)	(0.009)	(0.032)	(0.002)	(0.002)
Government spending	−0.26	0.426***	−0.349***	0.046***	0.0332
	(0.162)	(0.145)	(0.103)	(0.017)	(0.023)
Country fixed effects	Yes	Yes	Yes	Yes	Yes
Time dummies	Yes	Yes	Yes	Yes	Yes
#. of Observation	361	361	220	220	220
#. of countries	97	97	67	67	67
Adjusted R-squared	0.386	0.246	0.491	0.412	0.225

Source: Dabla-Norris et al. (2015: 25), based on Fraser Institute; IMF, *World Economic Outlook*; Solt Database; UNU-WIDER's World Income Inequality Database; World Bank's World Economic Indicators; World Economic Forum; and IMF Staff calculations

Note: Standard errors in parentheses, $*p < 0.1$; $**p < 0.05$; and $***p < 0.01$. Estimated using fixed-effects panel regressions with robust standard errors clustered at the country level. Additional controls include lagged GDP growth and share of employment in agriculture and industry. Income shares represent disposable (after tax) incomes or consumption based on household data. AEs = advanced economies

Table 6.3 Gender inequality and economic distribution, 1980–2010

Variables	*Dependent variable: Net GINI and income shares*				
	(1) *Net GINI*	*(2)* *Top 10*	*(3)* *Top 60*	*(4)* *Bottom 40*	*(5)* *Bottom 20*
United nation gender inequality index (GII)	9.761*	16.81*	10.09**	−9.367**	−5.934**
	(5.589)	(8.431)	(4.444)	(4.385)	(2.390)
Trade openness	−0.0109	−0.00942	−0.0146	0.0132	0.00588
	(0.0140)	(0.0121)	(0.0101)	(0.0102)	(0.00550)
Financial openness	0.0422***	0.0310***	0.0347***	−0.0291***	−0.0141**
	(0.0113)	(0.0115)	(0.00967)	(0.0100)	(0.00544)
Technology	−1.567	25.30	22.83*	−22.24*	−14.59**
	(18.53)	(20.74)	(12.21)	(12.45)	(6.187)
Financial deepening	0.0233**	0.0230***	0.0208**	−0.0200**	−0.00876**
	(0.00916)	(0.00785)	(0.00809)	(0.00800)	(0.00385
Financial deepening × AM interaction	−0.0286***	−0.0208**	−0.0315***	0.0296***	0.0132***
	(0.0101)	(0.00952)	(0.00847)	(0.00841)	(0.00408)
Educational attainment	−0.793**	−0.504	−0.481**	0.546***	0.292***
	(0.334)	(0.318)	(0.194)	(0.203)	(0.109)
Labor market institutions	0.688***	0.268	0.331**	−0.249*	−0.133*
	(0.197)	(0.172)	(0.133)	(0.140)	(0.0733)
Government spending	−0.320***	−0.356***	−0.112**	0.132**	0.0660**
	(0.102)	(0.105)	(0.0501)	(0.0533)	(0.0256)
Population over the age of 65	0.361**	0.206	0.251*	−0.292**	−0.140*
	(0.150)	(0.175)	(0.136)	(0.134)	(0.0709)
Observations (five-year averages)	338	208	244	244	244
Countries	97	66	89	89	89
Adjusted R-squared	0.236	0.421	0.359	0.345	0.305

Sources: Gonzales et al. (2015b: 24), based on Barro-Lee education attainment data set; Fraser Institute; IMF's *World Economic Outlook*; Solt Database; UNU-WIDER World Income Inequality Database; World Bank's World Development Indicators; World Economic Forum; and IMF Staff estimates

Note: Estimated using country and year fixed-effects panel regressions with robust standard errors clustered at the country level shown in parentheses, $*p < 0.10$; $**p < 0.05$; $***p < 0.01$

Appendix B

Table 6.4 Human development indicators

Health	*2015*
Life expectancy at birth, female (years)	76.3
Life expectancy at birth, male (years)	74.0
Mortality rate, under-5, female (per 1000)	14.9
Mortality rate, under-5, male (per 1000)	16.2
Births attended by skilled health staff (percent of total)	96.4
Education indicators	*2013*
Literacy rate, female (percent of females ages 15–25)	97.7
Literacy rate, male (percent of males ages 15–25)	98.3

Source: World Bank (2016b), World Development Indicators

Notes

1. "GII measures gender inequalities in three important aspects of human development—reproductive health, measured by maternal mortality ratio and adolescent birth rates; empowerment, measured by proportion of parliamentary seats occupied by females and proportion of adult females and males aged 25 years and older with at least some secondary education; and economic status, expressed as labor market participation and measured by labor force participation rate of female and male populations aged 15 years and older (UNDP, 2016)."
2. See Appendix B.
3. 100,000/year≈8000/month≈2000/week≈400/day.
4. Gross impact is percentage increase in per capita GDP assuming women having the same hours of work and productivity as men. Net impact is adjusted for productivity drag and part time work.

References

ActionAid. (2015). Close the gap? The cost of inequality in women's work. ActionAid UK, London. Retrieved March 30, 2016, from https://www.actionaid.org.uk/sites/default/files/publications/womens_rights_on-line_version_2.1.pdf

Aghion, P., Caroli, E., & García-Peñalosa, C. (1999). Inequality and economic growth: The perspective of the new growth theories. *Journal of Economic Literature, 37*(4), 1615–1660.

Aguirre, D. (2012). Empowering the third billion: Women and the world of work. Strategy, San Francisco. Retrieved March 30, 2016, from http://www.strategyand.pwc.com/media/file/Strategyand_Empowering-the-Third-Billion_Full-Report.pdf

Barro, R. J. (2000). Inequality and growth in a panel of countries. *Journal of Economic Growth, 5*(1), 5–32.

Becker, G. (1992). The economic way of looking at life. Nobel Lecture, December 9, 1992. Retrieved April 23, 2016, from http://www.nobelprize.org/nobel_prizes/economic-sciences/laureates/1992/becker-lecture.pdf

Cagatay, N. (1998). Gender and poverty. UNDP Working Paper No. 5. United Nations Development Programme, New York.

Carvalho, L. A., & Rezai, A. (2014). Personal income inequality and aggregate demand. Working Paper 2014–2023. Department of Economics, University of Sao Paulo, Sao Paulo.

Chamlou, N. (2008). *The environment for women's entrepreneurship in the Middle East and North Africa Region*. Washington, DC: The World Bank Group.

Chamlou, N., & Karshenas, M. (2016). *Women, work and welfare in the Middle East and North Africa: The role of socio-demographics, entrepreneurship and public policies*. London: Imperial College Press.

Cuberes, D. A., & Teignier, M. (2014). Aggregate effects of gender gaps in the labor market: A quantitative estimate. UB Economics Working Paper 2014/308.

Dabla-Norris, E., Kochhar, K., Suphaphiphat, N., Ricka, F., & Tsounta, E. (2015). Causes and consequences of income inequality: A global perspective. IMF Staff Discussion Note SDN/15/13. International Monetary Fund (IMF), Washington, DC.

Duflo, E. (2012). Women's empowerment and economic development. *Journal of Economic Literature, 50*(4), 1051–1079.

Elborgh-Woytek, K. A. (2013). *Women, work, and the economy: Macroeconomic gains from gender equity*. Washington, DC: International Monetary Fund.

Esteve-Volart, B. (2004). Gender discrimination and growth: Theory and evidence from India. LSE STICERD Research Paper DEDPS42, London School of Economics (LSE), London.

Gonzales, C., Jain-Chandra, S., Kochar, K., & Newiak, M., Zeinullayev, T. (2015a). Catalyst for change: Empowering women and tackling income inequality. IMF Staff Discussion Note SDN/15/20. International Monetary Fund, Washington, DC.

Gonzales, C., Jain-Chandra, S., Kochar, K., & Newiak, M. (2015b). Fair play: More equal laws boost female labor force participation. IMF Staff Discussion Note SDN/15/02. International Monetary Fund, Washington, DC.

IBRD [International Bank for Reconstruction and Development]. (2016). Women, business and the law: Getting to equal. Washington, DC: The World Bank Group. Retrieved March 30, 2016, from http://wbl.worldbank.org/~/

media/WBG/WBL/Documents/Reports/2016/Women-Business-and-the-Law-2016.pdf

ILO [International Labour Organization]. (2015). Key Indicators of the Labour Market (KILM). ILO, Geneva. Retrieved March 30, 2016, from http://www.ilo.org/global/statistics-and-databases/research-and-databases/kilm/lang--en/index.htm

ILO [International Labour Organization]. (2016). Women at work: Trends 2016. ILO, Geneva. Retrieved March 30, 2016, from http://www.ilo.org/wcmsp5/groups/public/---dgreports/---dcomm/---publ/documents/publication/wcms_457317.pdf

Jain-Chandra, S. (2015, October 27). Why gender and income inequality are linked. World Economic Forum, Geneva. Retrieved March 30, 2016, from https://www.weforum.org/agenda/2015/10/why-gender-and-income-inequality-are-linked/

Klasen, S. (1999). Does gender inequality reduce growth and development? Evidence from cross-country regressions. Policy Research Report on Gender and Development Working Paper No. 8. The World Bank Group, Washington, DC.

Moghadam, F. E. (2001). Iran's new Islamic home economics. In E. Mine Cinar, ed., *The economics of women and work in the Middle East and North Africa. Research in Middle East Economics.* Volume 4 of Research in Middle East Economics. Amsterdam and London: Elsevier.

OECD [Organization for Economic Co-operation and Development]. (2015). *In it together: Why less inequality benefits all.* Paris: OECD Publishing.

Piketty, T. (2014). *Capital in the twenty-first century.* Harvard: The Belknap Press.

Salehi Esfahani, H. (2015, August 6). Cheshmandaz-e bazar-e kar dar pasa-tahrim [Post-sanctions labor market prospects]. *Donya-ye eqtesad.* Retrieved March 30, 2016, from http://donya-e-eqtesad.com/news/909308/.

Salehi-Isfahani, D. (2009). Iran: Poverty and inequality since the revolution. Brookings, Washington, DC. Retrieved March 30, 2016, from http://www.brookings.edu/research/opinions/2009/01/29-iran-salehi-isfahani

Steinberg, C., & Nankane, M. (2012). Can women save Japan? IMF Working Paper No. 12/48. International Monetary Fund, Washington, DC.

Stotsky, J., Shibuya, S., Kolovich, L., & Kebhaj, S. (2016). Trends in gender equality and women's advancement. IMF Working Paper WP/16/21. International Monetary Fund, Washington, DC.

Taj Al-Saltana. (2003). *Crowning anguish: Memoirs of a Persian princess from the harem to modernity.* Translated by A. Vanzan, & A. Neshati. Edited, annotated, and introduced by A. Amanat. Washington, DC: Mage Publishers.

Taghato. (2015, January 28). Dar panj sal-e gozashteh, salaneh 100 hezar nafar az shoma-e zanan-e shaghel dar Iran kam shodeh ast [In the past five years, the number of female workers has decreased by 100,000 persons annually]. *Taghato.* Retrieved March 30, 2016, from http://taghato.net/article/9694

UNDP [United Nations Development Programme]. (2016). *Human Development Report* (data and definitions). Retrieved March 30, 2016, from http://hdr.undp.org/en

UNESCO [United Nations Educational, Scientific, and Cultural Organization]. (2016). Data tables on tertiary education. Retrieved March 30, 2016, from http://www.uis.unesco.org/Education/Pages/tertiary-education.aspx

Van der Weide, R., & Milanovic, B. (2014). Inequality is bad for growth of the poor (But Not for the Rich). Policy Research Working Paper 6963. The World Bank Group, Washington, DC.

Watson, B. (2015, January 23). Economic inequality for women costs $9tn globally, study finds. *The Guardian*. Retrieved March 30, 2016, from http://www.theguardian.com/sustainable-business/2015/jan/23/women-inequality-income-pay-actionaid-study-economy

World Bank. (2004). *Gender and development in the Middle East and North Africa Region: Women in the public sphere.* Washington, DC: The World Bank Group.

World Bank. (2012a). World development report: Gender equality and development. Washington, DC: The World Bank Group. Retrieved March 30, 2016, from https://siteresources.worldbank.org/INTWDR2012/Resources/7778105-1299699968583/7786210-1315936222006/Complete-Report.pdf

World Bank. (2012b). Accelerating progress on gender mainstreaming and gender related MDGs: Progress report. Washington, DC: The World Bank Group. Retrieved March 30, 2016, from http://www-wds.worldbank.org/external/default/WDSContentServer/WDSP/IB/2012/10/15/000333037_20121015011354/Rendered/PDF/731890BR0IDA0S0Official0Use0Only090.pdf

World Bank. (2016a). *Doing business 2016: Measuring regulatory quality and efficiency.* Washington, DC: The World Bank Group. Retrieved March 30, 2016, from http://www.doingbusiness.org

World Bank. (2016b). World Development Indicators (WDI). Washington, DC: The World Bank Group. Retrieved March 30, 2016, from http://data.worldbank.org

World Bank Group. (2015). *Women, business and the law 2016: Getting to equal.* Washington, DC: World Bank. Retrieved March 30, 2016, from https://openknowledge.worldbank.org/handle/10986/22546

WEF [World Economic Forum]. (2015). The Global Gender Gap Report 2015. WEF, Davos, Switzerland. Retrieved March 30, 2016, from http://reports.weforum.org/global-gender-gap-report-2015

CHAPTER 7

Aging and Gender Disparities in Contemporary Iran

Majid Koosheshi and Pooya Alaedini

Introduction

Iran has experienced a string of sociodemographic transitions during the last half a century. To start with, mortality rates have gradually declined since the 1960s (Khosravi et al. 2007). Furthermore, life expectancies for both sexes have steadily increased to register at 72 years in 2011 (UNDESA 2015). Yet, fertility rates in Iran have received a great deal of attention due to their rapid swings. In particular, it has been argued that the earlier fertility transition initiated in the 1970s was somewhat stalled through the first post-revolutionary decade due to the suspension of official family policies (Aghajanian 1991; Mirzaei 2005; Paydarfar and Moini 1995) as well as population momentum (Hakimian 2006). It has been further contended that the situation was spectacularly reversed through the resumption of the government's family planning programs as well as other shifting development variables (Aghajanian and Mehryar 2005; Mirzaei 2005; Abbasi-Shavazi et al. 2009). In any case, the fertility transition in Iran gained full force in the 1990s and ran its course through the 2000s, whereby total

M. Koosheshi (✉)
Department of Demography, University of Tehran, Tehran, Iran

P. Alaedini (✉)
Department of Social Planning, Faculty of Social Sciences, University of Tehran, Tehran, Iran

M.R. Farzanegan, P. Alaedini (eds.), *Economic Welfare and Inequality in Iran*, DOI 10.1057/978-1-349-95025-6_7

fertility rate of 6.53 births per woman, registered for the 1980–1985 period, dramatically dropped to 1.79 births per woman in the 2005–2010 period (UNDESA 2015). The combination of mortality and fertility transitions thus gave rise to the first signs of an age transition in the 2000s (Saraie 2009). These transitions have been further accompanied by unprecedented urbanization, rapid expansion of educational opportunities, and transformation of families (see Aghajanian and Thompson 2013; Foroutan 2014; Haghighat 2014).

An important outcome of recent demographic developments in Iran has been the relatively rapid growth of the elderly population. Indeed, Iran's elderly population has expanded in absolute and relative terms as a result of improving life expectancies, an earlier period of rapid population growth, and declining fertility rates in the more recent periods. Due to decreasing fertility, Iran's population growth rate declined from an annual average of 3.5 percent during 1966–1986 to an average of 1.7 percent per annum in the period 1986–2011 (SCI 1966, 1986, 2011a). Yet, the corresponding figures for the 65+ and 60+ age groups were, respectively, 2.2 and 2.5 percent in the first and 4.3 and 3.4 percent in the second period (ibid.). Thus, the expansion of the elderly population comprises a major feature of Iran's population dynamics. The current elderly population belongs to a generation with fertility rates in the order of six children that has benefited from improving health indicators to live significantly longer lives. Based on forecasts of the World Population Prospects (UNDESA 2015), Iran's 60+ age group, which totaled around 6 million persons in 2011, will become 30 million strong by 2050 to comprise a quarter of the country's population (see also Kiani et al. 2010).

In this chapter, we focus on the effects of these sociodemographic developments on elderly women. We start the next section with an examination of the growth and current population of the country's elderly as well as gender differences in life expectancy and literacy rate. We then turn to an investigation of gender gaps in employment and economic activity among the current elderly population as well as their significance for those who will join the elderly population in the future. Our discussion suggests that, against the backdrop of scarce job opportunities for females in Iran, the current rate of employment for elderly women hints at their increasing economic anguish. Low rates of employment among working-age females further confront the future generation of elderly women with the prospects of economic hardship. In another section, we treat the significantly lower marriage rates among elderly females in comparison with elderly males. We contend that the difference suggests potential gaps in support for elderly women, which is being exacerbated by changing family structures. In the second half of the chapter, we use the terminology and calculation methods of National Transfer Accounts (NTA) to investigate gender gaps for a number of parameters from an intergenerational perspective. NTA is an accounting system of economic flows between age groups or generations. Typically prepared for a national population in a given calendar year, the actual NTA has a macro approach and requires the calculation of measures for all economic flows and four behaviors of working, consuming, sharing, and saving. However, in this study, we only use individual-/household-level data for the year 2011—the last year for which the required data on Iran exist—to highlight certain economic differences among Iran's elderly men and women. Specifically, we employ data on labor income and those parts of transfers that are most beneficial for understanding gender differences as well as economic security of the elderly. Finally, in our conclusion, we summarize the chapter's findings as two sets of serious challenges faced by the current and future population of elderly women, which call for appropriate public policies.

Population, Literacy Rate, and Employment

Figure 7.1 compares the growth rates of Iran's elderly population (60+ and 65+) and the general population in 1986–1996 and 1996–2006. It indicates that Iran's total population of persons aged 65 years or older grew more than three and half times between 1976 and 2011 to reach 4.3 million. The population share of those in the 65+ age group increased from around 4 to about 6 percent in the period 1996–2011 (SCI 1996, 2006, 2011a). The latter figure is nonetheless small in comparison with other countries experiencing significant population aging. Furthermore, notwithstanding the rapid growth of the elderly population in Iran, old dependency ratios have remained relatively stable over the last four decades and have been decreasing during the 2010–2015 period as shown in Table 7.1. Thus, although the population segment with the highest rate of growth is associated with the elderly in Iran, the country's demographic profile remains quite young for now in proportional terms.[1]

Sex ratio for 65+ age group, which was 111.08 just before the Revolution, declined to 99.39 by 2011. Furthermore, the gender difference in life expectancies, given at age 65 in Table 7.2, has gradually widened to reach 1.6 years by 2011. These two indicators potentially hint at the feminization of Iran's elderly population in the future. At only around 36 percent in

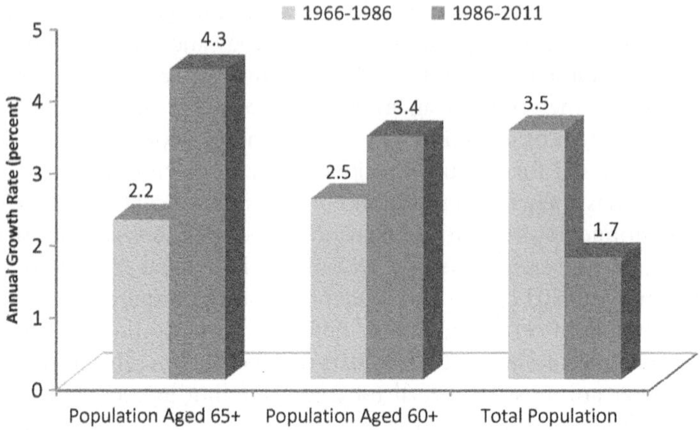

Fig. 7.1 Annual growth rates of the elderly and general populations, 1966–1986 and 1986–2011. *Source*: SCI (1996, 1986, 2011a) (National Censuses of Iran for 1966, 1986, and 2011)

Table 7.1 Total and old dependency ratios, 1975–2015

Category/Year	*1975*	*1980*	*1985*	*1990*	*1995*	*2000*	*2005*	*2010*	*2015*
Ratio of population 0–19 and 65+ per 100 population 20–64	134.8	133.1	140.6	143.9	134.0	110.5	79.3	61.3	55.3
Ratio of population 65+ per 100 population 20–64	7.5	6.9	7.1	8.1	8.8	8.9	8.8	8.0	7.9
Ratio of population 65+ per 100 population 25–64	9.5	8.8	8.9	10.2	11.1	11.4	11.5	9.9	9.1
Ratio of population 70+ per 100 population 20–69	4.0	3.8	3.7	4.1	4.8	5.0	5.4	5.2	4.8

Source: UNDESA, World Population Prospects (2015)

2011, the literacy rate for both sexes among the country's 65+ age group is quite low. Yet, it has been rising steadily since 1976 when it was only 13 percent and a mere 5.5 percent for women. The improvements are due largely to the gradual replacement of 65+ age group with increasingly more

Table 7.2 Characteristics of 65+ age group, 1976–2011

	Sex	*1976*	*1986*	*1996*	*2006*	*2011*
Population (1000)	Men and women	1186.47	1501.72	2595.18	3656.59	4296.77
	Men	624.39	767.92	1382.45	1928.38	2141.76
	Women	562.08	733.80	1212.73	1728.21	2155.01
Sex Ratio		111.08	104.65	113.99	111.58	99.39
Life expectancy at age 65	Men	11.5	12.3	13	13.6	13.9
	Women	12.4	13.4	14.1	15	15.5
	Gender gap	0.9	1.1	1.1	1.4	1.6
Literacy rate	Men	19.7	25.1	32.6	44	48.2
	Women	5.5	8.2	11.8	19.9	23.7
	Gender gap	14.2	16.9	20.8	24.1	24.5

Source: SCI (1976, 1986, 1996, 2006, 2011a) (National Censuses of Iran for 1976–2011); UNDESA, World Population Prospects (2015)

literate generations, but also to the efforts of Iran's literacy corps in including older populations in their campaign. However, the increasing literacy rate among the elderly in Iran has not been accompanied by a decline in its related gender gap. In fact, the gender gap in literacy rates for the 65+ age group grew significantly between 1976 and 2011, reaching 24.5 percent by the end of the period. This phenomenon will be reversed in the medium- to long-term, as literacy rates for both men and women are improving among the younger generations and their gender gap is diminishing. Nevertheless, in the near- to medium-term, the low rate of literacy associated with elderly women, which is also a measure of their human capital used to gain income in the past or at present, may have important implications for their quality of life.

Iran's post-revolutionary economic disruptions and the devastation experienced as a consequence of the war with Iraq had a significant negative impact on employment rates. Moreover, due to various reasons, presumably both sociodemographic and political economic, employment rates for either sex and almost all age groups—although fluctuating—have remained below those registered for 1976, as shown in Table 7.3. The sharpest decline has been experienced by both sexes in the 15–24 age group, which may be argued to have been partially influenced by expanding educational opportunities. Yet, employment rates for those between the ages of 25 and 64—expected to comprise the most economically productive part of one's lifecycle—have also declined considerably. As Table 7.3 indicates, between

1986 and 1996, coinciding with the period of so-called "reconstruction" after the Iran-Iraq War, the overall employment rate for the 25–64 age category improved from 47.5 to 49.3 percent. In 1986, 85 percent of men and 8 percent of women in this age group were employed; by 1996, these figures registered at 86 percent and 11 percent, respectively. The percentage of employed women further increased to 13.3 by 2006 but dropped back to 11.6 percent in 2011. The corresponding figure for men decreased throughout the 1996–2011 period. These trends have undoubtedly been influenced by an array of social and economic factors, including among others the structure of the Iranian economy and its capacity to create jobs as well as the rapid expansion of educational opportunities and attainments for both sexes.

Curiously, the only age-sex group whose position in terms of employment has improved in comparison with the 1976 figures comprises females 65 years or older. The employment rate of this group of women rose from 4.3 percent to 5.2 percent between 1976 and 2011. The positive trend should not necessarily be interpreted as a blessing. During the period under consideration, not only the retirement pension system in Iran expanded but also certain early-retirement programs were carried out by the government in response to unemployment woes faced by the country. The latter programs especially targeted women. Thus, the rise in the employment rate of elderly women is not likely to hint at their decreasing economic privation. Nor do the low employment and labor force participation rates of younger Iranian women in the formal economy support bright prospects for the future generation of elderly females.

A number of studies have investigated post-revolutionary trends in Iranian women's employment and labor force participation rates in the formal economy (e.g., Moghadam 1995; Alaedini and Razavi 2005; Mahmoudian 2006). Others have highlighted Iranian women's significant activities in the informal economy as well as advances in the types of formal-sector positions they hold despite the overall stability of their total share of employment (see Bahramitash and Salehi Esfahani 2011). These important issues notwithstanding, in the rest of this section, we focus on gender gaps in formal-sector employment by age groups and their significance for elderly women.

Table 7.3 shows that the gender gap in employment is most pronounced for those between the ages of 15 and 64, typically associated with the highest income-earning period of the lifecycle. In the most recent year for which data are available, that is 2011, despite the considerable decline of

Table 7.3 Percent of population employed by age group and sex, 1976–2011

Age/Year	*1976*	*1986*	*1996*	*2006*	*2011*
Men and women					
15–24	39.0	29.2	24.8	23.8	19.6
25–64	54.4	47.5	49.3	48.7	43.5
65+	29.9	23.7	27.2	21.3	20.9
Men					
15–24	62.3	51.5	42.0	40.2	33.9
25–64	93.8	85.1	86.3	83.1	75.1
65+	52.6	44.6	48.8	38.5	36.8
Women					
15–24	16.5	6.1	7.8	7.1	5.1
25–64	11.8	7.8	11.0	13.3	11.6
65+	4.3	1.9	2.5	2.2	5.2
Gender gap					
15–24	45.8	45.4	34.2	33.1	28.8
25–64	82.0	77.3	75.3	69.8	63.5
65+	48.3	42.7	46.3	36.3	31.6

Source: SCI (1976, 1986, 1996, 2006, 2011a) (National Censuses of Iran for 1976 through 2011)

men's employment rate as compared to 2006, for every 100 women 63 fewer employments than men were registered. The corresponding figures for 1996 and 2006 were around 80 and 70, respectively—indicating a gradual decline of the gender gap in employment for the age category under consideration. However, this gender gap has not narrowed nearly enough to have a society-wide lifecycle impact on women's welfare. Nor should we expect it to decline rapidly in the near future, if we take into account Iran's prevailing socioeconomic conditions. Aside from this, a number of factors may be speculated to have influenced the gradual decline of the gender gap in employment for the 25–64 age group. Later marriages and social changes associated with women's increasing independence may constitute one set of factors. Yet, the impact of education on narrowing the gender gap in employment may have been stronger, although educated women do not necessarily fare well in Iran's recession-hit job market.

In the five-year period between 2006 and 2011, only around 70,000 additional jobs were created on balance (SCI 2006, 2011a), in a country with a total employment of about 20.5 million and a working-age (25–64) population of around 38 million persons. Such low rates of job creation confront the growing population with serious unemployment prospects and may push them—especially women—out of the job market through

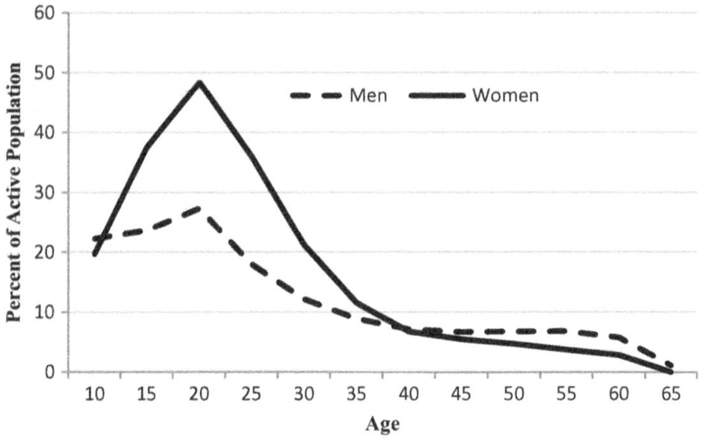

Fig. 7.2 Unemployment rate by five-year age group and sex, 2011. *Source*: SCI (2011a) (2011 Census)

disappointment. Graphs in Fig. 7.2 are drawn to show men's and women's unemployment rates by age, providing a snapshot of a single year—2011. The largest gender difference is registered for the 20–24 age group associated with those just out of high school or college. The gender difference then decreases and becomes zero just before age 40, as comparatively more women have left the job market altogether by then. After age 40, men's unemployment rate in fact becomes higher than women's.

Figure 7.3 depicts women's activity and employment rates by age, again in a single year—2011. While women's activity rate drops sharply after age 20, their employment rate peaks between the ages of 30 and 35—albeit at a low rate of around 15 percent—and then declines relatively quickly. These high rates of unemployment and low rates of economic activity for women in the age range associated with their highest economic potentials are an indication of their slim opportunities to earn income, save, and accumulate assets during their lifetimes. Figure 7.4 clearly depicts the differences between men and women in terms of these opportunities by constructing age pyramids for employed, economically active, unemployed, and total populations—which have important economic implications for women as they age and become elderly.

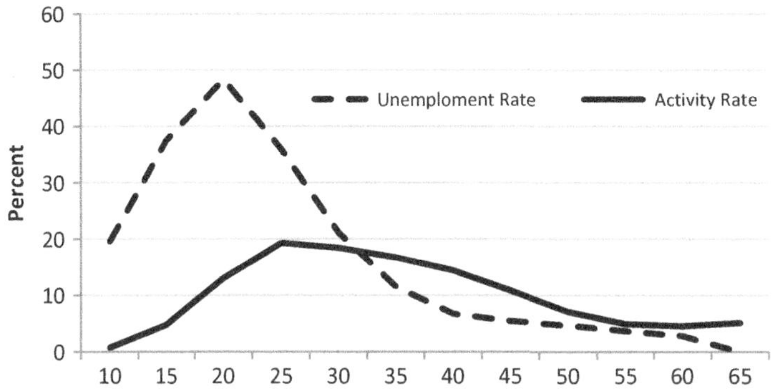

Fig. 7.3 Female activity and unemployment rates by five-year age groups, 2011. *Source*: SCI (2011a) (2011 Census)

Marriage and Family Support

In comparison to men, women get married younger in Iran, although the likelihood of one marriage before the age of 50 is the same for men and women (Torabi and Askari-Nodoushan 2012: 15). Due to the significant age differences between husbands and wives on the one hand and women's longer life expectancies on the other, elderly women are more likely to be without a spouse as compared to men. This is exacerbated with the higher likelihood of remarriage for elderly men. Against the background of Iran's patriarchal social structure, older widowers or divorced men may both lack the skills to live alone and be increasingly encouraged by the society to remarry. Table 7.4 underscores the significant gender differences among Iran's elderly population in terms of marriage status since 1976. From 1976 until around 2000, the difference was becoming smaller—which may be attributable to generational shifts—but the trend has gradually reversed since then. In 2011, whereas unmarried women (never married, divorced, or widowed) comprised 58.7 percent of the 65+ population, only 11.4 percent of men in the same age group were reportedly without a spouse. This considerable gap is the result of age differences between men and women at the time of first marriage—with women marrying at a younger age—as well as higher life expectancies for women and much higher rates of remarriage for older men as compared to women. As men continue to be the main holders of family wealth and assets, living husbands play crucial roles for elderly women's access to resources and quality of life. Thus, the

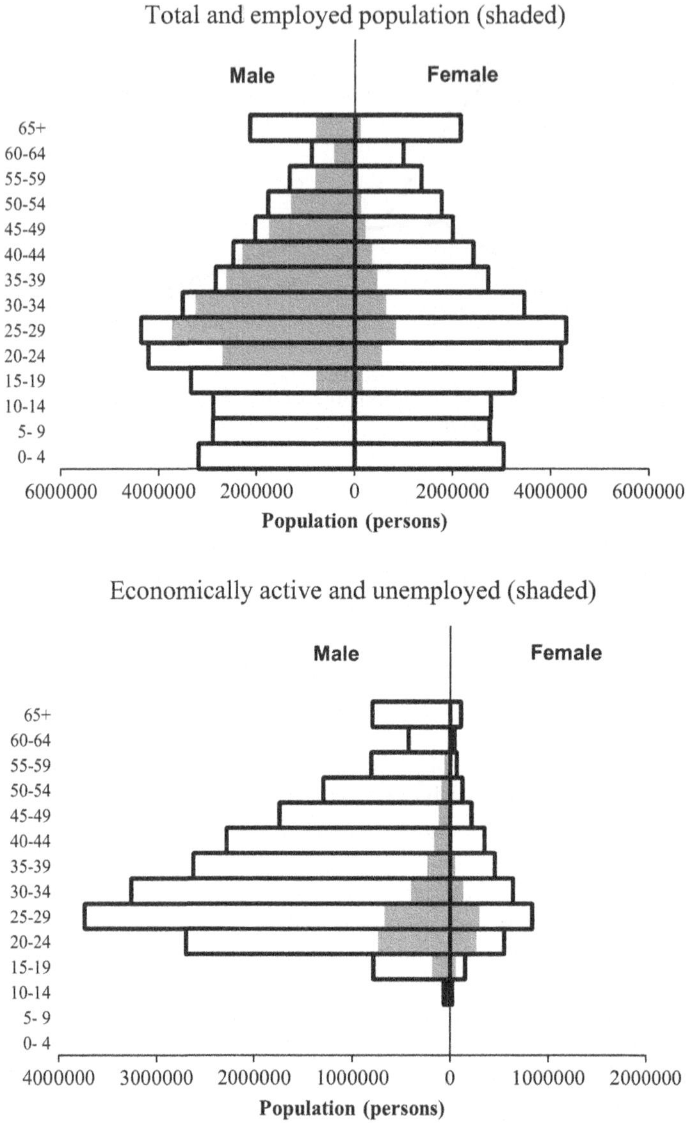

Fig. 7.4 Age pyramids of economically active, employed, and unemployed populations, 2011. *Source*: SCI (2011a) (2011 Census)

Table 7.4 Unmarried elderly and elderly living alone, 1976–2011

Year	*Percent of the elderly who are unmarried*			*Percent of the elderly who live alone*			
	Both Sexes	*Men*	*Women*	*Both Sexes*	*Men*	*Women*	*Gender gap*
1976	39.1	14.2	66.8	8.1	4.0	12.5	8.5
1986	37.5	14.9	61.2	–	–	–	–
1996	32.6	11.6	56.5	9.0	3.7	15.1	11.4
2006	33.3	11.6	57.4	–	–	–	–
2011	35.1	11.4	58.7	13.0	5.8	21.0	15.2

**Source*: SCI (1976, 1986, 1996, 2006, 2011a) (National Censuses of Iran for 1976–2011)
***Source*: UNDESA, 2005 for 1976 and 1996; SCI (2009) Time Use Survey, 2009

rise in the percentage of unmarried elderly women is not without significant implications. The quality of additional years of life for elderly women, who are much more likely to be unmarried as compared to men, depends on shifting socioeconomic conditions, including the amount of income and wealth at their disposal, the family relations and support they enjoy, and welfare and healthcare measures from which they can benefit.

Low life expectancies in pre-modern Iran meant that few people reached the old age. Furthermore, in the traditional context of the Iranian society, extended families featuring patriarchy and gerontarchy prevailed (Saraie 2007). In the absence of public support systems, extended families were supposed to wholly provide for elderly women. This was realized either by the husband's control of the extended family's resources and wealth or through intergenerational family commitments. In contemporary Iran, which is a society in transition, significant socioeconomic shifts are inexorably altering the functions and interrelationships of such informal social institutions. Rapid urbanization is inevitably resulting in the predominance of nuclear family households, a large number of elderly individuals who live alone, and ascendance of private norms. Figure 7.5 depicts trends in average household size and percentage of extended family households. In the period 1976–2011, the average household size decreased from around 5 to 3.6 persons. Somewhat more dramatically, between 1986 and 2011, the share of extended family households halved to comprise only around one tenth of all households. Furthermore, as indicated in Table 7.4, the percentage of elderly men and women who live alone has risen steadily since 1976. Yet, women have been much more likely to live alone in comparison with men. The gap between women and men in terms of the percentage of those who

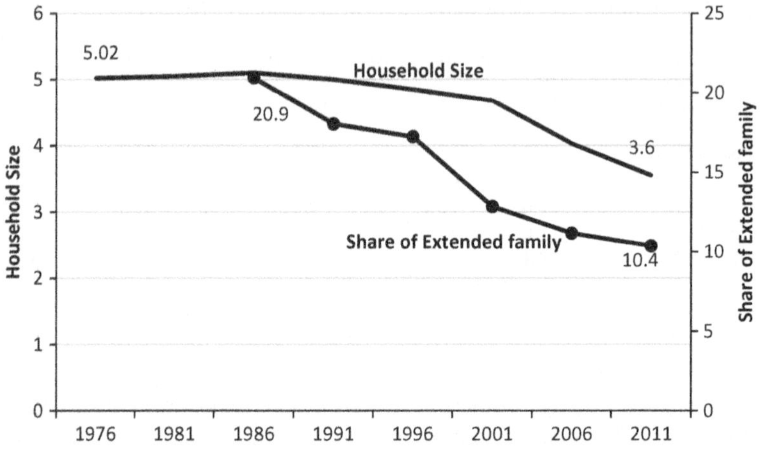

Fig. 7.5 Trends in average household size (1976–2011) and share of extended family households (1986–2011). *Source*: SCI (1976, 1986, 1996, 2006, 2011a) (National Censuses of Iran for 1976–2011); SCI (2011b) (2011 HEIS)

live alone has also been widening. This trend was unaffected by the narrowing gender gap from 1976 to around 2000 in the percentage of unmarried elderly. Declining household size and prevalence of nuclear families mean that adult children and their parents are becoming more likely to reside in separate domiciles. With this, intergenerational relationships are increasingly manifested between two separate rather than within a single household. The support structures of the earlier times—which were expected to be all-encompassing—are thus being replaced by a norm of assistance provided to elderly parents chiefly when there are serious needs (see Ghazi-Tabatabae et al. 2008).

In a research project conducted under the auspices of United Nations Population Fund (UNFPA) in Tehran (Koosheshi et al. 2014), the support networks of a total of 527 elderly men and women—chosen through a two-stage cluster sampling scheme—were investigated. Ten sources and four types of family and non-family informal social support were identified. Excluding parents and grandchildren, whose support was deemed negligible, the main members probed in the elderly's family network were spouse, child, son- or daughter-in-law, sister, brother, and extended relatives. Non-family included friend, neighbor, and colleague in the study. The gender differences in terms of dependence on family and non-family support for the investigated elderly sample—depicted in Figs. 7.6, 7.7, 7.8, and 7.9—are revealing. First, wives play crucial roles in their elderly husband's support network. As indicated in Fig. 7.6, female spouses are in fact the most important source of social support for elderly men in need of care, followed by children and daughters/sons-in-law. Yet, Fig. 7.9 shows that wives rank lowest in terms of sources of financial support for elderly men, which is a clear indication of their earlier low rates of employment and limited income-earning opportunities. Elderly men, when in need of financial support, rely mostly on their children and then almost equally on their children-in-law, siblings, extended family members, neighbors, friends, and colleagues. As indicated in Fig. 7.6, rather than their spouses, the main sources of caring support for elderly women are their children followed by sons/daughters-in-law. In terms of financial support, elderly women also rely on their children first and then on their husbands and children-in-law. It should be noted that the main focus of this study was on interfamily rather than intrafamily sources of financial support—hence, the relatively low rate of financial support given by husbands to elderly wives in Fig. 7.8.

Gender Disparities in Labor Income and Transfer Flows

In this section, we employ the National Transfer Accounts' (NTA) terminology and calculation methods (Lee and Mason 2011; UNDESA 2013) to further highlight gender disparities in terms of labor income, asset income, pension receipts, and inter-household transfers. NTA attaches age to National Income and Product Accounts to especially focus on the lifecycle deficit (LCD)—the difference between consumption occurring throughout the lifecycle and labor income earned only through a part of it.[2] This deficit must be addressed by reallocation through either private transfers (flows between households or from non-governmental institutions) or public transfers (social insurance or public-sector spending) or assets (inherited or accumulated earlier in life that may earn income or be dis-saved). In the economic lifecycle context of NTA, the ultimate source of all flows is labor income which is used by the individual and persons under his/her care (particularly in the younger or older generations) or alternatively is saved or transferred. At the macro level, if a population has surplus labor income, it is either saved or takes the form of public or private flows. Public and private transfers notwithstanding, surplus labor income may be saved as capital or property to address old age deficits. NTA is particularly capable of capturing old age deficits and highlighting poverty and lack of security experienced by

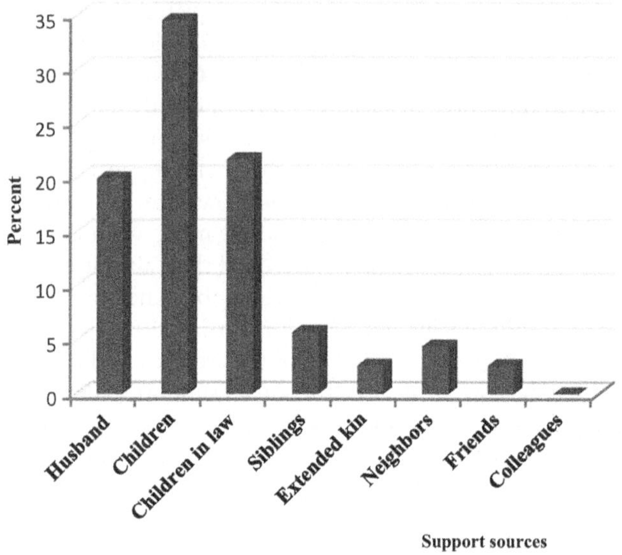

Fig. 7.6 Percentage shares of caring support sources for 60+ married elderly females, Tehran, 2007. *Source*: Based on Koosheshi et al. (2014)

the elderly population at the national level (see for example Narayana 2011; Mun Sim Lai and Tung 2015).

However, since the NTA for Iran is in the process of being developed—through a project registered with the global network of National Transfer Accounts (NTA 2016)—at this stage, we can only benefit from the use of data produced at the individual/household level. NTA's primary variables for the year 2011, extracted from the Household Expenditure-Income Survey (HEIS) of the Statistical Center of Iran (SCI), are thus reported here as preliminary results. HEIS' database contains raw household-level information with a unique code attached to each household member—through which age, sex, transfers, economic activities, and so on may be linked for each individual. The database has thus been used to calculate income values as well as total and per-capita transfers (incorporating sample weights and smoothing age profiles when drawing graphs in this section). NTA's income and transfer definitions used here are provided below:

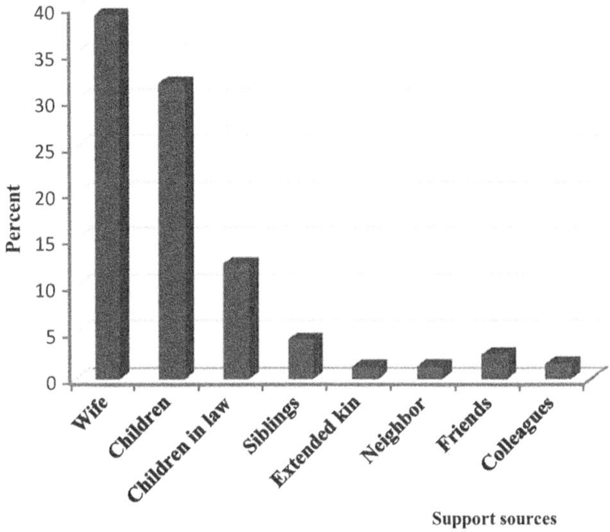

Fig. 7.7 Percentage shares of caring support sources for 60+ married elderly males, Tehran, 2007. *Source*: Based on Koosheshi et al. (2014)

1. Labor income (YL): Sum of wages, salaries, and self-employment income (gross earnings before taxes), and employee benefits (occasional or continuous as well as additional benefits for family [*haqq-e a'elemandi*]).
2. Private Asset Income—Property Income (YPF): Sum of rents, interest payments, and dividends from property.
3. Private Asset Income—Capital Income (YKF): Sum of earnings from savings accounts, certificates of deposit, stocks, and related insurance schemes.
4. Private Transfer Inflows (TFI): Cash or in-kind, educational or non-educational, assistance to households from non-public social and charity institutions.
5. Private Transfer Inflows—Inter-household (TFBI): All transfers received from other independent households; for instance, transfers received by adult children from parents or by parents from their adult children who have their own households independently.
6. Private Transfer Outflows—Inter-household (TFBO): All transfers provided to other independent households (age is attached to the

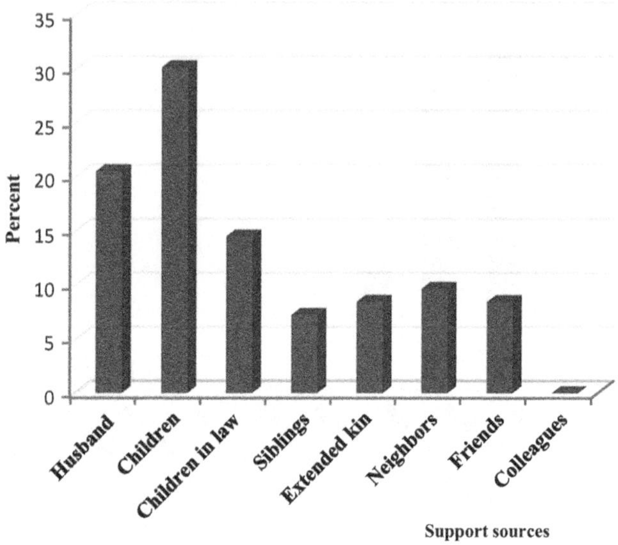

Fig. 7.8 Percentage shares of financial support sources for 60+ married elderly males, Tehran, 2007. *Source*: Based on Koosheshi et al. (2014)

head of household); for instance, transfers provided to parents or adult children by head of independent household.

7. Public Transfer Inflows—Pensions (TGSOAI): All forms of pension income and related stipends.

Table 7.5 summarizes our calculations for labor income (YL), property income (YPF), capital income (YKF), private transfer inflows (TFI), transfer inflows from other households (TFBI), transfer outflows to other households (TFBO), the difference between transfer inflows and outflows (TFBI-TFBO), and pensions (TGSOAI). It indicates that, in 2011, Iran's total labor income, comprising sum of all earnings including those from self-employment, was 1,556,000 billion rials. Women's share of total labor income was about 6.3 percent, and around 5.7 percent for the 25–64 age category, as shown in Table 7.6. Also, more than nine tenths of labor income was associated with the 25–64 age group.

As indicated earlier, not only women's employment rate in the 65+ age category in 2011 was historically the highest, it was the only employment

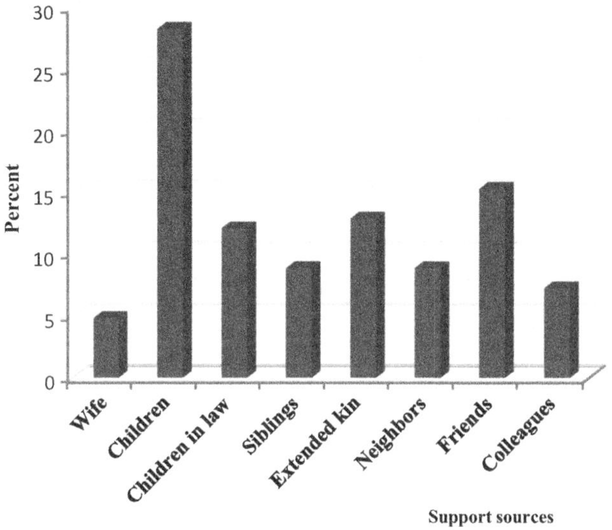

Fig. 7.9 Percentage shares of financial support sources for 60+ married elderly females, Tehran, 2007

rate for all age categories of women and men that had improved in comparison to its 1976 figure. Yet, considering the low level of human capital associated with women in the 65+ age category (as well as their old age), it is likely for them to receive low wages. Indeed, Table 7.7 shows that whereas 12.3 percent of the employed elderly are females, their share of labor income in the total income associated with the elderly population is only around 1.6 percent. Thus, improvements in the employment rate of elderly women should be attributed above all to increasing economic pressures they are experiencing.

When labor income is insufficient to cover lifecycle deficits, the needs may be addressed by two other means. One is though earnings from assets and the other is through transfers from the government or non-governmental organization and other households. Yet, as Iranian women's labor income during their economic lifecycle only accounts for 6 percent of the total labor income (with men's share being 94 percent), their share of income from capital (dividing 3806.7 by 13,948.7 in Table 7.5) is approximately 27 percent and their share of inter-household private transfer inflows (dividing 15,505.8 by 31,649.9 in Table 7.5) is

Table 7.5 Total and per-capita incomes by age groups and sex, 2011

Age	*Population*	*YL*	*YPF*	*YKF*	*TFI*	*TFBI*	*TFBO*	*TFBI-TFBO*	*TGSOAI*
Men, Total (billion rials)									
0–24		83,013.3	75.6	72.5	254.0	1895.4	617.1	1278.3	390.0
25–64		1,409,921.0	28,030.1	7531.0	5467.9	10,460.3	21,888.3	−11,428.0	156,994.0
65+		63,195.4	9963.6	2538.6	3577.3	3788.5	2587.8	1200.7	50,732.0
All ages		1,556,129.8	38,069.4	10,142.1	9299.2	16,144.1	25,093.2	−8949.0	208,116.0
Men, Per capita (million rials)									
0–24	16,528,270	5.0225	0.0046	0.0044	0.0154	0.1147	0.0373	0.0773	0.0236
25–64	19,207,121	73.4062	1.4594	0.3921	0.2847	0.5446	1.1396	−0.5950	8.1737
65+	2,141,760	29.5063	4.6521	1.1853	1.6703	1.7689	1.2082	0.5606	23.6871
All ages	37,877,151	40.9064	1.0798	0.2866	0.2744	0.4536	0.6625	−0.2089	5.8678
Women, Total (billion rials)									
0–24		17,918.4	45.0	75.8	335.4	1893.7	6.8	1886.9	696.2
25–64		84,991.1	5762.1	3232.2	4975.5	9509.0	1470.9	8038.0	64,338.2
65+		1021.9	2169.5	498.7	2927.8	4103.1	756.7	3346.4	21,143.0
All ages		103,931.5	7976.6	3806.7	8238.7	15,505.8	2234.5	13,271.4	86,177.5
Women, Per capita (million rials)									
0–24	16,055,048	1.1161	0.0028	0.0047	0.0209	0.1180	0.0004	0.1175	0.0434
25–64	19,016,139	4.4694	0.3030	0.1700	0.2616	0.5000	0.0774	0.4227	3.3833
65+	2,155,009	0.4742	1.0067	0.2314	1.3586	1.9040	0.3511	1.5529	9.8111
All ages	37,226,196	2.7007	0.1955	0.0952	0.2010	0.3876	0.0600	0.3276	2.1205

Source: SCI (2011b) (Household Income and Expenditure Survey)

Table 7.6 Total and employed population and share of labor income by sex, 2011

Age	*Total population*			*Employed population*			*Total labor income (billion rials)*		
	Number of persons	*Percent in sex category*	*Percent of total population*	*Number of persons*	*Percent in sex category*	*Percent of total employed*	*Amount*	*Percent of each sex*	*Percent of both sexes*
Men									
0–24	16,528,270	43.6	22.0	3,550,323	17.3	14.7	83,013.3	5.3	5.0
25–64	19,207,121	50.7	25.6	16,175,555	78.8	67.1	1,409,921	90.6	84.9
65+	2,141,760	5.7	2.9	797,508	3.9	3.3	63,195.4	4.1	3.8
Sum	37,877,151	100.0	50.4	20,523,386	100.0	85.2	1,556,130	100.0	93.7
Women									
0–24	16,055,048	43.1	21.4	730,207	20.4	3.0	17,918.4	17.2	1.1
25–64	19,016,139	51.1	25.3	2,733,305	76.5	11.3	84,991.1	81.8	5.1
65+	2,155,009	5.8	2.9	111,433	3.1	0.5	1021.9	1.0	0.1
Sum	37,226,196	100.0	49.6	3,574,945	100.0	14.8	103,931.5	100.0	6.3
Total	75,103,347		100.0	24,098,331		100.0	1,660,061		100.0

Source: Based on SCI (2011a) (2011 National Census); SCI (2011b) (Household Income and Expenditure Survey)

Table 7.7 Employed population and labor income by sex and age group, 2011

Age group	*Employed population (percent)*			*Total labor income (Percent)*		
	Men	Women	Both Sexes	Men	Women	Both Sexes
10–24	82.9	17.1	100.0	82.2	17.8	100.0
25–64	85.5	14.5	100.0	94.3	5.7	100.0
65+	87.7	12.3	100.0	98.4	1.6	100.0
sum	85.2	14.8	100.0	93.7	6.3	100.0

Source: Based on SCI (2011a) (2011 National Census); SCI (2011b) (Household Income and Expenditure Survey)

around 49 percent. Graphs in Figs. 7.10, 7.11, 7.12, 7.13, and 7.14 are further revealing in this regard. The largest gender gaps are in terms of labor income and asset income, which have resulted in lower gender gaps across other NTA parameters.[3]

The second age reallocation source after labor income is asset income, which includes income from property and capital. In 2011, capital constituted 25 percent of asset income while asset income was itself 25 percent of labor income plus asset income. A major gender difference is observed when comparing per-capita and total incomes from assets for men and women. As shown in Table 7.5, around three fourths of the total income from capital and more than four fifths of the total income from property are associated with men. Furthermore, per-capita income from assets flow in one direction toward men.

At the household level, after the death of one spouse, the accumulated wealth from labor income should theoretically be retained by the surviving wife or husband. Yet, this outcome is subject to inheritance laws, which in the Iranian context, clearly distinguish between men and women. A man solely inherits the assets of his deceased wife, whereas a woman inherits only one eighth of certain assets belonging to her deceased husband (one fourth if the husband is survived by his wife only)—as specified in Articles 905 and 949 of Iran's Civil Code (Majles 2016; Sadeghi Moghadam and Azizollahi, 2012: 188). Recent amendments have subjected more assets of the deceased husband to the one eighth (and one fourth) rule in favor of women, but they remain unequal based on the interpretation of Sharia (Rowshan et al. 2015: 167).

To shed further light on gender inequalities in terms of asset income, Table 7.5 and Fig. 7.11 may be analyzed in two scenarios. In the first scenario, we may assume that men and women have completely different

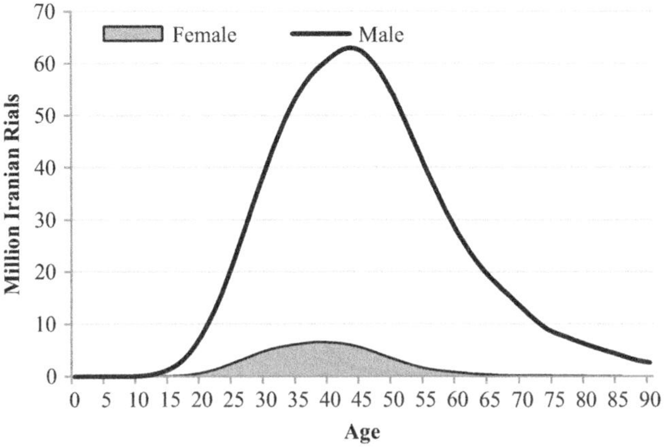

Fig. 7.10 Per-capita labor income by age and sex, 2011. *Source*: Calculated based on SCI (2011b) (Household Income and Expenditure Survey)

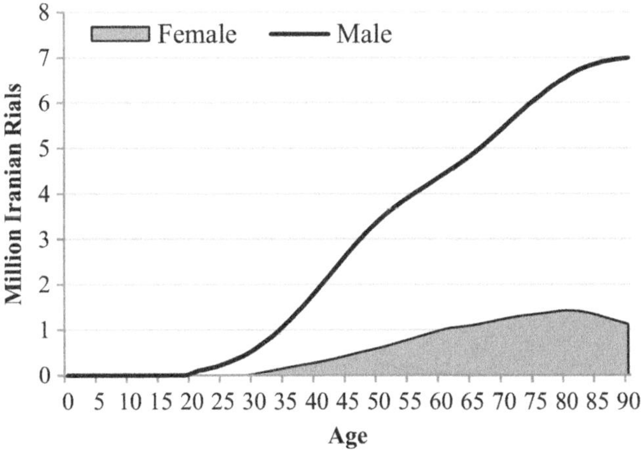

Fig. 7.11 Per-capita asset income by age and sex, 2011. *Source*: Calculated based on SCI (2011b) (Household Income and Expenditure Survey)

economic lifecycles. Then, as asset income itself is based on labor income, disparities in employment and per-capita labor income become the largest source of gender gap in asset income. If the assumption is correct, the

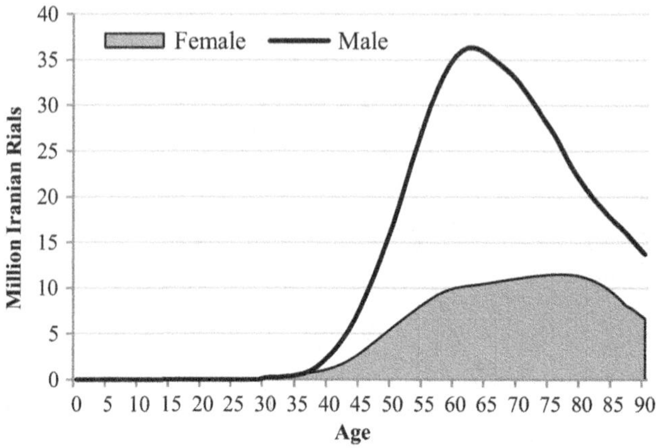

Fig. 7.12 Per-capita public transfer inflows—pensions by age and sex, 2011. *Source*: Calculated based on SCI (2011b) (Household Income and Expenditure Survey)

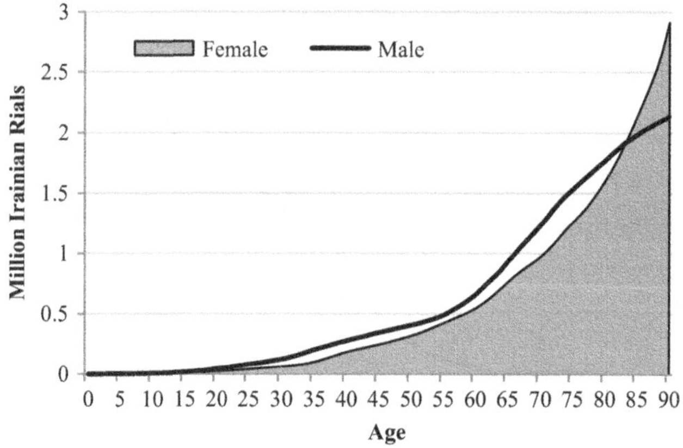

Fig. 7.13 Per-capita private transfer inflows by age and sex, 2011. *Source*: Calculated based on SCI (2011b) (Household Income and Expenditure Survey)

gender gap observed in Fig. 7.11 will be the smallest representation of gender inequality. The assumption in the second scenario is that men's and women's labor income independently shape household income. In

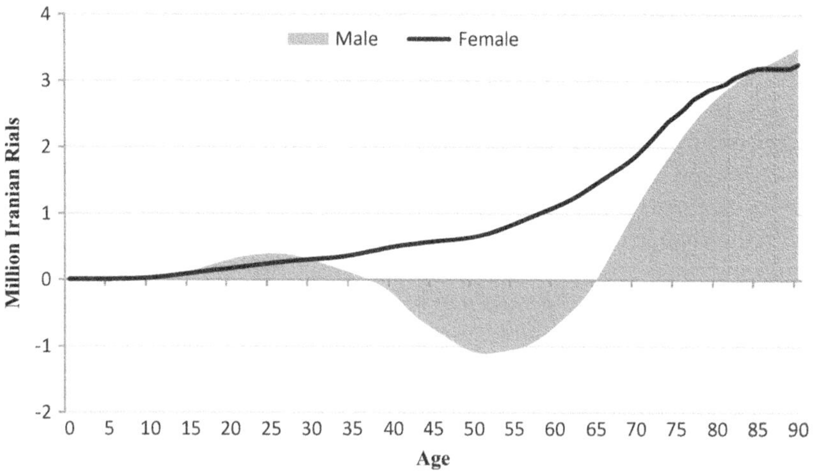

Fig. 7.14 Per-capita inter-household transfers (TFBI-TFBO) by age and sex, 2011. *Source*: Calculated based on SCI (2011b) (Household Income and Expenditure Survey)

this case, if we further assume that all women are married, as long as their husbands are alive, addressing deficits across different ages will not be a concern. However, as soon as the husband dies, the wife's share of asset income used to address lifecycle deficits will become subject to the inheritance law. Yet, considering how inheritance laws are specified in Iran's Civil Code, both scenarios lead to economic hardship for elderly women.

The case of public pensions (TGSOAI in Table 7.5) is similar to that of asset income, except that per-capita figures for such transfers are higher for both men (notwithstanding labor income) and women, especially in their old age. Public pension transfers constitute the most important source used by elderly women to address their needs and cover their lifecycle deficits, and the gender gap is smallest for them in this category of transfers. As indicated in Table 7.5, per-capita public pension transfers value for elderly women is about twice per-capita labor income of women between the ages of 25 and 64, that is, the peak of economic activity in the lifecycle. At approximately 9.8 million rials, elderly women's per-capita public pension transfers are less than half those of elderly men's. Based on figures in Table 7.5, per-capita pension transfer inflows for men are about 2.4 times those of women for both 25–64 and 65+ age categories. This suggests an apparent stability of gender gap across the ages. Yet, as Fig. 7.12 shows, starting at age 60, whereas the per-capita pension transfer inflow of men decreases, those of women increases slightly and remains stable through at least age 75. These trends have two roots. First, elderly individuals are survivors from earlier generations among whom pension schemes were not widespread—hence, decreasing pension transfer inflows. Second, part of the decrease in per-capita pension transfer inflows for men is associated with the change of rights to receive them from deceased husbands to their surviving wives—which is stipulated in Iranian pension laws. Figure 7.12 further shows that the gender gap in public pension transfers is much less pronounced than the case of labor income and asset income.

Per-capita figures for almost every source of income shown in Table 7.5 are lower for women in comparison with men, comprising a major set of gender disparities in Iran. The only exception is inter-household private transfer inflows, which are higher for women than men across all ages.[4] Yet, they also reflect the same type of gender disparity disfavoring females. Furthermore, as indicated in Table 7.5, the overall balances of inter-household transfers for men and women are negative (16,144.1–25,093.2 = −8949.0 billion rials) and positive (15,505.8–2234.5 = 13,271.4 billion rials), respectively. In per-capita terms, these respective balances translate to 0.21 and 0.33 million rials. The differences highlight women's dependence on receiving financial assistance from other households, which is in turn a reflection of employment and labor income inequalities they face. The per-capita balance of inter-household transfers becomes positive for men 65 years of age or older, while it becomes even larger for women in this age category. The corresponding figures are 0.56 and 1.5 million rials for men and women, respectively. Figure 7.14 further depicts the gender differences in terms of inter-household transfers. It shows that whereas the balance of inter-household transfers is negative for men between the ages of 30 and 70, it is positive for women across all age groups.

Furthermore, the gender gap in private transfer inflows (TFI, which is assistance to households from non-public social and charity institutions) is small. It is even reversed for the older age group among which few men survive. Figure 7.13 shows the rise of TFI after age 50 for both sexes. In fact, according to Imam Khomeini Relief Foundation (IKRF 2016), one quarter of the 6 million persons in Iran's 60+ age category rely on charity transfers from governmental or para-governmental organizations—which are nonetheless quite small in comparison with living expenses. This is indicative of the current economic challenges faced by older Iranians and especially elderly women. Although they are now enjoying significantly longer lives as compared to their previous generations, against the backdrop of their low levels of human capital, the relatively unfavorable economic environment they have faced in the post-revolutionary period, and their large number of children who required increasing amounts of expenditures for education, they have not been able to save or accumulate adequate assets.

Finally, Figs. 7.15 and 7.16 highlight the gender disparities in terms of total labor production and total asset income, respectively. Figure 7.15 shows that women's share of total labor production peaks around age 35 at slightly more than 15 percent. Moreover, women's share of the total pie is quite small as the Figure's snapshot capturing all ages clearly indicates. A slightly better pattern for women may be observed in Fig. 7.16, which concerns total asset income. Affected by their low share of total labor production, the female share of the total asset income is quite small and leaves elderly women with little to cope with their lifecycle deficits—hence, their heavier reliance on inter-household transfers as discussed earlier.

Conclusions

Our purpose in this chapter was to probe the interactions between economic and family lifecycles in Iran as they affect the lives of the elderly. The midlife onset of declining per-capita income from labor that continues through and becomes most pronounced in old age should equally affect the resources at the disposal of elderly men and women. Yet, we have shown that the impact is much more severe on elderly females in Iran. Women have fewer employment and income-earning opportunities, get married younger, live longer, and are more likely than men to lose their spouses and remain unmarried. Women's lower employment rates and per-capita labor incomes shape the main features of their economic lifecycle.

If we consider elderly women's lifecycle as independent, based on our calculations (not exactly the NTA approach), they face significant per-capita lifecycle deficits. Alternatively, if we take elderly women's economic positions as intimately tied to those of their families, in the best-case scenario, their welfare levels will only be sustained as long as their husbands are alive. After the death of their husbands, they neither have access to resources at the disposal of elderly men nor can inherit fully their husbands' wealth.

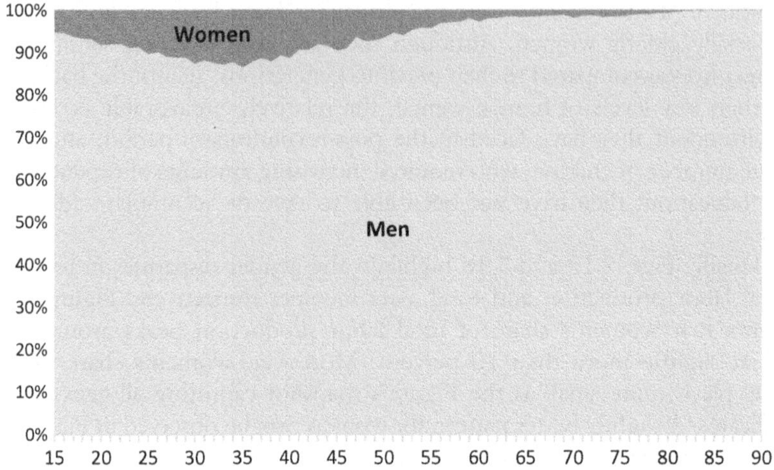

Fig. 7.15 Proportional total labor production by age and sex, 2011. *Source*: SCI (2011b) (Household Income and Expenditure Survey)

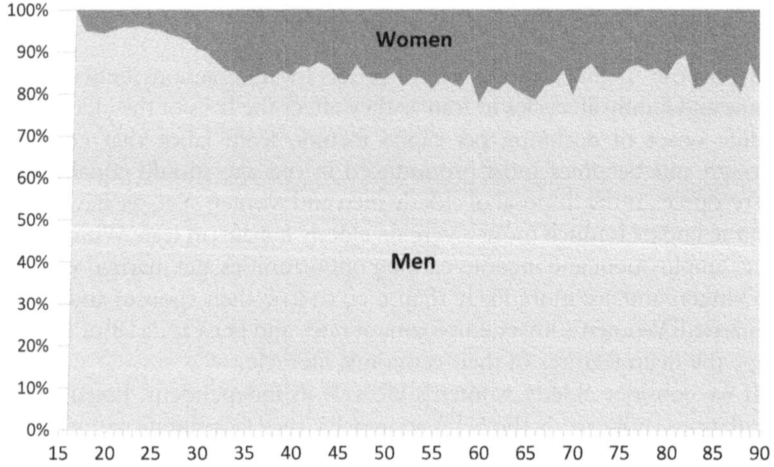

Fig. 7.16 Proportional total asset income by age and sex, 2011. *Source*: SCI (2011b) (Household Income and Expenditure Survey)

Notwithstanding those with autonomous pension rights as well as those who have the right to their deceased husbands' pensions, elderly women must rely on transfers from their children or governmental and non-governmental charity institutions. We have highlighted this clearly by showing the different sources of income and transfers for men and women. Whereas the balance of inter-household transfers is negative for working-age men, it is positive for women across all ages.

Two sets of challenges posed in relation to Iran's elderly population have thus been highlighted in this chapter, with differential implications for women and men. First, Iran's elderly population in the current period belongs to a generation associated with very low literacy rates and very high fertility rates. Members of this age group tended to have a large number of children that in their sociocultural and economic mindset would eventually translate into social mobility as well as social support for their families and themselves. Yet in the course of Iran's demographic transition, the current elderly population has experienced sociodemographic changes—with important economic ramifications—beyond its sociocultural expectations. For one thing, their large number of children—on whose education and upbringing they ended up spending handsomely—reduced their chances of saving and building assets to compensate their old age lifecycle deficits.

The second set of challenges has to do with the strong likelihood of rising economic poverty among the future generations of Iran's elderly. One indication of this possibility is the persistence of economic woes the country is facing in the current period, including high unemployment rates and very low rates of labor force participation that are additionally grave for the case of women. This means that the current working-age generation is missing significant opportunities to save and accumulate assets that are needed for the maintenance of their subsistence in the last part of their lifecycles. The gap must be filled by public or intergenerational transfers, the realization of either of which is under serious economic threats. Yet, further discussions on this issue and others related to the life and poverty cycles will be possible when Iran's NTA is completed.

Notes

1. This situation is termed "demographic window," which can potentially lead to "demographic dividend" under the right economic and employment circumstances (on demographic window in Iran, see Saraie, 2010).
2. Since Iran's NTA project is not complete yet, it is not possible at this time to calculate LCD. LCD is mentioned here only as a concept to set the stage for the rest of the discussion. Yet, using LCD as a national measure of economic lifecycle in societies like Iran, with complex wealth flows and associations between men and women, may not provide unambiguous results on gender gap and inequality.
3. As HEIS data used to calculate labor income are self-reported, they may be under-reported. Yet, our assumption when calculating per capita labor incomes is that any such effect is the same for men and women.
4. It should be stressed here that we only use inter-household transfers to further highlight gender disparities in terms of relying on others, particularly on children and other family members—as touched upon earlier in the chapter. Since the NTA data for Iran is yet to be fully developed, we are unable to discuss inter-household transfers in the context of the national economy. Furthermore, caution is necessary in the interpretation of our results, since inter-household transfers comprise just a small part of transfers of the national economy in terms of volume.

References

Abbasi-Shavazi, M. J., Macdonald, P., & Hosseini-Chavoshi, M. (2009). *The fertility transition in Iran: Revolution and reproduction.* New York: Springer.

Aghajanian, A. (1991). Population change in Iran, 1966–1986: A stalled demographic transition? *Population and Development Review, 17*(4), 703–715.

Aghajanian, A., & Mehryar, A. H. (2005). State pragmatism versus ideology: Family planning in the Islamic Republic of Iran. *International Journal of Sociology of the Family, 31*(1), 57–69.

Aghajanian, A., & Thompson, V. (Eds.). (2013). Household size and structure in Iran: 1976–2006. *The Open Family Studies Journal, 5,* 1–9.

Alaedini, P., & Razavi, M. R. (2005). Women's participation and employment in Iran: A critical examination. *Middle East Critique, 14*(1), 57–73.

Bahramitash, R., & Salehi Esfahani, H. (2011). *Veiled employment, Islamism and the political economy of women's employment in Iran.* Syracuse, NY: Syracuse University Press.

Foroutan, Y. (2014). Social change and demographic response in Iran (1956–2006). *British Journal of Middle Eastern Studies, 41*(2), 219–229.

Ghazi-Tabatabae, M., Mirzaei, M., & Koosheshi, M. (2008). Gender inequalities in family life of Tehrani elderly. *Journal of Cultural Studies and Communications, 11*(4), 19–42 in Persian.

Haghighat, E. (2014). Iran's changing gender dynamics in light of demographic, political, and technological transformations. *Middle East Critique, 23*(3), 313–332.

Hakimian, H. (2006). From demographic transition to fertility boom and bust: Iran in the 1980s and 1990s. *Development and Change, 37*(3), 571–597.

IKRF [Imam Khomeini Relief Foundation]. (2016). Retrieved March 1, 2016, from http://www.emdad.ir/news.asp?nu=137374

Khosravi, A., Taylor, R., Naghavi, M., & Lopez, A. D. (2007). Mortality in the Islamic republic of Iran, 1964–2004. *Bulletin of the World Health Organization, 85*(8), 607–617.

Kiani, S., Bayanzadeh, M., Tavallaee, M., & Hogg, R. S. (2010). The Iranian population is graying: Are we ready? *Archives of Iranian Medicine, 13*(4), 333–339.

Koosheshi, M., Khosravi, A., & Alizadeh, M. (2014). *Population ageing in Iran: Socio-economic, demographic and health characteristics of elderly.* Tehran: UNFPA. Retrieved from http://iran.unfpa.org/siuation.asp

Lee, R., & Mason, A. (Eds.). (2011). *Population aging and generational economy: A global perspective.* Cheltenham, UK: Edward Elgar.

Mahmoudian, H. (2006). Socio-demographic factors affecting women's labor force participation in Iran, 1976–1996. *Middle East Critique, 15*(3), 233–248.

Majles [Islamic Consultative Assembly]. (2016). Civil code of Iran [originally adopted in 1928]. Retrieved March 10, 2016, from http://rc.majlis.ir/fa/law/show/97937

Mirzaei, M. (2005). Swings in fertility limitation in Iran. *Middle East Critique, 14* (1), 25–33.

Moghadam, V. M. (1995). Women's employment issues in contemporary Iran: Problems and prospects in the 1990s. *Iranian Studies, 28.*

Mun Sim Lai, N., & Tung, A. C. (2015). Who supports the elderly? The changing economic lifecycle reallocation in Taiwan, 1985 and 2005. *The Journal of the Economics of Ageing, 5*, 63–68.

Narayana, M. R. (2011). Lifecycle deficit and public age reallocations for India's elderly population: Evidence and implications based on national transfer accounts. *Population Ageing, 4*(4), 207–230.

NTA [National Transfer Accounts]. (2016). Official website of National Transfer Accounts. Retrieved March 21, 2016, from http://www.ntaccounts.org
Paydarfar, A. A., & Moini, R. (1995). Modernization process and fertility change in pre- and post-Islamic Revolution of Iran: A cross-provincial analysis, 1966–1986. *Population Research and Policy Review, 14*(1), 71–90.
Rowshan, M., Sadeqnejad Naini, M., & Khalilzadeh, M. M. (2015). Analytical study of the wife inheritance from the husband's property in Imami jurisprudence and Iranian Law. [University of Shiraz]. *Journal of Legal Studies, 7*(1), 151–168. (in Persian).
Sadeghi Moghadam, M. H., & Azizollahi, M. M. (2012). The inheritance of a wife as sole inheritor. [University of Tehran]. *Law Quarterly, 42*(2), 187–197. (in Persian).
Saraie, H. (2007). Family and its evolution in the context of the demographic transition in Iran. *Journal of Population Association of Iran, 2*, 37–60. (in Persian).
Saraie, H. (2009). Second demographic transition with some references to the population of Iran. *Journal of Population Association of Iran, 6*, 118–140. (in Persian).
Saraie, H. (2010). The demographic window of Iran. *Social Development and Welfare Planning, 1*(1), 33–45. (in Persian).
SCI [Statistical Center of Iran]. (1966). 1966 Census results.
SCI [Statistical Center of Iran]. (1976). 1976 Census results.
SCI [Statistical Center of Iran]. (1986). 1986 Census results.
SCI [Statistical Center of Iran]. (1996). 1996 Census results.
SCI [Statistical Center of Iran]. (2006). 2006 Census results.
SCI [Statistical Center of Iran]. (2009). 2009 Time Use survey results.
SCI [Statistical Center of Iran]. (2011a). 2011 Census results.
SCI [Statistical Center of Iran]. (2011b). 2011 Household Expenditure and Income Survey [HEIS].
Torabi, F., & Askari-Nodoushan, A. (2012). Dynamics of the population age structure and changes in marriage in Iran. *Journal of Population Association of Iran, 13*, 5–23. (in Persian).
UNDESA [United Nations Department of Economic and Social Affairs]. (2015). World population prospects 2015 data files. Retrieved February 24, 2016, from http://esa.un.org/unpd/wpp/
UNDESA [United Nations Department of Economic and Social Affairs]. (2013). *National transfer accounts manual: Measuring and analyzing the generational economy*. New York: United Nations.
UNDESA [United Nations Department of Economic and Social Affairs]. (2005). *Living arrangements of older persons around the world*. New York: United Nations.

CHAPTER 8

Effects of Oil Sanctions on Iran's Economy and Household Welfare: New Evidence from A CGE Model

Mohammad Reza Farzanegan,
Mohammad Mohammadi Khabbazan, and Hossein Sadeghi

Introduction

This chapter[1] treats the economic and welfare consequences of Western-backed oil-export sanctions[2] against Iran. Oil sanctions were imposed on post-revolutionary Iran with the supposed goal of changing its government's political behavior. We aim to answer the following questions: (a) What were the likely effects of oil sanctions on the Iranian macroeconomic variables? (b) What were the likely effects of oil sanctions on Iran's household welfare?

M.R. Farzanegan (✉)
Center for Near and Middle Eastern Studies, School of Business & Economics, Philipps-Universität Marburg, Marbug, Germany

M.M. Khabbazan
Cluster of Excellence "Integrated Climate System Analysis and Prediction" (CliSAP) & Center for Earth System Research and Sustainability (CEN), University of Hamburg, Hamburg, Germany

H. Sadeghi
Tarbiat Modares University, Tehran, Iran

M.R. Farzanegan, P. Alaedini (eds.), *Economic Welfare and Inequality in Iran*, DOI 10.1057/978-1-349-95025-6_8

Sanctions-induced economic pressures are meant to effect change in the target state's political behavior. Yet, Hufbauer et al. (2007) show that in the long term, the success-to-failure ratio of sanctions in changing the target country's political behavior decreases significantly. The success-to-failure ratio is 2.4 during the first year after the sanction shock, reaches 2.3 in two years, and remains constant at 0.6 thereafter (Dizaji and van Bergeijk 2013).[3] The reason for the falling success ratio of sanctions is the targeted economy's process of adjusting to a new equilibrium. Indeed, an economy under sanctions can attempt to offset the reduction in its revenues (e.g., oil revenues, as is the case for Iran) by increasing taxes, reforming the subsidy system, or reallocating resources. If such painful policies are managed well and do not lead to political instability, then sanctions lose their effectiveness in the long term.

Iran has been the target of various sanctions ever since the 1979 Islamic Revolution. Yet, sanctions imposed on Iran became more severe beginning in 2006, coinciding with Mahmoud Ahmadinejad's presidential term. Between 2006 and 2010, sanctions mostly aimed to block the supply of heavy weapons and technologies that could be used in the Iranian military and nuclear projects. They did not target the Iranian economy in any particular way. The United Nations Security Council (UNSC) Resolution 1929, however, sent a strong signal that sanctions might be placed on Iranian oil (UNSC 2010). Whereas the Iranian government's right to diversify its energy portfolio was recognized, the resolution emphasized that "chemical process equipment and materials required for the Iranian petrochemical industry have much in common with those required for certain sensitive nuclear fuel cycle activities." This resolution was the basis of subsequent practical oil embargos imposed against Iran.

The Iranian government underplayed the threat, with President Ahmadinejad stating that: "From right and from left, they adopt sanctions, but for us they are annoying flies, like a used tissue" (The Telegraph, June 10, 2010). Soon, however, the European Union (EU) invoked UNSC Resolution 1929 to ban its member states from the sale and supply of equipment and technologies that could be used in the Iranian petrochemical industry. In July 2012, the EU banned the imports, purchase, and transport of Iranian crude oil. Oil sanctions were also combined with international financial, banking, and insurance sanctions.

Iran's oil production was reduced from more than 4 million bbl./d in 2005 to approximately 3 million bbl./d in 2012/2013 (U.S. Energy Information Administration 2013). According to the country's Minister of

Economic Affairs and Finance, Ali Tayebnia, Iran's GDP decreased by 5.8 percent in 2013. Taking into account population growth, this figure corresponds to a 7 percent reduction in per capita income (as a welfare driver) in a single year (BBC 2014). Yet, according to the Central Bank of Iran, the country's non-oil exports increased by approximately 25 percent from 2010 through 2012 (CBI 2015).[4]

On July 14, 2015 Iran signed an international agreement with P5+1 (the five permanent members of the United Nations Security Council—China, France, Russia, United Kingdom, United States—plus Germany) referred to as the Joint Comprehensive Plan of Action (JCPOA). Under JCPOA, Iran agreed to significant revisions in its nuclear program in return for the removal of the imposed sanctions. Pursuant to internationally agreed nuclear commitments, the EU and the UN Security Council lifted sanctions and the United States "ceased the application" of sanctions on many of the relevant sectors in Iran. In consequence, Iran's oil production and exports are expected to increase to pre-sanctions levels, while the country's reconnection to international banking will increase its foreign exchange revenues. Indeed, a recent report by the Economist Intelligence Unit on "assessing opportunities and risks in postsanctions Iran" (EIU 2016) highlights Iran's significant potential for growth and attracting international investors. In particular, Iran's GDP (adjusted for inflation) is forecasted to grow at approximately 5 percent per year in the period 2016–2020.

The implementation of JCPOA will most likely give a significant boost to the Iranian economy. However, its full realization is uncertain at the time being. According to Secretary of State John Kerry, Iran has only received $3 billion of its $100 billion frozen assets to date (CNSNews.com, 19 April 2016). In April 2016, the Governor of Central Bank of Iran met with US Treasury Secretary Jacob Lew to warn that banking-access problems were jeopardizing JCPOA (The Wall Street Journal, 15 April 2016). Furthermore, with uncertainty looming over policies to be pursued by the winner of upcoming US presidential elections vis-à-vis Iran, the impact of sanctions is likely to remain relevant in the foreseeable future.

In this study, we deviate from existing empirical analyses of economic sanctions against Iran (see next section) by utilizing a computable general equilibrium (CGE) model based on Iran's social accounting matrix (SAM). We estimate the impact of oil sanctions on a set of key macroeconomic indicators and household welfare. We show that under the scenario of oil sanctions imposed by the EU and Japan (our scenario three, which is a more realistic scenario than the others), there would be a dampening effect on

Iran's GDP of 2.2 percent, reducing total imports and exports by 20 percent and 16.5 percent, respectively, and decreasing private consumption by 3.9 percent. Furthermore, such a sanctions regime would increase net indirect taxes in Iran by almost 23.6 percent, the real exchange rate by 13 percent, and labor income by 8.7 percent. Most importantly, based on our simulation results, we suggest that such sanctions may increase non-oil exports by 61 percent and decrease consumer price index (CPI) by about 0.8 percent. Finally, we contend that richer households would experience greater welfare loss than poorer households.

The rest of the chapter is organized in the following way. The next section discusses the available literature on economic sanctions with a particular attention given to the case of Iran. In the third section, we present and discuss our empirical strategy and the data. The fourth section provides the empirical evidence and some robustness analyses. The final section concludes the chapter.

A Brief Review of the Literature on Sanctions

Overall, the literature is inconclusive about the effectiveness of economic sanctions in changing the target country's political behavior. Some studies, such as Eaton and Engers (1992, 1999) and Hufbauer et al. (2007), suggest that sanctions can be effective tools. Others, including Clawson (1998), Askari et al. (2001), and Torbat (2005), hold the opposite view. Dashti-Gibso et al. (1997) empirically examine the success determinants of economic sanctions, while Naghavi and Pignataro (2013) highlight the role of religious ideology in the economic sanctions/politics nexus. The latter's theoretical modeling shows that "...sanctions increase the magnitude and persistence of religious ideology in the target country," and thus enhance the legitimacy of the ruling state among the religious population.

Farzanegan (2013) explains how the sanctions have increased the size of Iran's shadow economy. Furthermore, Farzanegan (2011) investigates the Iranian government's budget allocations to different functions (such as military and non-military) in relation to the negative oil revenue shocks. As a proxy for oil sanctions, he uses the negative shocks on Iran's oil revenues. Employing unrestricted vector autoregressive (VAR) models and annual data from 1959 to 2007, his impulse-response analyses indicate that military and domestic security spending demonstrate a statistically significant negative response to negative oil shocks. That is, Iranian government's budget-allocation behavior is likely to change as a result of oil sanctions. Military and security spending also react positively and significantly at the time of increasing oil revenue shocks, whereas other non-military spending (e.g., education, health, and culture) do not show such a positive and statistically significant response. In another study using VAR models and a Granger causality analysis, Farzanegan (2014) finds a significant interaction between economic growth and military spending in Iran. By reducing military spending, economic sanctions cause lower economic growth in Iran because of strong linkages between Iran's military and its economy.

What is to be made of the effects of sanctions on Iran's domestic politics? Dizaji and van Bergeijk (2013) examine this issue using democracy indicators (e.g., Polity and Vanhanen indicators) and their response to oil revenue shocks as a proxy for oil sanctions. Their findings show that sanctions do change Iran's political behavior in the short term. Thus, lifting the sanctions may have negative short-term consequences for political rights.

On the methodological front, Siddig (2011) emphasizes that "simulation of economic sanctions using the CGE [computable general equilibrium] approach is particularly rare." The few studies of economic sanctions using CGE models include McDonald and Roberts (1998), Hubbard and Philippidis (2001), Philippidis and Hubbard (2005), and Siddig (2010, 2011). In the case of Iran, CGE has been mostly used in the trade-policy context, but not sanctions (see Sadeghi and Hassanzadeh 2011; Daneshjafari and Barghi Oskuei 2009; Mehrara and Barkhordari 2007). Therefore, our two-step methodological approach to the case study of Iranian oil sanctions using standard CGE (SCGE) is new and can provide further insight into the impact of sanctions on Iran's economy.

Model and Data

This section explains how we model the effects of oil sanctions as well as the applied dataset and elasticities.

Model Overview

We employ SCGE as this chapter's basic model. The multisectorial characteristic of SCGE (see Lofgren et al. 2002), together with an entirely specified economic trade side, makes it a rich model and facilitates the analysis of economic policies. Our contributions include both parameterizing SCGE on Iranian data and adjusting it to show how oil sanctions work.

The model is static, nonmonetary, and written as a collection of linear and nonlinear equations. The nature of the model is neoclassical and it follows a Walrasian general equilibrium theory inside a small, open country. It reflects the interactions between different economic performers at the same time. These performers include activities (represented as producers), commodities, factors, households, government, enterprises, and the rest of the world.[5] The entire system of equations must also meet a set of constraints covering macroeconomic aggregates and markets.

Optimal decisions about the amount of production are driven by activities that maximize profits as the difference between revenues and expenses on factors and intermediate inputs. Activities are not restricted to the production of only one commodity; two or more commodities can be simultaneously produced by an activity. In addition, commodities can be sold for domestic uses or exported. The model assumes that commodity and factor markets are completely competitive. Factors are mobile and fully employed where the total supply amount of factors is fixed at the level at which they are observed.

Our institutions include households, enterprises, government, and the rest of the world. Maximizing their utility function subject to budget constraints, households derive their amount of consumption through optimization. After paying taxes directly, households pay for marketed and nonmarketed commodities, save, and transfer some amount to other institutions. Selling factors to activities is the main source of households' income. Other income sources include transfers from other institutions such as enterprises, which do not consume but instead save, pay direct taxes, and receive from and transfer to other institutions. The government receives transfers from other institutions and tax revenues to save, buy commodities, and make transfers to other institutions. The final institution is the rest of the world and is known as the counterparty, that is, the destination of Iranian exports and the origin of Iranian imports. Except for exports and imports, all other transfers from and to the rest of the world are fixed in foreign currency. The difference between total foreign spending and receipts is foreign savings.

Three macroeconomic balances that should be satisfied by the entire system are government, external, and saving-investment balances. Here, we follow the "Johansen closure" (Johansen 1960). With respect to the government balance, the real government expenditure is fixed, whereas government saving is flexible given that it is the difference between government earning and spending. For external balance, whereas foreign saving is fixed in foreign currency, the real exchange rate is flexible. The trade balance and all transfers between the rest of the world and other institutions are also fixed in foreign currency. Finally, the macroeconomic closure related to saving-investment assumes that the quantities of real investment are fixed; thus, domestic nongovernment institutions (households and enterprises) must adjust their saving rates to equalize the savings needed to finance investment costs.[6] Although many macroclosures can be implemented in SCGE models, the macroclosures used in our static analysis are "preferable for simulations that explore the equilibrium welfare changes of alternative policies" (Lofgren et al. 2002), because it "avoids misleading welfare effects."

Moreover, there is empirical evidence to support the closure that we use for the case of Iran. For example, Farzanegan and Markwardt (2009) show that the oil price shocks have only a "marginal" effect on Iranian real government expenditures. In addition, despite the fact that the official exchange rate in Iran is fixed by the Central Bank, there has always been a free-market exchange rate that is a reference for most businesses, especially those without access to the subsidized exchange rate.[7] Indeed, Bahmani-Oskooee (1996) claims that in Iran, instead of the official exchange rate, "it is the black market rate (for foreign currency) that is co-integrated with money, income, and inflation rate." Moreover, the recent oil sanctions forced the Central Bank of Iran to raise the exchange rate, a move that serves as further evidence of exchange rate flexibility.[8]

Modeling Oil Sanctions: A Simple Theoretical Exposition

To model oil sanctions, we use a two-step approach. The first step provides us with the initial equilibrium value of oil exports under the no-sanctions condition; therefore, the amount of oil exports in the model is determined endogenously. This entails no major change to the SCGE model. Step two considers some scenarios in which the amount of oil exports is exogenously decreased. It is necessary to modify SCGE in order to show how sanctions work. Thus, in step two we introduce an equation which enables us to treat oil exports as an exogenous variable.

Step One

The SCGE model employs a constant elasticity of transformation (CET) function, Eq. 1, for commodity C, which is both exported and sold domestically. A CET function is identical to a constant elasticity of substitution

(CES) function except for the negative elasticity of substitution. Equation 1 provides the possibility of addressing the allocation of marketed domestic output for commodity C (QX_c) to two alternative destinations: domestic sale for commodity C (QD_c) and export for commodity C (QE_c).

$$QX_c = \alpha_c.\left(\delta_c.QE_C^{\rho_c} + (1-\delta_c).QD_C^{\rho_c}\right)^{\frac{1}{\rho_c}} \quad \text{(Eq.1)}$$

where

α_c = a CET function shift parameter for commodity C;

δ_c = a CET function share parameter for commodity C; and

ρ_c = a CET function exponent for commodity C.

$\Omega_C = \frac{1}{1+\rho_c}$, a transformation of ρ_c, is the elasticity of transformation between the two destinations. Because $-1 < \rho_c < \infty$, Ω_C varies from infinity to zero. In addition, for each domestically produced commodity, Eq. 2 shows the sum of the values of domestic sale and export, stating the marketed output value in producer price:

$$PX_c.QX_c = PDS_c.QD_c + PE_c.QE_c \quad \text{(Eq.2)}$$

where

PX_c = aggregate producer price for commodity C;

PDS_c = supply price for commodity C produced and sold domestically; and

PE_c = export price for commodity C in local currency. Suppliers maximize the sale revenues defined in Eq. 2 for any given aggregate output level subject to the imperfect transformability between domestic sales and exports expressed in Eq. 1. Eq. 3 defines the first-order condition that is the optimal mix between domestic sales and exports given the two prices PDS_c and PE_c[9]:

$$\frac{PDS_c}{PE_c} = \left(\frac{QD_c}{QE_c^*}\right)^{\rho_c - 1} . \frac{1-\delta_c}{\delta_c} \quad \text{(Eq.3)}$$

where

QE_c^* = the equilibrium amount of export for commodity C. It is useful to note that Eq. 3 assures that a decrease in the export-domestic price ratio generates a decrease in the export-domestic supply ratio, which represents a shift toward the destination that offers the higher return.

Step Two
Facing oil sanctions, the country is forced to reconsider finding the amount of QE^*_{oil} endogenously. Thus, it should consider the given quantity of oil exports after sanctions are imposed, $QE_{oil} = \overline{QE}^s_{oil} \leq QE^*_{oil}$, to be an exogenous variable. The maximization process then gives us Eq. 4 (see Appendix A):

$$\frac{PDS_{oil}}{PE_{oil}} = \left(\frac{QX^{\rho}_{oil}}{\delta.\alpha^{\rho}} - \frac{1-\delta}{\alpha}.QD^{\rho}_{oil}\right)^{\frac{1}{\rho}-1} . \frac{\delta}{1-\delta} QD^{\rho-1}_{oil} \qquad \text{(Eq.4)}$$

The model in step one should have the same number of single equations and variables. Because we are making QE_{oil} exogenous, we must omit one single equation in step two to maintain an identical number of single equations and variables. Thus, Eq. 1 for oil is excluded from the model in step two. We can test the correctness of the process in step two in the following manner: If the value of QE_{oil} is fixed at QE^*_{oil}, then the simulation results for both steps must be the same.

Data

Social Accounting Matrix (SAM)
We use the social accounting matrix (SAM) as the main dataset to provide an economy-wide, micro-consistent benchmark.[10] We employ a large disaggregated form of the SAM to best show the relationships between all of the players in the Iranian economy. To this end, we use the SAM modified by Mehrara and Barkhordari (2007) for the year 2001 and aggregate it.[11] The aggregated SAM has 151 accounts: 66 accounts representing commodities, 53 accounts representing activities, 20 accounts representing Iranian urban and rural households separated by income level, 2 accounts representing labor and capital, 3 accounts representing domestic, export and import transaction costs, and 3 accounts representing direct and indirect taxes and tariffs. In addition, there are four accounts representing enterprises, government, saving-investment, and the rest of the world. This SAM is balanced by using the iterative adjustment method provided in the SCGE.[12]

Elasticities

When dealing with the applied general equilibrium, it is typical to use components of integrated dataset as a benchmark to calibrate the parameters and exogenous variables for the base year. Although employing a calibration procedure provides us with most of the coefficients and exogenous variables in our analysis, the SCGE requires that we introduce Armington and CET elasticities,[13] the elasticity of substitution between factors (bottom of technology nest), the elasticity of substitution between aggregate factors and intermediate inputs (top of technology nest), the output aggregation elasticity for commodities, the Frisch parameter,[14] and the expenditure elasticity of goods. We invoke other studies, especially those that concern Iran, for these elasticities. Most studies that use CGE models have employed a number between 2 and 3 as the elasticity for the Armington function (e.g., McCalla and Nash 2007; Sadeghi and Hassanzadeh 2011). Likewise, we choose 3 for the Armington elasticity. For the CET function, 2 and 3 were used by Sadeghi and Hassanzadeh (2011) and Jensen and Tarr (2003), respectively. We use 2.5 for CET elasticity. Khodadadkashi and Jani (2011) and Akbarian and Rafiee (2006) show that substitution between factors as well as substitution between factors and intermediate inputs (such as energy) is nonelastic. Thus, we use 0.8 and 0.6 for the elasticity of substitution between factors and the elasticity of substitution between aggregate factors and intermediate inputs, respectively. AlShehabi (2013), De Melo and Tarr (1992), Jensen and Tarr (2003), and Rutherford et al. (1997) use 6 for the output aggregation elasticity, AlShehabi (2013) uses −1 for the Frisch parameter, and AlShehabi (2013) and Jensen and Tarr (2003) use 1 for the expenditure elasticity of most goods. Thus, we set the output aggregation elasticity at 6, the Frisch parameter at −1, and the expenditure elasticity of goods at 1.

Scenarios and Analysis

Scenarios

The geographic distribution of the destinations of Iranian oil exports from 1979 to 2009 is depicted in Fig. 8.1. During this period, Europe was the most important destination of Iranian oil exports, importing nearly 39 percent of Iran's oil. After Europe, the largest importing areas were Asia, except Japan (importing an average of 26 percent of Iran's oil exports), and Japan

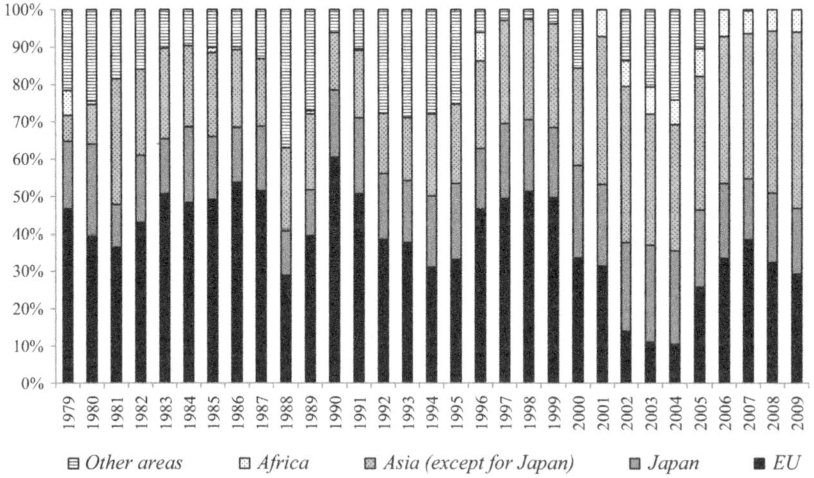

Fig. 8.1 Geographical distribution of Iranian oil exports (1979–2009). *Source*: CBI (2015)

(importing nearly 18 percent of Iran's oil exports). The remaining regions are categorized as Africa and other areas.

In this study, to show the effects of sanctions on the Iranian economy, *three scenarios* are built on the assumptions that the EU and Japan cut all of their imports of Iranian oil; given that the EU and Japan find another source of oil, we observe no major effect on world oil prices. Thus, the world price of oil in foreign currency is fixed.[15] The amount of Iranian oil exported to the EU and Japan fluctuates yearly, and thus, we use the average quantity of oil exported to these regions to model sanctions.

In the *first and second scenarios*, it is assumed that the amount of Iranian oil exports, QE_{oil}, decreases by 18 percent and 39 percent because of sanctions by Japan and the EU, respectively. The *third scenario* considers that both the EU and Japan implement sanctions at the same time, resulting in a 57 percent reduction in oil exports.

Simulation Results

Table 8.1 shows the impacts of the scenarios on macro-indicators in our general equilibrium model. Results are represented for *three conceptual scenarios*: sanctions by Japan, the EU, and both Japan and the EU. As

Table 8.1 Percent changes in macro-indicators due to oil sanctions

Indicators	*Oil sanctions by Japan*	*Oil sanctions by EU*	*Oil sanctions by Japan and EU*
Private consumption	−1.3	−2.8	−3.9
Total exports	−6.2	−12.3	−16.5
Total imports	−7.5	−14.8	−20.0
Non-oil export	16.5	39.0	61.1
Gross domestic production	−0.8	−1.6	−2.2
Net indirect tax	10.6	19.6	23.6
Real exchange rate	4.3	9.1	13.0
Consumer price index	−0.1	−0.4	−0.8
Labor income	2.5	5.7	8.7
Capital income	−1.1	−2.5	−3.8

Source: Authors' calculations

expected, our results indicate that the shock of oil sanctions in scenario three is bigger than the shock of sanctions by the EU, and these shocks are more significant than the shock of sanctions by Japan.

The shock of sanctions on oil starts with a decrease in total exports because oil exports constitute the major share of export revenues. In our SAM, the amount of oil exported is approximately 65 percent of total exports. Because oil exports are an important source of government revenues and are positively accounted for in GDP, a reduction in government oil income and a decrease in GDP are expected. Due to the dependence of imports on oil revenues, decreased oil earnings result in decreased imports. Foreign exchange rate appreciation aggravates the import situation. For example, the overall reduction in imports is 20 percent in scenario three.

The increase in exchange rate can have two different effects on activities' revenue. On the one hand, activities that demand imports as an intermediate input for their production line experience a higher import cost because of an increase in the exchange rate that forces them to produce less. On the other hand, for activities that involve selling products to the rest of the world, an increased exchange rate increases revenues and consequently provides the motivation to produce more.[16] The latter can be considered a blessing, as it mitigates the huge reduction in total exports; for instance, the total decrease in exports is 16.5 percent in scenario three with about 61 percent rise in non-oil export.

Regarding government, because of the assumption that its real expenditure is fixed at observed level, tax rates must grow to compensate for loss in oil revenues. Finally, as a result of sanctions, consumption by households—representing private sector consumption—decreases because import prices have increased and household incomes fall.

With respect to factor incomes, the results in Table 8.1 show that labor income rises by 8.7 percent, while capital income falls by 3.8 percent in scenario three. The reason is that as oil sanctions limit oil exports, oil production is logically reduced to prevent a huge loss to the oil industries. Therefore, producers do not need the same amount of the two factors anymore and those amounts are supplied in the factor market. The capital-intensive nature of oil production compared with Iran's other industries implies that the amount of capital supplied to the factor market exceeds the amount of capital demanded. In the SAM, the ratio of capital to the total factors employed by the oil industry is approximately 98 percent and this ratio for all other industries is 76 percent. Consequently, under the assumption of full employment, capital price drops because of an excess of supply in the capital factor market. This low-priced capital provides a good opportunity for other industries to increase the amount of their production. However, capital is not a complete substitution for labor in the technology nest and thus demand for labor rises. Finally, because the extra demand surpasses the extra supply of labor, labor wage increases and leads to increased labor income.

Regarding CPI, the simulation results show that oil sanctions not only do not raise the price index but also slightly decrease it. Under scenario three, for instance, CPI decreases by about 0.8 percent. On the one hand, reallocation of resources with lower price of capital compensates the loss to the supply side following the reduction of total import. On the other hand, due to decreases in household income, demand must fall. Therefore, the overall effect on the price index can be negative.

In Figs. 8.2a and b, we show the percentage changes in household welfare caused by oil sanctions. To capture welfare changes, SCGE employs the equivalent variation (EV) indicator that, at base prices, measures the changes in income needed to avert the simulated induced changes. All households experience welfare loss because of the sanctions as their earnings decrease. Although labor income rises as capital income drops, the overall result is a reduction in total factor income since the share of labor income is approximately 20 percent of Iran's total factor income in our SAM.

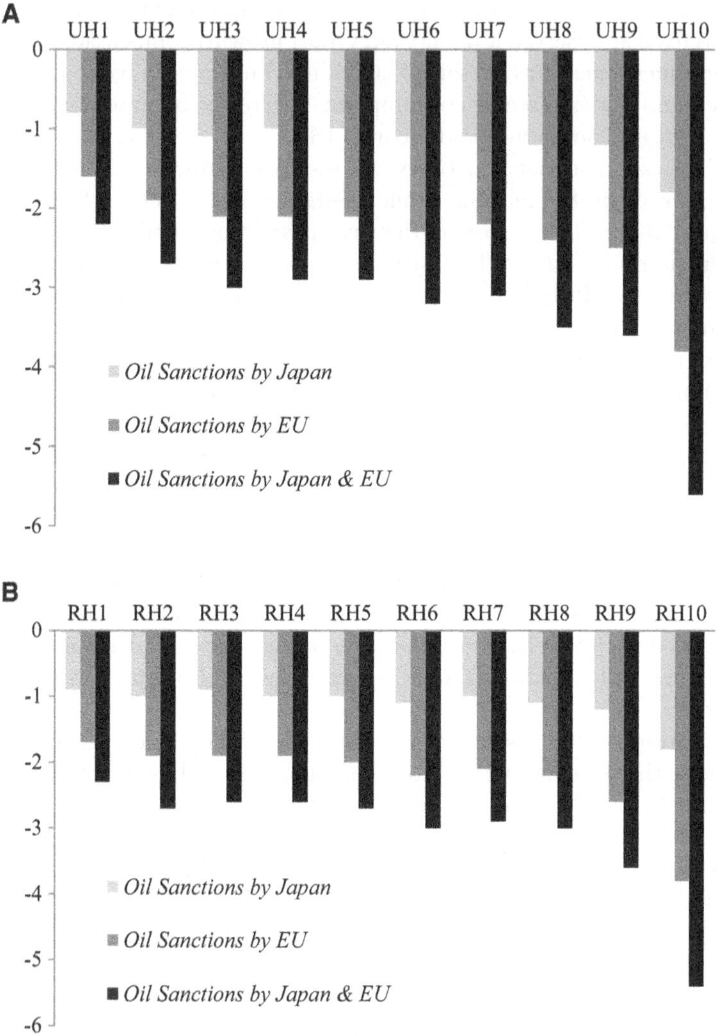

Fig. 8.2 (**a**) Percent changes in urban households' (UHs') welfare due to oil sanctions. Source: Author's calculations. (**b**) Percent changes in rural households' (RHs') welfare due to oil sanctions. *Source*: Author's calculations

Because a major source of household income is based on factor income, reduced factor income reduces income. Given that for each household the share of revenue from the factor income is fixed at the base simulation, the percentage decrease in household income is the same for all households. However, this means that the absolute decrease in income for richer households is greater than for poorer ones; in general, then, richer households suffer more from sanctions.

The SCGE assumes that utility functions are "Stone-Geary."[17] Therefore, in the SCGE, first-order conditions that show optimal household consumption are linear functions with respect to total consumption expenditure—known as the linear expenditure system (LES). One differentiable characteristic among households is their subsistence use of commodities. It is rational to suppose that, in general, this amount of consumption is larger for upper-income households. In addition, richer households may use greater share of imported commodities and services (e.g., international vacations) than do poorer ones. Under the aforementioned circumstances, oil sanctions result in decreased welfare for all households, with larger negative effects on upper-income households.

Sensitivity Analysis

Hitherto, we have presented our central results for the basic dataset included in the SAM. However, these results may be sensitive to the choice of key parameter levels or treatment of closures. How and to what extent do changing previous assumptions affect the results? We present our sensitivity tests in the following subsections. To investigate the sensitivity of our simulation, we consider the two following questions: Will the sign of the results of altering earlier assumptions differ from the central case? In addition, will the order of magnitudes for results change as a result of changing these assumptions?

Results of Altering Key Elasticities

The key elasticities that are the most strongly expected to affect the simulation results are the elasticity of substitution between factors in the bottom of the technology nest and the Armington and CET elasticities of substitution. As mentioned above, these parameters in our core analysis are 0.8, 3, and 2.5, respectively. The second column in Table 8.2 provides the central results for the scenario of oil sanctions by the EU and Japan (scenario three); it exactly duplicates the relevant results in Table 8.1, Figs. 8.2a

Table 8.2 Sensitivity analysis on key elasticities

Indicator	*Scenario 3*	*ESB (low)*	*ESB (high)*	*Arm (low)*	*Arm (high)*	*CET (low)*	*CET (high)*
Private consumption	−3.9	−4.0	−3.9	−4.2	−3.7	−4.5	−3.5
Total exports	−16.5	−16.6	−16.5	−14.7	−18.0	−18.4	−14.9
Total imports	−20.0	−20.0	−20.0	−17.8	−21.8	−22.3	−18.0
Non-oil export	61.1	61.0	61.1	66.5	56.7	55.5	65.9
Gross domestic production	−2.2	−2.3	−2.2	−2.4	−2.1	−2.6	−2.0
Net indirect tax	23.6	24.6	22.8	27.4	21.5	20.5	25.0
Real exchange rate	13.0	13.0	13.0	14.4	11.9	14.8	11.7
Consumer price index	−0.8	−1.0	−0.7	−0.8	−0.9	−0.8	−0.9
Labor income	8.7	11.2	7.0	8.7	8.7	8.6	8.9
Capital income	−3.8	−4.4	−3.4	−3.8	−3.8	−3.9	−3.7
Urban household 1	−2.2	−2.1	−2.3	−2.4	−2.1	−2.7	−1.9
Urban household 2	−2.7	−2.6	−2.7	−2.9	−2.5	−3.2	−2.3
Urban household 3	−3.0	−2.9	−3.0	−3.2	−2.8	−3.5	−2.6
Urban household 4	−2.9	−2.9	−3.0	−3.1	−2.7	−3.5	−2.5
Urban household 5	−2.9	−2.9	−3.0	−3.2	−2.8	−3.5	−2.6
Urban household 6	−3.2	−3.2	−3.2	−3.4	−3.0	−3.8	−2.8
Urban household 7	−3.1	−3.0	−3.1	−3.3	−2.9	−3.6	−2.7
Urban household 8	−3.5	−3.5	−3.5	−3.7	−3.3	−4.0	−3.1
Urban household 9	−3.6	−3.6	−3.6	−3.8	−3.4	−4.2	−3.2
Urban household 10	−5.6	−5.8	−5.4	−5.9	−5.3	−6.3	−5.1
Rural household 1	−2.3	−2.3	−2.3	−2.4	−2.2	−2.8	−1.9
Rural household 2	−2.7	−2.7	−2.7	−2.8	−2.5	−3.2	−2.3
Rural household 3	−2.6	−2.6	−2.6	−2.7	−2.4	−3.1	−2.2
Rural household 4	−2.6	−2.6	−2.6	−2.8	−2.5	−3.1	−2.3
Rural household 5	−2.7	−2.7	−2.7	−2.8	−2.6	−3.2	−2.3
Rural household 6	−3.0	−3.1	−3.0	−3.2	−2.9	−3.5	−2.7
Rural household 7	−2.9	−2.9	−2.9	−3.0	−2.7	−3.3	−2.5
Rural household 8	−3.0	−3.1	−3.0	−3.2	−2.9	−3.5	−2.7
Rural household 9	−3.6	−3.7	−3.5	−3.8	−3.4	−4.1	−3.2
Rural household 10	−5.4	−5.7	−5.2	−5.7	−5.2	−6.1	−4.9

Source: Authors' calculations

and b under the third scenario. We use the central results in scenario three as a comparative point to determine how the results of altering key elasticities will vary. The next columns show the results when each elasticity deviates from its fixed initial level by 20 percent (either lower or higher).[18]

The third and fourth columns in the table show that the results are not sensitive to altering the elasticity of substitution between factors at the bottom of the technology nest elasticity of substitution (ESB). However, as expected, there are some minor changes in the results; the greatest change is found in labor and capital income. Because the elasticity of substitution between factors at the bottom of the technology nest is at the lower level, changes in labor and capital income are 11.2 percent and −4.4 percent, respectively. Conversely, with a higher elasticity of substitution between factors at the bottom of the technology nest, labor income increases by 7 percent while capital income decreases by 3.4 percent. The reason is that when this elasticity is higher, factors at the bottom of the technology nest can be substituted more easily, thus mitigating the effects of oil sanctions.

The Armington (CET) elasticity reflects substitutability between commodities that are produced domestically and commodities that are imported (exported). The sign and order of magnitude for none of the results vary from our central results. Thus, our results are considered insensitive to varying Armington and CET elasticities.

Furthermore, higher elasticities decrease the effect of oil sanctions on macro-indicators and household welfare (although this effect is rather small) and vice versa for the case of lower elasticities. Meanwhile, there are two exceptional cases for each of the Armington and CET elasticities. The lower Armington elasticity decreases the effect of oil sanctions on total exports and imports, whereas the higher elasticity increases that effect. In addition, lower CET elasticity decreases net indirect tax and labor income, whereas higher elasticity has an increasing effect on them. In sum, our results are robust when we change the initial elasticities by +/−20 percent.

Results of Enforcing Other Closures

The treatment of the government sector, the exchange rate, and the saving-investment ratio are the other important features of our core simulation. The current results are based on a closure involving the government in which the tax rates and government expenditure are fixed, while government saving is flexible. In the SCGE, there are two alternative closures with respect to government: Gov. 2 and Gov. 3. In both Gov. 2 and Gov. 3, government saving and expenditure are fixed and direct tax rates of domestic institutions are adjusted endogenously to generate that fixed level of government saving. The difference between these two closures is that for Gov. 2, the same numbers of percentage points are used to

Table 8.3 Sensitivity analysis on other closures

Indicator	*Scenario 1*	*Government*		*External balance*	*S-I*
		Gov. 2	*Gov. 3*		
Private consumption	−1.33	−1.33	−1.33	3.97	−0.05
Fixed investment	–	–	–	–	−2.93
Total exports	−6.17	−6.17	−6.17	−10.53	−6.23
Total imports	−7.46	−7.46	−7.46	2.23	−7.54
Non-oil export	16.5	16.5	16.5	3.8	16.3
Foreign saving	–	–	–	67.71	–
Gross domestic production	−0.75	−0.75	−0.75	−0.41	−0.81
Net indirect tax	10.60	10.61	10.60	−16.84	−0.69
Real exchange rate	4.30	4.30	4.30	–	4.10
Consumer price index	−0.1	−0.1	−0.1	0.0	−0.1
Labor income	2.51	2.51	2.51	2.09	1.98
Capital income	−1.11	−1.11	−1.11	−0.99	−0.99
Urban household 1	−0.80	−0.90	−0.90	3.90	0.30
Urban household 2	−1.00	−1.00	−1.00	4.00	0.20
Urban household 3	−1.10	−1.10	−1.10	4.20	0.20
Urban household 4	−1.00	−1.00	−1.10	4.00	0.20
Urban household 5	−1.00	−1.10	−1.10	3.90	0.20
Urban household 6	−1.10	−1.10	−1.10	3.90	0.10
Urban household 7	−1.10	−1.10	−1.10	3.70	0.10
Urban household 8	−1.20	−1.20	−1.20	3.90	0.0
Urban household 9	−1.20	−1.20	−1.20	3.70	0.0
Urban household 10	−1.80	−1.80	−1.80	4.50	−0.30
Rural household 1	−0.90	−0.90	−0.90	3.40	0.20
Rural household 2	−1.00	−1.00	−1.00	3.50	0.10
Rural household 3	−0.90	−1.00	−0.90	3.30	0.10
Rural household 4	−1.00	−1.00	−1.00	3.30	0.10
Rural household 5	−1.00	−1.00	−1.00	3.30	0.0
Rural household 6	−1.10	−1.10	−1.10	3.40	0.0
Rural household 7	−1.00	−1.10	−1.00	3.20	0.0
Rural household 8	−1.10	−1.10	−1.10	3.20	0.0
Rural household 9	−1.20	−1.30	−1.20	3.50	−0.10
Rural household 10	−1.80	−1.70	−1.70	4.60	−0.20

Source: Authors' calculations

endogenously adjust the base-year direct tax rate of selected domestic nongovernment institutions, whereas for Gov. 3, the tax rates are adjusted through multiplying by a flexible scalar.[19] In Table 8.3, under columns Gov. 2 and Gov. 3, these closures are used to simulate the effects of sanctions for scenario one. A comparison shows that, in general, our results are not significantly affected; therefore, the simulation is not sensitive to altering the government closure.[20]

For external balance, our core simulation employs a *flexible* real exchange rate together with fixed foreign saving. In Table 8.3, under the column External Balance, another way of addressing external balance is employed; that is, the exchange rate is *fixed*, whereas foreign saving is left flexible.

The results are sensitive to the assumption about the *external balance*. Under this condition, households do *not* suffer from oil sanctions but instead *benefit* from a much higher welfare level compared with the pre-sanction situation. The results show that the changes in private consumption, import, and household welfare are positive. The reason behind these findings is that the huge reductions in total exports caused by oil sanctions are mostly compensated with an enormous increase in foreign saving, 67.71 percent, instead of an increase in the real exchange rate, 4.3 percent. Hence, the investment-driven characteristic of saving-investment balance implies that household saving decreases. Consequently, factors that are not needed in the oil industry are employed by other activities, and the increased production and consumption of other commodities increase households' welfare.

Another alternative closure that significantly affects the results is the *saving-investment balance*. In the core model, an investment-driven closure is used. This closure assumes that real investment quantities are fixed. To equalize savings with investments, the base-year saving rates for households and enterprises are modified by the same number of percentage points. In Table 8.3, under the column S-I (Saving-Investment), a saving-driven closure is employed. By using a saving-driven closure, the saving rates for nongovernment institutions are fixed; to equalize between the investment cost and the savings value, a flexible scalar is multiplied by the quantity of each commodity in the investment bundle. Although real exchange rate, export, and import are not much different from those of the core simulation, the results regarding welfare level show deviations. In this case, after the shock of oil sanctions affects the Iranian economy's trading sector, the other parts of the system primarily react to it by reducing the amount of fixed investment instead of the amount of private consumption.

With respect to welfare levels, all households are at least as well-off as they were before the sanctions except for the highest income group of urban households and the two highest income groups of rural households. The overall consequence for private consumption is a minor reduction.

It should be repeated that the results for the circumstances under which the exchange rate is fixed and/or the saving-investment balance is saving-driven are *misleading*, especially when a single-period model is used. As argued in relation to the empirical strategy and data section, the macroclosures used here are more in line with macroconditions in Iran. In addition, as oil sanctions are imposed, the use of a fixed exchange rate forces the model to raise foreign savings to reach an equilibrial solution regardless of what will happen subsequently. The welfare gained under this condition is misleading because, eventually, foreign investment is increased as foreign debts have to be repaid, and households will incur welfare losses. The use of a savings-driven closure in a single-period model also reduces investments since oil sanctions prevent the model from correctly capturing welfare changes. Indeed, reductions in investments will reduce production capacities in the future, eventually leading to welfare losses.

Conclusion

This chapter has focused on analyzing the economic effects of oil sanctions on the Iranian economy, including changes in household welfare and macro-indicators. The framework of our analysis is the CGE model, based on Lofgren et al. (2002), and we have used the Iranian social accounting matrix (SAM) in 2001 as an economy-wide database. We have modified Lofgren et al. (2002) in a manner that allows for the inclusion of oil sanctions in the model. The model is closed under the Johansen closure rule. Three scenarios in which the exportation of crude oil from Iran to the rest of the world is banned have been developed. In addition, sensitivity analysis of results to key elasticities and other macroclosures has been carried out.

Our results show that the Iranian economy and households are affected enormously by sanctions. The third scenario (i.e., sanctions by the EU and Japan) bans 57 percent of Iranian oil exports. Macro-indicators that are *negatively* affected are (in order) total imports by 20 percent, total exports by 16.5 percent, private consumption by 3.9 percent, capital income by 3.8 percent, GDP by 2.2 percent, and CPI by 0.8 percent. Other macro-indicators that *positively* change (i.e., increase) are (in order) non-oil export by 61 percent, net indirect tax by 23.6 percent, the real exchange rate by 13 percent, and labor income by 8.7 percent. The rise in non-oil exports can be considered an adjustment process to sanctions, as it mitigates the huge reduction in total exports.

In addition, all household income groups in urban and rural areas suffer from oil sanctions and welfare declines. An interesting finding is that, in general, richer households lose more than poorer households. Furthermore, sensitivity analysis indicates that our model is robust and insensitive to the Armington and CET elasticities, along with the elasticity of substitution between factors at the bottom of the technology nest. However, although other government closures do not have a major effect on the findings, the use of other closures regarding *exchange rate* and *saving-investment* has misleading effects in simulations and can destabilize the model.

Our model may also be used to investigate the effects of lifting sanctions on the Iranian economy. In addition, small changes in the model structure may allow for the inclusion of sanctions on exports or imports of other commodities. Finally, the model can be applied to other sanctioned economies.

Appendix A

Proof of Eq. 4.

Allocation of domestic output of oil (QX_{oil}) follows a CET function (Eq. B) addressing oil production between two destinations, export (QE_{oil}) and domestic use (QD_{oil}). Oil producers experience sanctions and must consider the amount of oil export as a given. Therefore, an oil producer must maximize his revenues (Eq. A) given prices (PDS_{oil}, PE_{oil}, and PX_{oil}) and subject to the CET function and a fixed quantity of domestic output (QX_{oil}) and export (QE_{oil}):

$$\text{Max}: \quad PX_{oil}.QX_{oil} = PDS_{oil}.QD_{oil} + PE_{oil}.QE_{oil} \qquad \text{(Eq.A)}$$

$$\text{S.T.}: \quad QX_{oil} = \alpha.\left(\delta.\ QE_{oil}^{\rho} + (1-\delta).\ QD_{oil}^{\rho}\right)^{\frac{1}{\rho}} \qquad \text{(Eq.B)}$$

Since Eq. B can be written as the following equation:

$$QE_{oil} = \left(\frac{QX_{oil}^{\rho}}{\delta\alpha^{\rho}} - \frac{1-\delta}{\delta}\,QD_{oil}^{\rho}\right)^{\frac{1}{\rho}} \qquad \text{(Eq.b)}$$

Then, to maximize Eq. A subject to Eq. B, we have to solve the following equation:

$$\frac{d\left[PDS_{oil}.QD_{oil} + PE_{oil}.\left(\frac{QX_{oil}{}^{\rho}}{\delta\alpha^{\rho}} - \frac{1-\delta}{\delta}\ QD^{\rho}_{oil}\right)^{\frac{1}{\rho}}\right]}{dQD_{oil}} = 0$$

The result is Eq. 4 (mentioned in this chapter):

$$\frac{PDS_{oil}}{PE_{oil}} = \left(\frac{QX^{\rho}_{oil}}{\delta.\alpha^{\rho}} - \frac{1-\delta}{\alpha}.\ QD^{\rho}_{oil}\right)^{\frac{1}{\rho}-1} \cdot \frac{\delta}{1-\delta}\ QD^{\rho-1}_{oil}$$

Notes

1. This chapter is the extension of an earlier working paper (Farzanegan et al., 2015).
2. We follow Askari et al. (2003: 14) in defining sanctions as "coercive measures imposed by one country or coalition of countries, against another country, its government or individual entities therein to bring about a change in behavior or policies."
3. For a historical review of economic sanctions, see Daoudi and Dajani (1983) and Hufbauer et al. (2007).
4. We have not found any reliable data about non-oil exports after 2013.
5. For a complete description of SCGE, see Lofgren et al. (2002).
6. According to Lofgren et al. (2002), the implicit assumption is that "the government is able to implement policies that generate the necessary private savings to finance the fixed real investment quantities."
7. The gap between formal and informal (free) exchange rates is known as the black market premium, or BMP. See Farzanegan (2009, 2013).
8. See Farzanegan (2013) for an economic examination of recent sanctions in Iran.
9. This equation is the same as that of Lofgren et al. (2002).
10. For general discussions of SAMs, see Pyatt and Round (1985) and Reinert and Roland-Holst (1997); for perspectives on SAM-based modeling, see Pyatt (1988) and Robinson and Roland-Holst (1988).

11. The source of the SAM modified by Mehrara and Barkhordari (2007) is the SAM for 2001 which is published by the former Iranian Organization of Management and Planning.
12. The SAM is available upon request from authors.
13. In SCGE, a CES aggregation function that shows domestic market demand captures imperfect substitutability between imports and domestic output. This function is often called the Armington function after Paul Armington, who first introduced the use of the CES function for this purpose (Armington 1969).
14. The Frisch parameter measures the elasticity of the marginal utility of income with respect to income.
15. For a recent study on the response of international oil prices to negative shocks in Iranian oil exports, see Farzanegan and Raeisian Parvari (2014). In summary, Farzanegan and Raeisian Parvari (2014) show that oil sanctions do not increase international oil prices; instead, the supply of non-Iranian oil increases.
16. Financial and banking sanctions that can offset the increase in exports as an outcome of an increased exchange rate are not included among the goals of this study and therefore are not simulated.
17. For details, see Blonigen et al. (1997: 223–225) and Dervis et al. (1982: 482–485).
18. The Armington and CET elasticities of substitution are 2.4 and 2 at their low level and 3.6 and 3 at their high level, respectively. For the elasticity of substitution between factors in the bottom of the technology nest, the lower level is 0.64 and the higher level is 0.96.
19. For more explanation on the difference between the two alternative closures, see Lofgren et al. (2002: 14).
20. Unlike our sensitivity analysis on key elasticities, we have chosen scenario one as the central case to compare between closures. The reason is that making the exchange rate fixed in our model has a large effect on the results and in scenario three, we have not reached an equilibrium situation.

References

Akbarian, R., & Rafiee, H. (2006). An estimation of capital-labor substitution elasticity: A case of Iran manufacturing. *Faslnameh Barresiha-ye eghtesadi, 3*, 5–21. (in Persian).

AlShehabi, O. H. (2013). Modeling energy and labor linkages: A CGE approach with an application to Iran. *Economic Modelling, 35*, 88–98.

Armington, P. S. (1969). A theory of demand for products distinguished by place of production. *IMF Staff Papers, 16*, 159–178.

Askari, H., Forrer, J., & Teegen, H. (2003). *Economic sanctions: Examining their philosophy and efficacy*. Westport, CT: Praeger.

Askari, H., Forrer, J., Teegen, H., & Yang, J. (2001). US economic sanctions: Lessons from the Iranian experience. *Business Economics, 36*, 7–19.

Bahmani-Oskooee, M. (1996). The black market exchange rate and demand for money in Iran. *Journal of Macroeconomics, 18*, 171–176.

BBC [British Broadcasting Corporation]. (2014, March 6). Vazir-e eqtesad: Tarikib-e tavarrom va roshd-e manfi dar tarikh-e eqtesad-e keshvar bi-sabeqeh ast [Economy minister: Combination of inflation and negative growh is unprecidentd in the history of the countr's economy]. Retrieved March 29, 2016, from http://www.bbc.co.uk/persian/business/2014/03/140306_tayebniya_economy_iran.shtml (in Persian).

Blonigen, B. A., Flynn, J. E., & Reinert, K. A. (1997). Sector-focused general equilibrium modeling. In J. F. Francois & K. A. Reinert (Eds.), *Applied methods for trade policy analysis: A handbook* (pp. 189–230). Cambridge: Cambridge University Press.

CBI [Central Bank of Iran]. (2015). Time series data tables. Retrieved December 15, 2015, from http://tsd.cbi.ir

Clawson, P. (1998). Iran. In R. N. Haass (Ed.), *Economic sanctions and American diplomacy* (pp. 85–106). New York: Council on Foreign Relations Press.

CNSNews.com. (2016). Kerry: Iran has only received $3 billion, not $100B, as a result of nuclear deal. Retrieved April 24, 2016, from http://www.wsj.com

Daneshjafari, D., & Barghi Oskuei, M. (2009). Survey of the effects of implementing general principle 44 policies on macroeconomic variables using a CGE approach. *Pazhuheshha-ye-Eghtesadi, 10*, 15–38. (in Persian).

Daoudi, M. S., & Dajani, M. S. (1983). *Economic sanctions: Ideals and experience*. Boston, MA: Routledge and Kegan Paul.

Dashti-Gibso, J., Davis, P., & Radcliff, B. (1997). On the determinants of the success of economic sanctions: An empirical analysis. *American Journal of Political Science, 41*, 608–618.

De Melo, J., & Tarr, D. (1992). *A general equilibrium analysis of US foreign trade policy*. Massachusetts: MIT Press.

Dervis, K., De Melo, J., & Robinson, S. (1982). *General equilibrium models for development policy*. New York: Cambridge University Press.

Dizaji, S. F., & Van Bergeijk, P. A. G. (2013). Potential early phase success and ultimate failure of economic sanctions: A VAR approach with an application to Iran. *Journal of Peace Research, 50*, 721–736.

Eaton, J., & Engers, M. (1992). Sanctions. *Journal of Political Economy, 100*, 899–928.

Eaton, J., & Engers, M. (1999). Sanctions: Some simple analytics. *American Economic Review, 89*, 409–414.

EIU. (2016). All that glitters: Assessing opportunities and risks in postsanctions Iran. The Economist Intelligence Unit, London. Retrieved April 22, 2016, from http://www.eiu.com/public/topical_report.aspx?campaignid=IranRe-engagement

Farzanegan, M. R. (2009). Illegal trade in the Iranian economy: Evidence from a structural model. *European Journal of Political Economy, 25*, 489–507.

Farzanegan, M. R. (2011). Oil revenue shocks and government spending behavior in Iran. *Energy Economics, 33*, 1055–1069.

Farzanegan, M. R. (2013). Effects of international financial and energy sanctions on Iran's informal economy. *The SAIS Review of International Affairs, 33*, 13–36.

Farzanegan, M. R. (2014). Military spending and economic growth: The case of Iran. *Defence and Peace Economics, 25*, 247–269.

Farzanegan, M. R., & Markwardt, G. (2009). The effects of oil price shocks on the Iranian economy. *Energy Economics, 31*, 134–151.

Farzanegan, M. R., & Raeisian Parvari, M. (2014). Iranian-Oil-Free Zone and international oil prices. *Energy Economics, 45*, 364–372.

Farzanegan, M. R., Mohammadikhabbazan, M., & Sadeghi, H. (2015). Effect of oil sanctions on the macroeconomic [indicators] and household welfare in Iran: New evidence from a CGE model. MAGKS working paper No. 07-2015, Marburg.

Hubbard, L. J., & Philippidis, G. (2001). General equilibrium and the ban on British beef exports. *Journal of Agricultural Economics, 52*, 87–95.

Hufbauer, G. C., Schott, J. J., Elliott, K. A., & Oegg, B. (2007). *Economic sanctions reconsidered* (3rd ed.). Washington, DC: Peterson Institute for International Economics.

Jensen, J., & Tarr, D. (2003). Trade, exchange rate and energy pricing reform in Iran: Potentially large efficiency effects and gains to the poor. *Review of Development Economics, 7*, 543–562.

Johansen, L. (1960). *A multi-sectoral study of economic growth*. Amsterdam: North-Holland Publishing Company.

Khodadadkashi, F., & Jani, S. (2011). Dynamic study of producers' behavior in using institutions based on a two-stage CES production function, with emphasis on reforming energy consumption in production and development of employment. *Faslnameh Motaleat-e-Energy, 30*, 97–124. (in Persian).

Lofgren, H., Harris, R., Robinson, S., Thomas, M., & El-Said, M. (2002). A Standard Computable General Equilibrium (CGE) Model in GAMS. *TMD Discussion Paper*, 75. International Food Policy Research Institute, Washington, DC.

McCalla, A. F., & Nash, J. (2007). *Reforming agricultural trade for developing countries: Volume 1. Key issues for a pro-development outcome of the doha round*. Washington, DC: The World Bank Group.

McDonald, S., & Roberts, D. (1998). The economy-wide effects of the BSE crises: A CGE analysis. *Journal of Agricultural Economics, 49*, 458–471.

Mehrara, M., & Barkhordari, S. (2007). The effects of Iran's accession to WTO on employment and value added in economic sectors. *Majalleh Tahghighat-e-Eghtesadi, 80*, 171–194. (in Persian).

Naghavi, A., & Pignataro, G. (2013). Theocracy and resilience against economic sanctions. Presentation at the International Symposium: Sanctions and the Iranian Political Economy. CNMS, Philipps-University of Marburg, Marburg.

Philippidis, G., & Hubbard, L. J. (2005). A dynamic computable general equilibrium treatment of the ban on UK beef exports: A note. *Journal of Agricultural Economics, 56*, 307–312.

Pyatt, G. (1988). A SAM approach to modeling. *Journal of Policy Modeling, 10*, 327–352.

Pyatt, G., & Round, J. (1985). *Social accounting matrices: A basis for planning*. Washington, DC: The World Bank Group.

Reinert, K. A., & Roland-Holst, D. W. (1997). Social accounting matrices. In J. F. Francois & K. A. Reinert (Eds.), *Applied methods for trade policy analysis: A handbook* (pp. 94–121). New York: Cambridge University Press.

Robinson, S., & Roland-Holst, D. W. (1988). Macroeconomic structure and computable general equilibrium models. *Journal of Policy Modeling, 10*, 353–375.

Rutherford, T., Rutström, E., & Tarr, D. (1997). Morocco's free trade agreement with the EU: A quantitative assessment. *Economic Modelling, 14*, 237–269.

Sadeghi, H., & Hassanzadeh, M. (2011). Survey of probable effects of world financial crisis on Iranian rural and urban households' income: A computable general equilibrium approach. *Majalleh Tahghighat-e-Eghtesadi, 95*, 79–102. (in Persian).

Siddig, K. H. A. (2010). Macroeconomy and agriculture in Sudan: Analysis of trade policies, external shocks, and economic bans in a computable general equilibrium approach. Retrieved April 22, 2016, from http://ssrn.com/abstract=1684084

Siddig, K. H. A. (2011). From bilateral trade to multilateral pressure: A scenario of European Union relations with Sudan. *Middle East Development Journal, 3*, 55–73.

The Telegraph. (2010). *Iran dismisses new UN sanctions as 'a used hanky'*. Retrieved April 27, 2016, from http://www.telegraph.co.uk/news/worldnews/middleeast/iran/7816395/Iran-dismisses-new-UN-sanctions-as-a-used-hanky.html

The Wall Street Journal. (2016). Iran's Central Bank Chief Warns Banking-Access Issues Jeopardize Nuclear Deal. Retrieved April 27, 2016, from http://www.

wsj.com/articles/irans-central-bank-chief-warns-banking-access-issues-jeopardize-nuclear-deal-1460745930

Torbat, A. E. (2005). Impacts of the US trade and financial sanctions on Iran. *The World Economy, 28*, 407–434.

U.S. Energy Information Administration. (2013). *Sanctions reduced Iran's oil exports and revenues in 2012*. Retrieved April 24, 2016, from http://www.eia.gov/todayinenergy/detail.cfm?id=11011

UNSC [United Nations Security Council]. (2010). *Resolution 1929*. Retrieved April 24, 2016, from http://www.un.org/en/ga/search/view_doc.asp?symbol=S/RES/1929%282010%29

CHAPTER 9

Household Welfare in Iran Under Banking Sanctions: From Open Economy Toward Autarchy

Mohammad Mohammadi Khabbazan and Mohammad Reza Farzanegan

Introduction

Over the last three decades, the role of economic sanctions in foreign policy has rapidly expanded. Economic sanctions are non-military measures that aim to change a target state's behavior (Kaempfer and Lowenberg 2007). Some analysts argue that economic sanctions are incapable of achieving their goals, because they have no real influence on the target economy's rulers (Drezner 1999; Elliott 1998; Hufbauer et al. 1990; Pape 1997). Others suggest that whereas sanctions may have a relatively high chance of success in the immediate period after their implementation (Dizaji and van Bergeijk 2013), over time, the target economy is likely to adjust to the

M.M. Khabbazan
Cluster of Excellence "Integrated Climate System Analysis and Prediction" (CliSAP) & Center for Earth System Research and Sustainability (CEN), University of Hamburg, Hamburg, Germany

M.R. Farzanegan (✉)
Center for Near and Middle Eastern Studies, School of Business & Economics, Philipps-Universität Marburg, Marbug, Germany

M.R. Farzanegan, P. Alaedini (eds.), *Economic Welfare and Inequality in Iran*, DOI 10.1057/978-1-349-95025-6_9

imposed constraints by reallocating its resources (see Chap. 8; Dizaji and van Bergeijk 2013; Siddig 2011).

Post-revolutionary Iran has been a main target of international sanctions. A major reason for the imposition of sanctions on Iran has been to reduce the country's strategic power (Katzman 2013), while the stated goal has been to stop Iran from pursuing its nuclear program. The most important sanctions imposed on Iran include those affecting the country's oil exports and international banking.

In 2015, Iran and the P5+1 (the five Permanent Members of the UN Security Council plus Germany) reached a final agreement after much negotiation and signed the Joint Comprehensive Plan of Action that requires the lifting of nuclear-weapons-related[1] economic sanctions imposed on Iran. Many observers naturally attribute this agreement, at least partly, to economic pressures placed on Iran through the sanctions. Yet, it has also been shown (e.g., in Chap. 8) that although oil sanctions impose significant economic pressure on Iran, the economy may be able to partially alleviate their harmful effects through such adjustments as increasing non-oil exports.

There is little doubt about the welfare costs of embargoes on the target economies (Kaempfer and Lowenberg 2007). However, the question remains how and to what extent the sanctions have imposed welfare losses on Iran. Quantitative answers to this key question are of great interest as they shed light on the mechanisms of and differences among sanctions. To provide a reliable answer for one of the sanction types, namely, *banking sanctions*, we use in this chapter the SAM-based standard computable general equilibrium (SCGE) model by Lofgren et al. (2002) to pursue the following goals: (1) investigating the effects of banking sanctions on household welfare and macro-indicators in Iran, (2) detailing the effects of banking sanctions by decomposing them into three sub-banking sanctions (export-only, import-only, and financial-only sanctions), and (3) highlighting the differences between oil sanctions and banking sanctions in terms of welfare losses.

Through our simulations, we show that banking sanctions significantly reduce household welfare in Iran for all income groups in both urban and rural areas—with richer households generally losing more welfare than poorer households. Our decomposition of the effects of banking sanctions further indicates that bans on exports can be more harmful to Iranian households than embargos on imports and foreign investments. In addition, banking sanctions affect Iran's macro-indicators—such as GDP and private consumption—negatively and significantly, while they raise the exchange rate and consumer price index (CPI). We also show that banking sanctions disrupt some adjustment processes—for example, increase in non-oil exports—that can take place under oil sanctions.

In the next section, we review the sanctions imposed against Iran as well as the reactions of the Iran's economy to them. In the third section, we introduce our stylized model and data used to simulate banking sanctions for various scenarios. In the fourth section, we explain our analyses and discuss our results. The final section concludes the chapter by discussing the implication of our results as well as outlooks.

Sanctions and Iran's Economy

In 2012, Iran became the target of more international financial sanctions that made the international financial system inaccessible to Iran's Central Bank. These sanctions meant that Iranian individuals, enterprises, and the government could no longer engage in any international transaction in which the Central Bank of Iran was involved. Iranian businesses were thus forced to find alternative means to conduct business, such as working with black market dealers or paying and receiving funds in gold or the national currency of the other party (Katzman 2012). This resulted in higher transaction costs. Furthermore, some countries have been able to buy Iranian oil at major discounts (Van de Graaf 2013: 152), thus reducing Iran's take. Corruption was yet another consequence, instances of which have been featured prominently by the Iranian media. For example, Babak Zanjani, blacklisted by both the USA and the EU for helping the Iranian government circumvent sanctions, was arrested for withholding nearly two billion dollars in oil revenues.

Although Iran's rulers have tended to downplay the impact of sanctions publicly,[2] they have also called for precautionary measures, under the rubric of a "resilience economy," to reduce the economy's vulnerability to the sanctions and to prevent socio-economic and political crises. The principles of the resilience economy are: (1) to increase non-oil exports (such as gas, electricity, petrochemicals, and petroleum by-products) in place of crude oil and other raw materials; (2) to reform consumption patterns and address corruption; and (3) to reduce the reliance of public budget on oil revenues by among other things diverting more of the oil revenues into the National Development Fund of Iran (Khamenei.ir 2014). Yet, part of the vulnerability of Iran's economy is attributable to corruption and public-sector mismanagement (Hufbauer and Schott 2006; Katzman 2013; Plaut 2013) which remain major problems.

As expected, sanctions created major trouble for Iran. Subsequent to their implementation, Iran's exports of crude oil dropped by around 40 % within a year, from approximately 2.5 million barrels per day (bbl/d) in 2011 to around 1.5 million bbl/d in 2012 (U.S. Energy Information Administration 2013). The country's GDP shrank as a result. The exchange value of the Iranian rial also dropped by more than 80 % (Monshipouri and Dorraj 2013) while Iran's inflation rate soared by 32 % in 2013 (Statistical Center of Iran 2016). According to Iran's Central Bank, the supply of money increased by more than 30 % between 2011 and 2012 (CBI 2015). However, non-oil exports from Iran increased by approximately 25 % from 2010 through 2012 (CBI 2015).[3] Hufbauer et al. (2012) note that Iran's average welfare loss caused by the sanctions was around $5.7 billion or approximately 1–3 % of Iranian GDP between 2006 and 2012. Yet, the agreement between Iran and P5+1 on July 14, 2015 dubbed Joint Comprehensive Plan of Action (JCPOA) calls for sanctions relief in return for the suspension of some of Iran's nuclear-related activities. Although prospects for significant sanctions relief are relatively bright at the moment, the implementation of JCPOA has faced some hurdles in practice. Probing the effects of the sanctions on Iran's economy thus continues to remain a relevant endeavor.

Using the SAM-based standard CGE (SCGE) model by Lofgren et al. (2002), Chap. 8 probed the effects of oil sanctions on Iran's macroeconomic indicators and household welfare, positing that banking sanctions exert no pressure on the economy. It modeled oil sanctions in a two-step *quantity* approach that works better when only one commodity is (or few commodities are) the target of sanctions. It indicated that although oil sanctions impose significant economic pressures on Iran (by among other things reducing its GDP, total exports, total imports, and household welfare), the country's economy may be able to partially alleviate these harmful effects through such adjustments as reallocating resources and increasing non-oil exports. However, these adjustment processes may be disrupted when banking sanctions are taken into account. For instance, even if the exchange rate soars, Iran may not be able to increase non-oil exports under banking sanctions; therefore, household welfare may further decrease.

Research Design

Model and Data

We follow Chap. 8's methodological approach by using the SCGE and employing the "Johansen closure" (Johansen 1960) rules for macro closures of the model. To "avoid the misleading welfare effects" (Lofgren et al. 2002), Johansen closure requires that: (1) the real government expenditure is fixed, whereas government saving is flexible; (2) the real exchange rate is flexible, whereas foreign saving is fixed in foreign currency; and (3) savings are investment-driven.[4] Based on a Walrasian general equilibrium theory, SCGE is a static non-linear model that is representative of a single open economy. SCGE is suitable for analyzing the effects of external shocks on heterogeneous households and follows the neo-classical approach. Labor and capital are fully employed in the model. Household welfare is measured by the equivalent variation (EV) indicator, which is the variation in income required to avert the simulated induced changes at base prices.[5]

To make it easier to report the results on activities, we use an aggregated version of the SAM used in Chap. 8. We aggregate the SAM according to the standard of Central Product Classification (CPC) Ver.2 (UNSD 2013) in its first level, where there are ten classes of commodities. For the aim of this chapter, there are three exceptions in our SAM. First, oil must have a distinct account in the SAM, so it is disaggregated from its mother class (ores and minerals, electricity, gas, and water). Second, we aggregate the last two classes (business and production services; community, social, and personal services) into a single class for activity (services). Third, we disaggregate the produced services into two groups including tradable and non-tradable services. The aggregated SAM has 52 accounts: 10 accounts for activities, 11 accounts for commodities, 20 accounts representing Iranian urban and rural households separated by income level, 4 accounts, each for enterprises, government, saving-investment, and rest of the world, 2 accounts for labor and capital, 3 accounts for tariff and direct and indirect tax, and 2 accounts showing domestic and export transaction costs. In this way, the size of the model (the number of single equations/variables) is reduced by almost a factor of eight, providing numerical solutions much faster. However, the accuracy of our results may be affected when the size of the model is reduced. To test the reliability of our results, we replicate the results of Chap. 8 using the aggregated SAM. Although the sizes of the models differ, the results are largely similar, thus justifying the use of the aggregated SAM.[6] In addition, we employ the same amounts of elasticities and exogenous variables as in Chap. 8 to calibrate the model. By conducting a thorough sensitivity analysis, the previous chapter showed that the simulated results are insensitive to reasonable variations in the elasticities and the exogenous variables.

Set up of Simulations and Scenarios for Banking Sanctions

Adopting scenarios, we simulate the effects of the increasingly strict application of banking sanctions against Iran. To do so, we employ the *sanction parameter S*, which simultaneously decreases the relative received price for exports, increases the relative price paid for imports, and reduces the percentage of foreign savings in total saving. By introducing *S*, we implicitly suppose Iran, a small-open economy, can potentially circumvent sanctions at the expense of receiving less per quantity of export and paying more per quantity of import than before. That is, circumvention of sanctions compels Iranian trade activity to pay dealers a certain proportion of world price of the commodity being traded. In this sense, *S* can serve as a transaction cost which is imposed due to banking sanctions. Compared to Chap. 8, our current approach can be called a *price approach*.

In detail, an *increase* in *S decreases* the relative received price for exports through Eq. 1, *increases* the relative price paid for imports through Eq. 2, and *reduces* the percentage of foreign savings in total saving through Eq. 3:

$$PE_c = pwe.(1 - te_c - S).EXR + \sum_{c'} PQ_{c'}.ice_{c'c} \quad \text{(Eq.1)}$$

$$PM_c = pwm.(1 + tm_c + S).EXR + \sum_{c'} PQ_{c'}.icm_{c'c} \quad \text{(Eq.2)}$$

$$FSav^* = \overline{Fsav}.(1 - S) \quad \text{(Eq.3)}$$

where

PE_c = export price for commodity c in local currency;

pwe = f.o.b. (free on board) export price for commodity c in foreign currency;

te_c = export tax rate;

EXR = exchange rate;

$PQ_{c'}$ = price of commodity c' used as trade input;

$ice_{c'c}$ = quantity of commodity c' used as trade input per unit of traded commodity c.

PM_c = import price for commodity c in local currency;
pwm = f.o.b. (free on board) import price for commodity c in foreign currency;
tm_c = import tax rate;
$Fsav^*$ = (equilibrium) foreign saving after sanctions are implemented; and
$\overline{Fsav}$ = (equilibrium) foreign saving before sanctions; The optimal mix between domestic sales and exports for the commodity *c* in SCGE is expressed in the following equation:

$$\frac{QE_c}{QD_c} = \left(\frac{PE_c}{PDS_c} \cdot \frac{1-\delta_c^t}{\delta_c^t}\right)^{\frac{1}{\rho_c^t - 1}} \quad \text{(Eq.4)}$$

where
QE_c = quantity of export for commodity c;
QD_c = quantity of domestic sale for commodity c;
PDS_c = supply price for commodity c produced and sold domestically;
δ_c^t = a CET function share parameter for commodity c; and
ρ_c^t = a CET function exponent for commodity c. This equation assures that a decrease in the export-domestic price ratio generates a decrease in the export-domestic supply ratio. In addition, in SCGE the optimal mix between domestic sales and imports for the commodity *c* is expressed in the following equation:

$$\frac{QM_c}{QD_c} = \left(\frac{PDD_c}{PM_c} \cdot \frac{\delta_c^q}{1-\delta_c^q}\right)^{\frac{1}{1+\rho_c^q}} \quad \text{(Eq.5)}$$

where
QM_c = quantity of import for commodity c;
PDD_c = demand price for commodity c produced and sold domestically;
δ_c^q = an Armington function share parameter for commodity c; and
ρ_c^q = an Armington function exponent for commodity c. This equation assures that a decrease in the domestic-import price ratio generates a decrease in the import-domestic demand ratio.

We develop three scenarios in order to capture banking sanctions. We set *S* to *0.25*, *0.50*, and *0.75* as representative of *low*, *moderate*, and *strict* banking sanctions, respectively. It is worthwhile to note that here, our intention is not to reduce exports, imports, and foreign investments exactly as those events have occurred but to develop three scenarios of increasingly strict application of banking sanctions. First, in reality, not all reductions can be attributed to sanctions. For example, part of the reductions in exports and imports after imposition of sanctions can be due to energy reforms which Iran experienced simultaneously with sanctions. Second, using *S*, we are able to simulate various magnitudes of sanctions that are more informative in terms of showing the effects under various intensities of sanctions. In fact, we emphasize *the way and the pressure* through which banking sanctions force Iran's economy to move toward an autarchy.

Furthermore, to thoroughly investigate how banking sanctions affect household welfare, we divide the banking sanctions into three scenarios: *export-only*, in which sanctions are only imposed against exports; *import-only*, in which sanctions are only imposed against imports; and *financial-only*, in which sanctions reduce foreign savings only. In addition, to make the differences between these scenarios more visible, we use the parameters *E*, *I*, and *FS*', respectively, for export-only, import-only, and financial-only scenarios.

Results

The Macroeconomic and Welfare Effects of Banking Sanctions

The effects of banking sanctions on Iran's macroeconomic indicators are shown in Table 9.1. Because of their obvious importance, oil exports and production values are also reported. The results capture the effects of the successive tightenings of banking sanctions from $S = 0.25$ to $S = 0.75$, which are representative of low banking sanctions to strict banking sanctions, respectively. As shown, the economy suffers significantly from banking sanctions; absorption, private consumption, total exports and imports, GDP, capital income, and household welfare fall, whereas net indirect tax, exchange rate, CPI, and labor income rise. Furthermore, the results indicate that Iran's economy becomes inflexible when banking sanctions are tougher.

We have simulated banking sanctions such that sanctions accompany decreases in total imports, exports, and foreign investment. Here, the results for the medium case ($S = 0.50$) are presented. The overall reduction in total exports is approximately 59 %, whereas the total reduction in total imports is approximately 82 %. Although declines in total imports negatively affect the exchange rate, the net effect of reductions in total exports and imports is an

Table 9.1 Percentage changes in macro-indicators due to banking sanctions

Macro-indicators	S = *25 %*	S = *50 %*	S = *75 %*
Absorption	−3.36	−9.87	−17.70
Private consumption	−5.70	−16.76	−30.05
Total export	−38.81	−58.88	−66.37
Oil export	−47.42	−67.52	−73.46
Total non-oil export	−22.30	−42.32	−52.79
Total import	−52.49	−82.32	−96.92
Oil production value	−44.9	−62.2	−67.3
Net indirect tax	12.99	14.75	26.54
GDP	−2.25	−7.54	−14.09
Exchange rate	20.2	63.6	208.0
CPI	2.16	3.76	4.93
Labor income	3.57	4.35	4.47
Capital income	−6.81	−11.31	−14.24
Total households' welfare	−5.6	−16.3	−29.1

Source: Authors' calculations

increase of approximately 63 % in the exchange rate. Under banking sanctions, oil exports also fall by approximately 68 %, which leads to a reduction of around 62 % in oil production value. Because oil exports constitute the major source of Iran's government funding, their reduction results in an increase of approximately 15 % in net indirect taxes to preserve current government expenditures. The model's full employment assumption implies that when oil activity, which is indeed capital-intensive, decreases oil production, the activity uses less capital. As unused capital flows to other activities, capital income falls by more than 12 %. This is an opportunity for non-oil activities to increase.

Meanwhile, activities that need imported commodities for their manufacturing processes decrease their production because of the sanctions, which also implies more use of labor, leading to an increase in labor income of more than 4 %. The sanctions' overall effect is to decrease GDP by more than 7 %. In addition, the loss of foreign savings must be compensated with increases in private savings, which causes additional reduction in household consumption. Overall, absorption and private consumption fall by 9.87 % and 16.76 %, which result in approximately 16 % losses in household welfare. Although, as mentioned, some activities may gain from the reduced price of capital and increase their production, such increases cannot compensate for the vast, sanctions-induced loss of supply to domestic markets; the economy will experience a positive inflation rate of approximately 3.7 %.

Additionally, the simulation results indicate that Iran's economy becomes inflexible when banking sanctions are stronger. Most of the macro-indicators vary widely (nonlinearly) during successive tightening of sanctions. For example, when S is 0.25, reductions in total exports and total imports are approximately 39 % and 52 %, respectively, which subsequently causes GDP to fall by 2.2 %. However, when S rises to 0.50, reductions in total exports and total imports are approximately 59 % and 82 %, respectively, causing a 7.5 % decrease in GDP. For the extreme case, when $S = 0.75$, total imports decrease by more than 96 % while total exports decrease by approximately 66 %. In this case, GDP decreases by more than 14 %. In addition, the exchange rate increases under banking sanctions. For instance, the exchange rate soars by a factor of almost three for the extreme case. This increase in the exchange rate is an incentive for exporters and a hindrance for importers; this can explain the difference in the reduction of total exports and total imports. For the consecutive tightening of banking sanctions, total household welfare decreases by 5.6 %, 16.3 %, and 29.1 %. We interpret these nonlinear changes in macro-indicators as the inflexibility of Iran's economy in response to banking sanctions when banking sanctions become tougher. Indeed, such reductions also imply that banking sanctions may threaten Iranian households, which may lose more than 30 % of their consumption in the extreme case.

The most important difference between banking sanctions and oil sanctions arises out of the pressure that banking sanctions—but not oil sanctions—put on non-oil exports. This is a crucial assumption that explains why under oil sanctions, CPI may decrease, whereas it increases with banking sanctions. Under oil sanctions, a soaring exchange rate and reduced capital wages are two strong motivations for non-oil exporters to increase their exports and production. Because it is assumed that exports are related to domestic supply through a constant elasticity of transformation (CET) function, increased exports of non-oil products must be accompanied by increased domestic supply. Therefore, assuming there is no pressure on non-oil exports, there is not only a possibility that CPI increases will be low but also a possibility that it will decrease. However, this adjustment process is disrupted by banking sanctions. As the simulation results show, although some activities may increase their level of production in the presence of banking sanctions (see Table 9.2 in Appendix A), the shocks to the supply side of the economy cannot be fully offset, logically leading to inflation.

Figure 9.1 shows the welfare effects of three scenarios simulating successive tightening of banking sanctions against Iran on urban households (UH) and rural households (RH) grouped in income levels. When *S* rises from 0.25 to 0.75, Iranian households may lose welfare in a range between 4 % and 35 %. In general, the reason for this finding is that national production (and national income) decreases because of banking sanctions, resulting in reductions in welfare losses through the decrease in private consumption. In the low banking sanctions' scenario ($S = 0.25$), losses in urban and rural households' welfare are almost the same, with a slightly increasing effect for upper-income levels. This pattern is nearly the same for the stricter banking sanctions' scenario. However, the results indicate that the richest households in both urban and rural areas suffer significantly more from sanctions than do other households. The reason for this finding is that upper-income households are the major owners of capital; therefore, decreases in capital income directly influence them. In addition, it is assumed that upper-income households are major users of imported commodities. Given the assumption that upper-income households have a stronger effect on Iran's decision-making process, our findings hint at the impetus on Iran's part for the realization of JCPOA in 2015.

The Welfare Effects of Sub-banking Sanctions

In this sub-section, we decompose the effects of banking sanctions on households' welfare into its sub-scenarios of export-only, import-only, and financial-only sanctions. In this way, we can investigate the working mechanisms of the banking sanctions in detail and study which scenario may have the most significant impact on households. Figures 9.2, 9.3, and 9.4 demonstrate the effects of export-only, import-only, and financial-only sanctions against Iran, respectively, on household welfare in both urban and rural areas. In the export-only scenario, it is assumed that the sanctions are only imposed on exports (both oil and non-oil products). Under the import-only scenario, only Iran's importation of products is the target of sanctions, and in the financial-only scenario, only foreign savings are affected by sanctions.

Simulations for the low sanctioning scenario ($E = I = FS = 0.25$) indicate that financial-only sanctions are stronger than export- and import-only sanctions in reducing Iranian household welfare. Under the low sanctioning scenario, the losses in household welfare range from 1.3 % to 2.1 %, from 0.7 % to 1.9 %, and from 0.4 % to 1.3 in financial-only, export-only, and

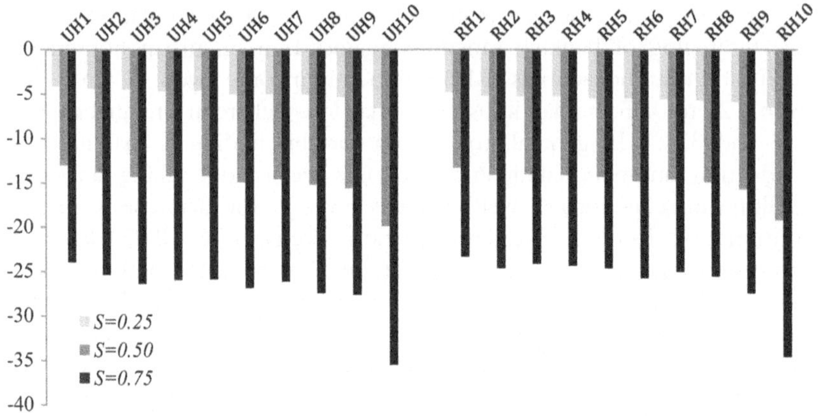

Fig. 9.1 Percentage changes in household welfare due to banking sanctions. *Note*: UH = Urban household; RH = rural households

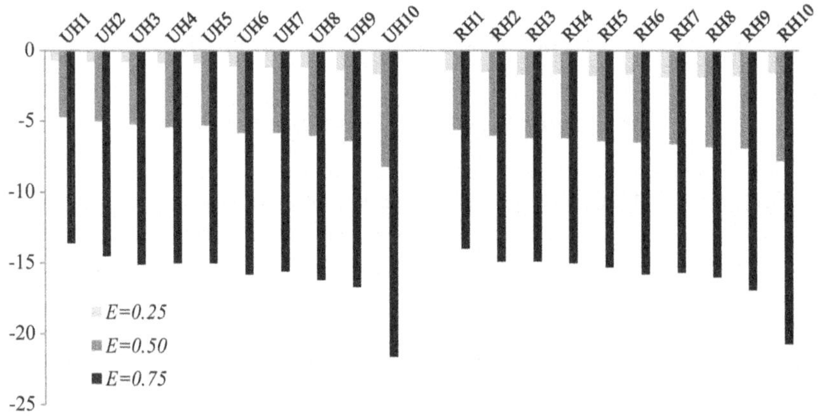

Fig. 9.2 Percentage changes in household welfare due to export-only sanctions. *Note*: UH = Urban Household; RH = rural Households

import-only scenarios, respectively. However, as sanctions become harsher, the export-only scenario has more harmful effects on household welfare. In the strict scenarios ($E = I = FS = 0.75$), export-only sanctions reduce household welfare by more than 13 %, whereas financial-only and import-

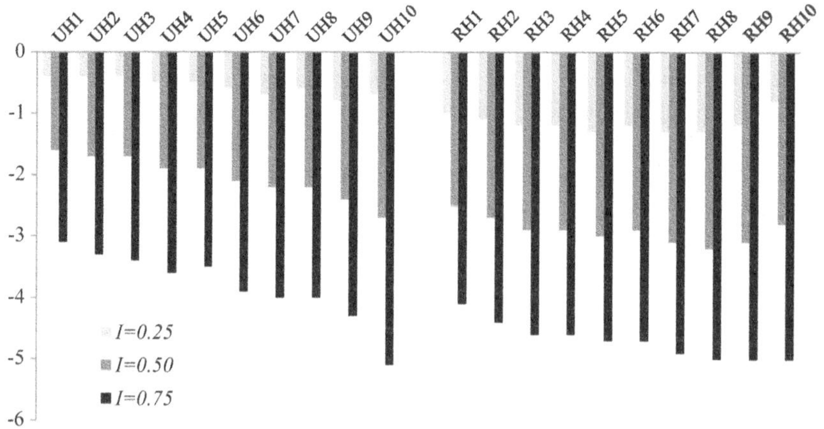

Fig. 9.3 Percentage changes in household welfare due to import-only sanctions. *Note*: UH = Urban Household; RH = rural Households

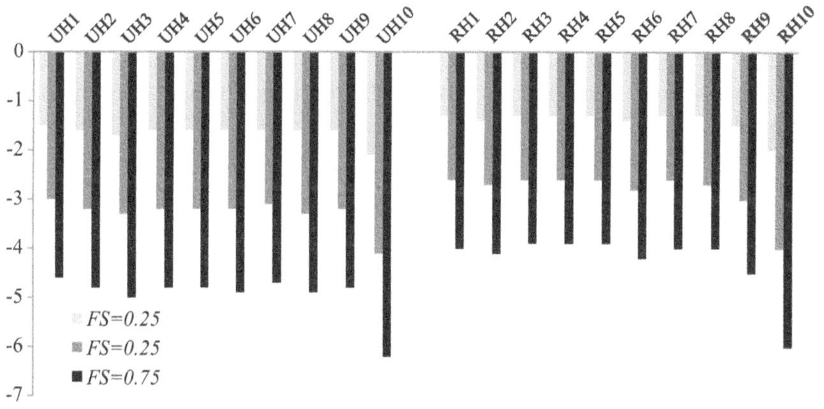

Fig. 9.4 Percentage changes in household welfare due to financial-only sanctions. *Note*: UH = Urban Household; RH = rural Households

only scenarios decrease household welfare in a range of 3.9–6.2 % and 3.1 %–5.1 %, respectively. There is an interesting pattern of sanctions-induced welfare change among households. In general, welfare loss increases among richer households both in urban and rural areas. However, this loss is more significant for the richest households. In addition, although rural households are more vulnerable than urban households to import-only sanctions, under low ($I = 0.25$) and moderate sanctions ($I = 0.50$), welfare loss is more significant for rural middle-income households.

Although all three sub-banking sanctions have decreasing effects on household welfare, it is worthwhile to restate that the mechanisms underlying such decreases are completely different (see Table 9.3, in Appendix A). Under export-only sanctions, the pressure on exports increases the exchange rate, leading to a reduction in imports. Such sanctions affect household welfare through income reductions, which leads to consumption losses. Moreover, under export-only sanctions, increased CPI exacerbates the situation by making domestic production even more expensive. In contrast, in the import-only scenario, the exchange rate falls. This appreciation in Iranian rial against international currency discourages exporters by reducing their received monetary value. The shortage in domestic supply caused by reduced imports, however, again results in increased CPI. As noted, foreign saving is the only decreased indicator in the financial-only simulation. Because the saving-investment closure implies that the amount of savings must be equivalent to the amount of investments, decreased foreign savings must be compensated by increased private savings.[7] Therefore, household consumption should be reduced, which consequently decreases household welfare.

Conclusion

In this chapter, we investigated the economic effects of banking sanctions on Iranian household welfare and macroeconomic indicators. We also highlighted the differences between banking sanctions and oil sanctions in terms of their effects on household welfare and macroeconomic indicators. Moreover, by decomposing banking sanctions into three sub-banking sanctions (export-only, import-only, and financial-only sanctions), we shed light on its working mechanisms.

Our results show that banking sanctions significantly affect Iranian macroeconomic indicators and cause enormous economic hardship. Macroeconomic indicators that *decrease* include absorption, private consumption, total export and import, GDP, and capital income. Macroeconomic indicators that *increase* include net indirect tax, exchange rate, CPI, and labor income. Depending on the intensity of sanctions, the changes in macroeconomic indicators vary over different scenarios. For example, the decrease in

GDP varies from 2.25 % under low sanctions to 14.09 % under high sanctions economy, whereas the increase in exchange rates ranges from 20.2 % to 208 %. The simulation results suggest that Iran's economy becomes inflexible when sanctions are stricter.

Our results further indicate that all urban and rural households suffer from banking sanctions regardless of income group. Depending on the intensity of a given banking sanction, Iranian households may experience welfare loss in a range between 4 % and 35 %, with the higher losses pertaining to the richer households. With respect to sub-banking sanctioning scenarios, whereas the results indicate welfare reductions in all scenarios, the export-only scenario is more stringent than the others. The financial-only scenario is also more stringent than the import-only scenario. The greater loss of welfare by middle-income households in rural areas under low and moderate import-only scenarios is an important result of this chapter.

Oil sanctions and banking sanctions can influence Iranian household welfare and macro-indicators differently. In general, banking sanctions disrupt some adjustment processes (such as increasing non-oil exports) that may take place under oil sanctions to alleviate the harms. The stricter limitations under banking sanctions suggest that this type of sanctions is more effective than oil sanctions. This shows clearly in the consumer price index, which decreases under oil sanctions and increases under banking sanctions. Our results are in line with the political and economic reality in Iran since the beginning of banking sanctions and may provide an ambitious explanation for the Iranian government's recent political actions, such as entering negotiations and reaching a nuclear deal in 2015.

In this work, we assume both that sanctions do not reduce Iran's government expenditures and that upper-income households have more influence on Iran's government. Given these assumptions, we conclude that banking sanctions have been effective because they resulted in significant welfare loss for rich households. However, one may argue that government welfare must be separately considered. Although this can be the case, here two questions arise: (a) How can we measure government welfare? (b) What is the relationship between government income and household income?

We support our results by arguing that our assumptions are adequate because Iran's government can use its National Development Fund in the case of negative revenues shocks. Moreover, because household income can be derived from work for government, any reduction in government revenues should be reflected in reduced household income.

Appendix A

Table 9.2 Percentage changes in activities' quantity, price, and levels due to banking sanctions

Activities	*Quantity (Q)*			*Price (P)*			*Level (P.Q)*		
	S = *25 %*	S = *50 %*	S = *75 %*	S = *0.25*	S = *0.50*	S = *0.75*	S = *25 %*	S = *50 %*	S = *75 %*
Agricultural	1.2	−5.9	−16.6	−3.2	−5.4	−6.9	−2.1	−11	−22.4
Mining	17.3	34	51.2	−2.8	−4.8	−6.1	14	27.6	42
Oil	−41.1	−57.6	−62.2	−6.4	−10.7	−13.5	−44.9	−62.2	−67.3
Food	7.7	5.6	−2	−0.5	−1.3	−2.1	7.1	4.2	−4
Transportation	13.2	20.8	24.7	1.8	2.7	2.8	15.3	24.1	28.1
Industrial	33.3	70.9	111.8	5.9	11.5	16.7	41.1	90.5	147.2
Construction	−1.2	−2.5	−3.7	4.5	8	11	3.2	5.3	6.9
Distribution	13	20.3	25	−3.5	−5.8	−7.4	9.1	13.2	15.7
Financial	−10	−24.2	−39.9	−4.5	−7.5	−9.5	−14	−29.9	−45.6
Services	−0.9	−3.8	−7.4	0.1	−0.4	−0.7	−0.9	−4.2	−8.1

Source: Authors' calculations

Table 9.3 Percentage changes in macro-indicators due to sanctions

Macro-indicators	*Export-only*			*Import-only*			*Financial-only*		
	E = *0.25*	E = *0.50*	E = *0.75*	I = *0.25*	I = *0.50*	I = *0.75*	FS = *0.25*	FS = *0.50*	FS = *0.75*
Absorption	−0.8	−4.0	−10.7	−0.4	−1.5	−2.7	−1.0	−2.0	−3.0
Private Consumption	−1.4	−6.8	−18.1	−0.8	−2.5	−4.5	−1.7	−3.4	−5.1
Total export	−27.0	−52.3	−73.2	−21.8	−35.6	−45.0	3.4	6.9	10.3
Oil export	−34.3	−62.2	−80.7	−28.0	−44.4	−54.7	5.1	10.2	15.4
Total non-oil export	−13.1	−33.3	−58.8	−10.0	−18.9	−26.4	0.3	0.5	0.7
Total import	−32.7	−63.3	−88.6	−26.4	−43.1	−54.5	−1.4	−2.8	−4.1
Oil production	−32.9	−57.5	−72.1	−27.0	−41.9	−50.9	4.7	9.5	14.4
Net indirect tax	5.0	7.0	12.9	12.9	16.0	16.2	2.0	4.0	6.0
GDP	−0.8	−3.9	−10.3	−0.4	−1.4	−2.6	0.0	0.0	0.0
Exchange rate	25.2	71.4	197.0	−4.8	−8.5	−11.5	0.4	0.7	1.1
CPI	1.2	2.5	3.9	1.0	1.7	2.2	0.1	0.2	0.4
Labor income	3.1	4.9	5.5	2.4	3.6	4.2	−0.8	−1.6	−2.5
Capital income	−4.4	−8.9	−13.2	−3.5	−5.8	−7.4	0.2	0.4	0.7
Total households' welfare	−1.4	−6.6	−17.5	−0.7	−2.4	−4.4	−1.7	−3.4	−5.1

Source: Authors' calculations

Notes

1. According to JCPOA, only sanctions imposed against Iran because of its attempt to obtain nuclear weapons will be lifted, conditional upon a report by the International Atomic Energy Agency (IAEA) indicating that Iran has fulfilled the terms of the JCPOA. Other sanctions may remain.
2. "From right and from left, they adopt sanctions, but for us they are annoying flies, like a used tissue" (Mr. Ahmadinejad, on an official visit in Tajikistan, The Telegraph, 10 June 2010).
3. We have not found any reliable data on non-oil exports after 2013.
4. For a complete description of the SCGE and the treatment of closures, see Lofgren et al. (2002).
5. We believe that SCGE is sophisticated enough to investigate the effects of banking sanctions. Although we admit that there are more sophisticated models than SCGE, we argue that their complexity creates more uncertainty, which we wish to avoid here.
6. The test results are derived by employing the two-step approach introduced in Chap. 7 for the scenario in which oil exports are placed under sanctions by Japan and the EU. To preserve the brevity of this study, we do not show that test here.
7. Decreases in foreign savings can also be partly compensated by increases in the exchange rate. As we use the Johansen closure, the welfare effects of reductions in foreign savings are correctly measured. However, because we use a static model, the effects of reductions in foreign savings on macro-indicators may be misleading.

References

CBI [Central Bank of Iran]. (2015). Time series data tables. Retrieved December 15, 2015, from http://tsd.cbi.ir

Dizaji, S. F., & Van Bergeijk, P. A. G. (2013). Potential early phase success and ultimate failure of economic sanctions: A VAR approach with an application to Iran. *Journal of Peace Research, 50*, 721–736.

Drezner, D. W. (1999). *The sanctions paradox: Economic statecraft and international relations.* Cambridge: Cambridge University Press.

Elliott, K. A. (1998). The sanctions glass: Half full or completely empty. *International Security, 23*, 50–65.

Hufbauer, G. C., Schott, J. J., & Elliott, K. A. (1990). *Economic sanctions reconsidered: History and current policy.* Washington, DC: Peterson Institute.

Hufbauer, G. C., & Schott, J. J. (2006). Can sanctions stop the Iranian bomb? Peterson institute for international economics, Washington, DC. Retrieved March 22, 2016, from http://www.iie.com/publications/papers/paper.cfm?ResearchID=606

Hufbauer, G. C., Schott, J. J., Elliott, K. A., Muir, J., & Cosic, M. (2012). Case 2006-1 UN, US [EU] v. Iran (2006-: Proliferation). In G. C. Hufbauer, J. J. Schott, K. A. Elliot, J. Muir, & M. Cosic (Eds.), *Case studies in economic sanctions and terrorism*. Washington, DC: Peterson Institute for International Economics.

Johansen, L. (1960). *A multi-sectorial study of economic growth*. Amsterdam: North-Holland Publishing Company.

Kaempfer, W. H., & Lowenberg, A. D. (2007). The political economy of economic sanctions. *Handbook of Defense Economics, 2*, 867–911.

Katzman, K. (2012). Iran sanctions. *CRS Report for Congress*, 7-5700.

Katzman, K. (2013). Iran sanctions. *CRS Report for Congress*, 7-5700.

Khamenei.ir. (2014). Eblagh-e syasatha-ye kolli-e "eqtesad-e moqavemati" [Communication of the general policies of the "resilience economy]. Office website of the Supreme Leader. Retrieved April 30, 2016, from http://farsi.khamenei.ir/news-content?id=25370 (in Persian).

Lofgren, H., Harris, R., Robinson, S., Thomas, M., & El-Said, M. (2002). A Standard Computable General Equilibrium (CGE) Model in GAMS. TMD Discussion Paper No. 75. International Food Policy Research Institute, Washington, DC.

Monshipouri, M., & Dorraj, M. (2013). Iran's foreign policy: A shifting strategic landscape. *Middle East Policy, 20*, 133–147.

Pape, R. A. (1997). Why economic sanctions do not work. *International Security, 22*, 90–136.

Plaut, S. (2013). The Collapse of Iran's Rial. Gatestone Institute International Policy Council, New York. Retrieved March 22, 2016, from http://www.gatestoneinstitute.org/3597/iran-rial-collpase

Siddig, K. (2011). From bilateral trade to multilateral pressure: A scenario of European Union relations with Sudan. *Middle East Development Journal, 3*, 55–73.

SCI [Statistical Center of Iran]. (2016). Excel data tables on Inflation Rate. Retrieved November 16, 2016, from www.amar.org.ir

The Telegraph. (2010). Iran dismisses new UN sanctions as a "used hanky." Retrieved April 27, 2016, from http://www.telegraph.co.uk/news/worldnews/middleeast/iran/7816395/Iran-dismisses-new-UN-sanctions-as-a-used-hanky.html

UNSD [United Nations Statistics Division]. (2013). Central Product Classification (CPC) Ver.2. Retrieved April 24, 2016, from http://unstats.un.org/unsd/cr/registry/cpc-2.asp

U.S. Energy Information Administration. (2013). *Sanctions reduced Iran's oil exports and revenues in 2012.* Retrieved April 24, 2016, from http://www.eia.gov/todayinenergy/detail.cfm?id=11011

Van De Graaf, T. (2013). The "oil weapon" reversed? Sanctions against Iran and US-EU structural power. *Middle East Policy, 20*, 145–163.

Index

Note: Page numbers followed by 'n' denote notes

M.R. Farzanegan, P. Alaedini (eds.), *Economic Welfare and Inequality in Iran*, DOI 10.1057/978-1-349-95025-6

E

F

G

The manufacturer's authorised representative in the EU is Springer
Nature Customer Service Centre GmbH, Europaplatz 3, 69115 Heidelberg,
Germany. If you have any concerns regarding our products, please
contact ProductSafety@springernature.com

Printed and bound by CPI Group (UK) Ltd, Croydon, CR0 4YY
10/10/2026
02231221-0004